# DAILY
# CELEBRATION
## VOLUME 2

# DAILY
# CELEBRATION
## VOLUME 2

DEVOTIONAL READINGS FOR
EVERY DAY OF THE YEAR

## William Barclay

Edited by
Denis Duncan

WORD BOOKS, Publisher
Waco, Texas

The publishers are grateful to the following for permission to include quoted extracts:

Faber & Faber for T. S. Eliot, Choruses from 'The Rock' VIII.
A. P. Watt for Rudyard Kipling, 'If'.
The Society of Authors for A. E. Housman, 'Last Poems' XIII.

*Printed and bound in the United States of America.*

# *Contents*

|  | page |
|---|---|
| The Magic of William Barclay, by Denis Duncan | 9 |
| JANUARY | 11 |
| FEBRUARY | 35 |
| MARCH | 59 |
| APRIL | 81 |
| MAY | 103 |
| JUNE | 125 |
| JULY | 147 |
| AUGUST | 169 |
| SEPTEMBER | 193 |
| OCTOBER | 215 |
| NOVEMBER | 239 |
| DECEMBER | 263 |

*Daily Celebration, Volume 2* is a companion volume to *Daily Celebration* published in November 1971. It contains a Barclay "thought" for each day of the year. These items appeared originally in an extended form in "Obiter Visa" and "Seen in Passing" in *British Weekly*. They have been edited into their present form and sequence, and given their titles by Denis Duncan, editor of *British Weekly* from 1957 to 1970.

# The Magic of
# William Barclay

You cannot analyse magic. Break it up into what seem to be its component parts as you will, you still won't find out what makes magic magic. There's an elusive indefinable something somewhere that makes the parts into a magical whole.

This is true of William Barclay. As a totality he has—or is—magic. But reduce him to labelled elements—brilliant mind, humble heart, massive brain, childlike faith, capable musician, football fan, railway enthusiast, theologian, thinker, thorough worker—and that which makes William Barclay what he is, isn't revealed by the bits. Yet it gleams in the whole person. The magic *is* there.

I called this man Barclay a modern miracle in my *Through the Year with William Barclay* published in 1971. I did this because his record and output, diligence and expository brilliance are unequalled by any contemporary writer I know. I outlined there the basic biographical facts of his life and his attainments as preacher, writer, broadcaster, etc. The response to that book has been so impressive that Hodder and Stoughton felt the inexhaustible Barclay material could bring further blessing.

What is it that contributes to the magic of William Barclay? First, surely that he speaks the most profound thoughts in the language of the people.

William Barclay is a great human being. Nearly all his life (except for his first five years in Wick in Caithness) has been spent in the vital earthiness of the West of Scotland, a place where humanity is real. To those at a distance from Glasgow, the thought of life in that great city seems daunting. But to those who "belong to Glasgow" there is no more human, warm, friendly place on earth. Life has often been hard there, but it has made real character and real people.

William Barclay lived as a boy in Motherwell in industrial Lanarkshire and near to the Glasgow in which he has taught with such distinction. To hear William Barclay speak is to feel the earthiness and reality of life. So he speaks to humanity with understanding. Distinct from man because of the brilliance of his mind, he is, at heart, one of "Jock Tamson's bairns". He is a man who knows men, their feelings and their needs.

The magic of Barclay comes out too in his common inheritance with suffering humanity. He is deaf and has been so deaf for so long (but don't pity him please for that which he calls a blessing!). That makes him part of human pain.

He and Mrs. Barclay lost a daughter in a drowning accident off Northern Ireland. That was a terrible blow, perhaps the hardest he had to bear. But it gave him an understanding of human sorrow that helps him bring comfort to people in pain. So when William Barclay appears on television, there comes through the earthy voice and sympathetic heart, the accents of authenticity. This man speaks with authority. He knows, as an academic but also as a human being, what he is talking about. Men listen.

Perhaps most of all the magic of William Barclay is in his humility. He can stand level with the greatest man in his professional sphere, yet he is everybody's friend and available to whoever wants him or needs him. This is not always true of those whom men call "great". It is part of the greatness of William Barclay.

So I offer you a little more of the Barclay magic. Some items will speak to one, some to another. All will not like everything. Most will like something.

It has been hard to avoid repetition of some of Dr. Barclay's favourite illustrations as he does often repeat incidents over a period of years. Where I have found a reference back to *Through the Year with William Barclay* (or *Daily Celebration* as it is published in the U.S.A.), I have mentioned it. Some minor repetition of favourite texts and tales may take place. But from the inexhaustible treasures of the photographic mind of this "modern miracle", there will I hope be given to you another blessing.

It has been an extended privilege to work with these thoughts once again. I hope it will be an added blessing to use them as you will.

Denis Duncan

# January

## GET CRACKING!

I was cleaning my car in the street at my front door, using one of these amazing brushes which lift off the dust like magic.

A very small girl came up and watched me.

"My daddy's got one of these brushes to clean his car too," she said.

"That's very nice," I replied. And, with a view to making conversation, added, "And what kind of car has your daddy got?"

"Oh," said the little girl, "he hasn't got the car yet, but he's got the brush to clean it."

If you can't get all you want, start with what you can get!

If you can't achieve the big thing of which you dream, "get cracking" on what you *are* able to do.

TODAY!

## MIRACLES!
January 2

One of the most alarming parables Jesus ever spoke was the Parable of the Talents (Matt. 25:24–30). In that parable the striking thing is the condemnation of the man who hid his talent in the earth and did nothing with it.

No doubt that man said to himself: "It's all very well for these lads with five and two talents; but I've only got one talent. What's the use of me trying to do anything? It's hopeless to do anything with one talent; it's not worth trying."

That is the kind of thing that a Christian never dare say.

Once Jesus said: "Go ye therefore, and teach all nations" (Matt. 28:19). To whom did he say it?

He said it to eleven ordinary men.

What if *they* had said, as they had every right, humanly, to say: "It's hopeless"?

Once the risen Lord said: "Ye shall be witnesses unto me both in Jerusalem, and in all Judaea, and in Samaria, and unto the uttermost part of the earth."

To whom did he say that? To one hundred and twenty men (Acts 1:8, 15).

What if *they* had said: "It's useless for us to set out on a campaign to win the world"?

The characteristic of the Christian is that he always "gets cracking" on what he can do.

The result?

Miracles!

In his book *An Unfinished Autobiography*, H. A. L. Fisher tells how, when he was a student, he spent some time in France. There he met many famous men.

Among them was Rodin, the famous sculptor.

They were talking about the strange barrenness which at that time affected the productions of literature and of art.

In one sentence Rodin gave his explanation of it.

"My compatriots have lost the art of admiration," he said.

One of the most tragic features of life is the loss of wonder.

When we are young, we live in a thrilling and wonderful world. As we grow older, we begin to live in a world which has grown grey and commonplace.

But the change is not in the world. It is in ourselves.

The classic expression of this loss of wonder is in Wordsworth's "Ode, Intimations of Immortality". We come into this world "trailing clouds of glory from God who is our home". And then the shadows begin to close:

> Shades of the prison-house begin to close
>   Upon the growing boy ...
> The youth who daily from the east
>   Must travel, still is Nature's priest,
> And by the vision splendid

Is on his way attended;
At length the man perceives it die away,
And fade into the light of common day.

The vision is lost, and the wonder is gone.
How tragic!

A poet who expressed deep pessimism was A. E. Housman.
He writes:

When first my way to fair I took
Few pence in purse had I,
And long I used to stand and look
At things I could not buy.
Now times are altered; if I care
To buy a thing, I can
The pence are here, and here's the fair,
But where's the lost young man?

Life had brought him many things, but on the way something had been lost.
That something was himself and the wonder of youth.
When *that* wonder is gone, all is gone.
W. B. Yeats tells how John Davidson, the poet, said to him: "The fires are out; and I must hammer the cold iron."
His days of greatness were at an end.

Fielden Hughes has written a most interesting book called *Down the Corridors*, in which he sets out his experience as a schoolmaster. He writes:

I should aim not to kill life with pedantry, but, as my business was to produce whole men, nothing that happened to awake wonder and pleasure in me was likely to be wasted. Besides, the worst thing that can happen to a schoolmaster is that he should lose his own sense of wonder, and should cease to be excited about living.

If that should happen to him, all he has is his dreary stock-in-trade, which boys only want if he can set it on fire. They won't have it damp or dead, or when it has nothing to appeal to the excitement and fire which live in their hearts and minds . . .

We go on with our job till we are sixty at least; and it may be till we are sixty-five. But there is in every teacher's life a day when he ought to retire, and he probably knows it. That may be his sixty-fifth birthday, or it might occur when he is in his thirties. It is the day when the fire goes out.

It is sad.
But it is a reality which has to be faced, for everybody's sake.


AMAZING LOVE                                                     January 5

Somehow we must keep the sense of wonder alive. It is, in fact, not so very difficult to do this.

The more we know about this astonishing world the more we are bound to wonder.

As Hendrik van Loon reminds us, an ordinary passenger train going day and night without stops would take about nine years to reach the moon, 300 years to reach the sun, 8,300 years to reach the planet Neptune, 75,000,000 years to reach Alpha Centauri, which is the nearest of the fixed stars, and 700,000,000 years to reach the Pole Star.

Who will not be astonished in a universe like that?

There is a text in one of the Psalms: "Thou hast made us to drink of the wine of astonishment" (Ps. 60:3).

It is a draught of that wine that all men need the more as the years begin to close about them. But, if we look at God's world, and even more, if we look at God's love, we too will be lost in wonder, love and praise.

For the more we know of the love of God, so amazing, so divine, the more we must stand astonished.


WAITING ON GOD                                                  January 6

We are living today in a world which is in a hurry, a world which worships speed. The tempo of life has never been faster, and the pressure of life has never been more intense.

There is something fundamentally wrong about all this.

Newman once described culture as a "wise receptivity".
There is far too little time in life when we wait passively to receive.

Yeats writes in his autobiography: "Can one reach God by toil? He gives himself to the pure in heart. He asks nothing but our attention."

But so many of us are living a life in which there is no time to glance at God, much less to contemplate him.

Everyone knows the lines which W. H. Davies the tramp-poet wrote with such a simple loveliness:

> What is this life if, full of care,
> We have no time to stand and stare?

That is what very few people in this modern world have time to do. Which is sad.

MAKE TIME!                                                      January 7

There are certain things in life for which we *must* make time.

*We must make time to think.*
So many people are so busy living that they have no time to think *how* they are living.
Plato said that the unexamined life is the life not worth living.
No business could ever survive if sometimes it did not take stock, and if sometimes it did not check up on the whole policy and purpose behind it.
Time to think is essential to life, if life is to be what it was meant to be.

*We must make time to pray.*
John Buchan once described an atheist as "a man with no invisible means of support".
The tragedy of life is that so many people who would resent being called atheists are trying to live life without contact with the invisible world and with God.
This is the age of nervous breakdowns, where the insanity statistics are frightening. We live in a worried and frightened age, and many of these things are due to no other cause than that men have lost contact with the eternal strength.

*We must make time to talk.*
Samuel Johnson, who knew John Wesley quite well, used to say that Wesley had only one fault—he had no time to sit back, cross his legs, and have his talk out.
One of the strange phenomena of modern life is that good talk is very nearly a thing of the past. A visit which once meant an evening of stimulating

interchange of ideas has now become a silent session at the television set, during which even a whisper is hushed into silence.

It would stimulate our thoughts and bring us nearer each other, if we took a little more time to talk.


BE STILL! January 8

But we must make time for one thing more.
*We must make time to do nothing.*


Pascal once said that more than half this world's ills come from the fact that people cannot sit in a room alone.

There is a place in life for complete relaxation, for a deliberate letting go of the tensions, for a wise idleness, for a restful passivity.

Many a man's mental and physical troubles would be eased, and possibly ended, if only he could persuade himself for a little time to relax and to do nothing.


The Bible is full of advice to us to do this very thing.

"Be still," said the Psalmist, "and know that I am God" (Ps. 46:10).

"Stand still," said Moses to the people scurrying about in their terror, "and see the salvation of the Lord" (Exod. 14:13).

"Come ye yourselves apart into a desert place," said Jesus, "and rest awhile" (Mark 6:31).


God grant us more stillness in this hurried life of ours.

Only so, will life become what it is meant to be.


FROM NOWHERE TO NOWHERE January 9

I have come across a whole series of sayings which might serve as verdicts upon life.


Yeats tells how a certain critic described Ibsen's play, *The Doll's House*, as "a series of conversations terminated by an accident".

To some people, that would accurately enough describe life. They meet. They talk. The chances and the changes of life meaninglessly intervene. They pass on.


Edwin Muir tells of the refugees whom he saw on the German roads after the war: "They seemed to be on a pilgrimage from nowhere to nowhere."

To some people, that would accurately describe life. Whence they came, they do not know. Whither they go, they cannot tell.

There can be no progress in a life in which there is no goal, for there is nowhere to reach.

Let us look at some verdicts on life.

Macbeth, as the shadows close about him in Shakespeare's play, says:

> Life's but a walking shadow, a poor player,
>> That struts and frets his hour upon the stage,
> And then is heard no more; it is a tale
>> Told by an idiot, full of sound and fury,
> Signifying nothing.

Life to Macbeth was a drama of unrelated moments with no sense and no plot.

Robert Louis Stevenson wrote:

> I have trod the upward and the downward slope;
>> I have endured and done in days before;
> I have longed for all, and bid farewell to hope;
>> And I have lived and loved and closed the door.

To Stevenson, at that moment, life was the way to the closed door beyond which there lay only the hope and the love and the life itself that were dead. What poor verdicts!

THE CHRISTIAN'S VERDICT                                    January 10

But neither of the verdicts quoted yesterday is the Christian verdict on life.

In one flashing sentence Paul gave the Christian verdict on life when he was writing to his friends at Philippi: "For me to live is Christ" (Phil. 1:21).

*For the Christian, life begins with Christ.*

In a modern novel, there is a scene between two people who have fallen deeply and truly in love. One says to the other: "I never knew what life was until I saw it in your eyes."

It is the Christian conviction that life only becomes life more abundant when Christ enters into it; that Jesus Christ gives to life an adventure and

17

a meaning and a significance and a relevance and an aim and object which it never had before he entered into it.

*For the Christian, life continues in Christ.*
Life is lived in his presence and in his company.
No task is faced alone.
No sorrow is borne in isolation.
No journey is made as a lonely pilgrim.

*For the Christian, life ends in Christ.*
In the end he goes, not to the dark, but to Jesus Christ, the light of the world.
To live in the light *is* life abundant.


A DESTINY                                                        January 11

Sir Philip Gibbs tells how, between the wars, he was at a debate in London-derry House.
The debaters were a distinguished company—Rose Macaulay, Margaret Irwin, C. Day Lewis, Margaret Kennedy, T. S. Eliot.
The subject of the debate was: "I find this is a good life, or, I do not."
Sir Philip says: "Not one of them could find a good word to say about this life. True, they jested; but they jested like jesters knocking at the door of death."

There is nothing other than the Christian faith which can give life real value.
Christianity supplies man with a task, the task of serving God and serving his fellow men.
Christianity supplies man with a standard, the standard of the perfection of Jesus Christ.
Christianity supplies man with a strength, the strength of the continual presence of the Risen Lord.

Christianity supplies man with a destiny and when this life is done, life in the presence of God.


WHEN A MISTAKE IS MADE                                           January 12

If I have time, I like to go to football matches.
I was in London on a certain Saturday when two of the most famous clubs in England were playing, so I went to see the match.

It was a thriller. One of the clubs is very famous and had been very much up against it at that time. In an attempt to get on to the rails again, they had signed on some new young players at very large transfer fees.

One of the great handicaps against which a young player signed at a colossal fee has to fight is the struggle to be worth his fee. He is always conscious of what the club paid for him.

One of these young players was playing at centre-forward (as they used to call it!) and he was trying with all his heart and soul and strength. He did get one magnificent goal, then a short time afterwards he missed a chance which a child could have accepted. He blazed the ball past an open goal from about three yards out from the goal.

He stood there the picture of dejection, his head bowed and his shoulders drooped.

In the same forward line there was a forward who was a famous international, and who had played for that team very much longer. When this famous international saw the dejection of his young colleague, he ran up to him and flung a comforting arm round his shoulder, gave him a pat on the back, and said a few words of encouragement to him. The young centre-forward squared his shoulders, shook himself and charged into the game to play twice as hard as before.

What an example to Christian people!

"Brethren," said Paul, "if a man be overtaken in a fault, ye which are spiritual, restore such an one in the spirit of meekness; considering thyself, lest thou also be tempted" (Gal. 6:1).

That is indeed the Christian way.


RESTORE THAT MAN! January 13

Once, in the House of Commons, Gladstone made a most important speech. In the course of it he had to quote certain figures, and the figures he quoted were quite wrong and quite inaccurate. His opponents were not slow to seize on his mistake and to make things very difficult for him.

Now the figures had been supplied to Gladstone by his private secretary, whose duty it was to brief his chief, so Gladstone might well have turned and rent that young man for involving him in this public humiliation.

But, instead, that night Gladstone wrote him a very gracious and kindly letter telling him not to worry, that all men made mistakes, that, as far as he was concerned, the matter would never be mentioned again.

If a man be overtaken in a fault—what happens usually? So often he is criticised, torn to pieces, cold-shouldered, even ostracised!

A teacher can do an infinite amount of damage by coming down savagely, sarcastically, or over-severely on a pupil's mistake, when a word of encouragement might have sent the child out to do better in the days to come.

A parent can do infinite damage by an over-critical attitude to his or her children.

"Restore such an one . . ."
That is the Christian way

## "BELIEVISM"                                                January 14

In his youth he sunk to every iniquity both on land and as a sailor on the ship of a slave-trader. But every now and again something would happen, an event like a shaft of lightning, a storm at sea, a preservation, and John Newton would be left looking at God.

But then the effect would die and the old life would engulf him; and again, so John Newton writes:

"I forgot; I so soon forgot."

Most of us are like that.
The moment we are sorry, we forget.
We forget so soon.

Goodness is too often a spasmodic thing. The chart of our goodness is like the temperature chart of a patient with a high fever. We are capable of reaching the heights of goodness, and we are just as capable of taking a sudden nose dive into the depths.

There are young people who bank on the love and the kindness of their parents. They know that, whatever they do, they will get away with it; and, often unconsciously, they trade on that knowledge. Most of us are a little like that with God.

Everyone knows the well-worn saying of Heine. He had not been a good man, and yet he seemed not in the least worried. When he was asked why he was so unworried, he answered: "God will forgive. *C'est son métier.*" It is his trade.

Consciously and unconsciously we trade on the mercy of God.

But the New Testament is clear. "Bring forth therefore fruits meet for repentance" (Matt. 3:8).

"By their fruits ye shall know them" (Matt. 7:20).

J. D. Drysdale complained about what he called the danger of "only believism".

The Christian belief is belief that issues in action, that is proved by action.

If it isn't, it is not belief at all.

## 999 WORKS!

We had a fire in our house, a fire which brought along the fire-brigade. The paraffin stove in my study went up in flames—the fault was mine not the stove's!

My wife and I succeeded in dealing with the flames, so that the worst of the danger was averted, but the stove itself and the rugs in which we had smothered it were still smouldering, and, for safety's sake, we decided to telephone for the fire-brigade.

I rang 999, told the voice at the other end of my trouble, and received the answer: "We'll deal with it."

In six minutes, the fire-brigade arrived.

The firemen dealt with the situation with extreme efficiency and with courtesy—they even asked for something with which to wipe up the mess—and the situation which might have caused a very great deal of damage was cleared up with practically no damage at all.

I discovered parables and symbols that night!

I discovered that, in certain situations in life, if you are wise, you *shout for help*. You may feel very silly, and more than a bit of a fool doing it, but, if you want to avoid worse trouble, you ask for help.

That is the way it should be with God. Many of our troubles in life come from the fact that we try to do things by ourselves, when we ought to call in the help of God.

For many years I have seen on my telephone the words "Emergency Calls. For fire, police or ambulance dial 999". I had never had occasion to dial 999 before, and I often wondered what would happen, if I did.

Now I know it works!

That it is a discovery that it is open to any of us to make about God.

We know that God is there. We have heard that, if we call upon him, he helps.

Maybe we have never tried.

But if we call on God, and ask for his help, we shall find that, like dialling 999, it works too.

CALL FOR HELP!                                    January 16

Over that fire I discovered too that, when I asked for help, it comes *with speed*.

When we ask for God's help, time and time again God answers, and answers at once, as many can testify.

One of the loveliest things in life, and in human nature, is the way that a mother hears a child's cry in the night. The mother may be asleep, but let the child cry, and immediately the mother is awake, and on the way to see what the matter is.

"Before they call," says God, "I will answer; and while they are yet speaking, I will hear" (Isa. 65:24).

I discovered another thing.

Once all the bother was over, and there was time to speak to the firemen, I was very apologetic about it. I was specially apologetic about sending for the fire-brigade when the worst had past, and when there was nothing left but the smouldering remains to deal with.

But the firemen were insistent that we had done the right thing.

"If you are in the slightest doubt," they said, "never hesitate to send for us. That is what we are here for."

When in doubt, it is always safer to call for help.

The God whose glory it is to help, knows nothing but joy when we call.

THE BOOK                                         January 17

A short time after the firemen had left, we had the routine visit which follows from the officer of the salvage corps. He came into my study, made a note of the trifling damage, and looked at my desk.

The open Bible was lying there.

"I see you've got the Book," he said. "You'll not come to much harm so long as you have that there."

I don't know that man's name, but, out of our fire, there came again a great truth.

There are things which can wreck a life even more disastrously than a fire can wreck a house.

But no one will find it easy to wreck our lives, so long as we have "the Book".

And so long as we have beside us and within us, the One of whom the Book tells.

COMPENSATION											January 18

There is a Glasgow church in which I have sometimes preached. In it the organist was blind.

I have always been amazed by the fact that you only needed to tell him once the hymns you wished sung. And he knows the whole order of service.

You can't hand him a list. He couldn't read it. But simply repeat the hymn-list once, and it is firm in his memory.

I was preaching there one morning, and with me was the minister of the church. After I had fixed up the morning list of hymns, the minister was arranging the evening praise list with this amazing blind man.

The minister said: "I would like this evening to have 'For those we love within the veil'. That's hymn number 216."

"No," said the blind organist in his soft Highland voice, "not 216, 218."

This blind man carried in his memory the number of every hymn in the hymn book.

But when I spoke to him about his amazing memory, he refused to think of it as amazing at all.

He simply felt it was a compensation for his blindness.

It was therefore his blessing.

GOD'S COMPENSATIONS										January 19

I was once with a Youth Fellowship in one of the Church Extension churches on the south side of Glasgow. There must have been at least 200 young people there, many of them from a housing scheme which is alleged to be a rather tough spot.

I never got a better hearing from any audience in all my life.

One of my questioners was a young lad who was a spastic. It was an amazing thing, a thing commanding unbounded admiration, that this lad, with his terrible handicap and his awkward unco-ordinated movements, could possibly take part in an open discussion like that, and could openly witness as to how he prayed to God to help him to conquer his handciap—and God had helped him most amazingly.

I talked to the boy afterwards, and he told me that he had only one ambition, to be a minister. Then he said to me: "I'll bet you I can do what you can't do." I said: "I wouldn't be surprised at that. What is it you can do?"
He said: "I can read a page of any newspaper once, and then repeat it by heart."
If, by the grace of God, that lad ever becomes a minister, he has got a gift that is going to stand him in good stead.

God always gives compensations.
If something is taken away, he seems to give something else instead.
Much had been taken from the spastic lad and the blind organist, but he gave them memories capable of amazing things.
These, surely, are God's compensations.

MY COMPENSATION                                              January 20

I happen, as you know, to be deaf, so deaf that, without a very wonderful hearing aid, I am quite helpless and cannot hear anyone. But there is one tremendous advantage in being deaf. If you are deaf, your power of concentration is far more than doubled, for the very simple reason that you never hear all the sounds which are so distracting for other people!
There is a big compensation for a writer in being deaf!

I think that if we worked this out a bit, we might get a surprise.
If God has taken something from us, he gives us something else back. For, as we said yesterday, it would do some of us good to start counting our blessings instead of brooding on our losses.

That was one of the great discoveries that Paul made.
Paul was a sick man, a man with a trouble which was like a stake (it is a "stake" rather than a "thorn") turning and twisting in his body. He prayed to God to take that terrible pain away. Again and again he prayed that it should be taken away. It wasn't taken away. But out of that terrible experience of pain and agony, which was to haunt him all his life, Paul discovered something—he discovered the grace which is sufficient for all things and the strength which is made perfect in weakness (2 Cor. 12:1–10).

We will often find compensations if we think more of what life has given us and less about what life has taken away.

Once a man came to Spurgeon and told him that he was saved, and that now that he was saved, he wanted to help to bring people to Jesus Christ.

Spurgeon looked at him.

"What are you?" said Spurgeon.

"I'm an engine driver," said the man.

"Is your fireman a Christian?" asked Spurgeon.

"I don't know," said the man.

"Well," said Spurgeon, "find out; and if he's not, start on him."

A man who lived in a tenement in a respectable artisan district in a certain great city was touched for Christ. He immediately began to go to a church which was near at hand.

In that church about the first person he met was the man who lived in the house across the landing. That man was an elder in that church, and never in years had he mentioned the church to his next-door neighbour, and never had he made any attempt to guide him or lead him or persuade him into it.

What a failure in Christian responsibility!

Christians ought to be missionaries.

If they aren't, they are failures.

So start ...

Just where you are!

Start there!

*As a Church member, you are one of a community pledged to the spread of the gospel.*

Do you realise that serious fact, that a Church member *is* one of a community pledged to the spread of the gospel?

Do we ever pause to think why we are members of the Church at all?

Is it to obtain the rites of the Church at marriage and baptism and death?

Is it to have the right to expect a visit from the minister when we are ill, and to have the equal right to complain bitterly if we do not receive such a visit?

Is it—a little better—to gain help and strength for the days of the week?

We are members of the Church because we are pledged to the spread of the gospel.

Where are we going to spread it?

I know of many cases where people were, as they claimed, "converted". They were asked what they were going to do tomorrow, now that they were converted. The answer invariably was: "I'm going to say my prayers and read my Bible."

That is a very inadequate description of the Christian life. You could do that and never move outside of your own house or room. That could be sheer escapism.

Of course we must say our prayers and read our Bibles—but the object of doing so is to go out into the world and to live for Christ in the shop, the office, the factory, the school.

It is there that our Christianity is seen—or not seen.

We are in the Church, not only for what we can get out of it, but also for what we can bring out of it to others.

VULNERABILITY                                                                    January 23

One of the strange features of human life is its vulnerability. Nor is that vulnerability a purely physical thing. Everyone knows how vulnerable the human frame is, how (as Pascal said so long ago), a drop of water or a draught of air can kill a man. That kind of vulnerability we all know and recognise.

But there is also a vulnerability in the sphere of the mind and the heart and the spirit.

*A man is vulnerable to goodness.*

O. Henry, that master of the short story, has a tale about a lad who used to stay in a country town, and who had once been a good boy.

He came to the great city, fell in with bad company, and learned to walk the wrong way—and to walk it very successfully. He was an excellent pickpocket and a thief. He had done well and he had never been caught. He was pleased with himself. For he was at the top of his thieving profession!

One day he was going down one of the city streets. He had done well. He had just stolen a wallet and snatched a bag, and he was pleased with himself.

All of a sudden he saw a girl of his own age. He looked again, and he recognised her. She had sat beside him in the same class in the village school, in the old days when he had been young and good and innocent. He had only to look at her to see that she was still the same sweet, simple girl that she had always been.

She didn't see him; but the very sight of her suddenly made him catch a glimpse of himself. He suddenly saw himself for the petty sneak-thief that he was. He leaned his burning forehead against the cool iron of a lamp standard. "God!" he said, "how I hate myself."

In spite of what he was and of what he had done, he was still vulnerable to goodness.

To find we still have that vulnerability is something for which we ought to thank God.

## THE DIVINE PURSUIT                                    January 24

Life would be much simpler if we could sin in peace.

Life would be much easier if there were no such things as shame and regret and remorse.

Life would be much easier, if a man had no conscience, and if God would let him alone.

But that never happens.

*A man is vulnerable to God.*

You can never tell when suddenly God will break in.

You remember Browning, so often quoted because it is so often true:

> Just when we are safest, there's a sunset-touch,
>   A fancy from a flower-bell, someone's death,
> A chorus ending from Euripides,
>   And that's enough for fifty hopes and fears
> As old and new at once as nature's self,
>   To rap and knock and enter in our soul.

No man is ever safe from memory. No man is ever safe from goodness. And least of all is any man safe from God.

That is, I think, what Augustine meant when he said that God has made us for himself, and our hearts are restless till they rest in him.

That is what the Psalmist meant when he said: "Whither shall I go from Thy Spirit? or whither shall I flee from Thy presence? If I ascend up into heaven, Thou art there: if I make my bed in hell, behold, Thou art there. If

I take the wings of the morning and dwell in the uttermost parts of the sea, even there shall Thy hand lead me, and Thy right hand shall hold me. If I say, Surely the darkness shall cover me, even the night shall be light about me. Yea the darkness hideth not from Thee; but the night shineth as the day; the darkness and the light are both alike to Thee" (Ps. 139:7-12).

There is no escaping the divine pursuit.

GOD'S MAN                                               January 25

During the Second World War I had something to do with a canteen which was run for the troops in the town in which I was then working. Early in the war, we had billeted with us in our town a number of Polish troops who had escaped from Poland.

Among them there was a Polish airman. When he could be persuaded to talk, he would tell the story of a series of hair-breadth escapes. He would tell of how somehow he had escaped from Poland, how somehow he had tramped his way across Europe, how somehow he had crossed the Channel, how he had been shot down in his aeroplane once and crashed on another occasion.

He always concluded the story of his encounters with death with the same awe-stricken sentence: "I am God's man."

Here was a man who felt that God had dealt so wondrously with him that he belonged henceforth to God.

Every one of us is God's man.

W. M. McGregor used to have a favourite beginning to his prayers: "Thou hast made us and we are Thine; Thou hast redeemed us and we are doubly Thine."

Or as Paul had it: "Know ye not that . . . ye are not your own? For ye are bought with a price" (1 Cor. 6:19, 20).

THIS DANGEROUS LIFE                                     January 26

*We are God's because God has created us.*

The Jews had a lovely thought. They believed that no child could ever come into being without the action of the Holy Spirit of God.

"There are three partners in every birth," they said, "the father, the mother and the Holy One, blessed be He."

God alone is the creator of life, and this life which we enjoy was given to us by God.

*We are God's because God has preserved us.*

Whoever we are and wherever we are, God has brought us through all the chances and the changes of life to this present hour.

Sometimes when we look back and see what we have come through, we are compelled to say: "If I had known what was coming, I would have said that I could never face it."

But God brought us through it all, still on our feet and still able to bear up.

H. G. Wells tells of an experience of his. He was on a liner which was entering the port of New York in a dense fog. The ship was creeping forward, feeling her way through the fog. Suddenly out of the fog there loomed another vessel, and the two vessels glided past each other with hardly a yard to spare.

"It made me think," said Wells, "of the general large dangerousness of life."

Life is indeed a dangerous thing, but God has preserved us in danger, has upheld us in sorrow, has healed us in sickness, has brought some of us back even from the gates of death.

God has preserved us.
We belong to God.

REDEEMED—AT A PRICE                                      January 27

This too is true.

*We are God's because God has redeemed us.*

The essential fact of Christianity is that God thought all men worth the sacrifice of his Son. God thought it worth the life and the death of Jesus Christ to bring men home to himself.

When we are using something which we have borrowed and which belongs to someone else, we are specially careful of it. We do not much care if we crack or scrape or tear or damage something which belongs to ourselves. That does not matter. But if the thing belongs to someone else we exercise a double care.

We ought to be like that with life.

This life of ours does not belong to us. We did not create it, and very certainly we did not redeem it. When we look back, we see very clearly that by ourselves we could never have sustained it.

This life belongs to God. That is why we should use it with reverence and with care, because it does not belong to us.

There was that Polish airman I mentioned who looked back across the adventurous panorama of his life and said with awe in his voice: "I am God's man."

We should all be saying that.

We should also remember that we dare not waste or soil that which does not belong to us, that which cost so much.

HAND IN HAND                                                    January 28

A churchman told me of something that he himself had seen at Kelvin Hall during Billy Graham's crusade there.

He was in the audience with his wife. Into the seats beside them came a man and a woman. They were obviously well-to-do and in the higher reaches of the social scale. The man was the very picture of a successful business-man. He looked the last possible kind of man to make any public declaration for Jesus Christ.

As my preacher friend sat there, he could not help noticing that this man and his wife were not on good terms. It was not that they were quarrelling or anything like that; but they were treating each other with the frigid courtesy of almost complete strangers. There was obviously a barrier between them; it was clear that this was a marriage which had failed.

The service went on, and the time for decisions was reached. For a minute or two nothing happened. Then this well-dressed, hard-headed business-man turned to his wife and said, still with the courtesy which one uses to strangers: "Excuse me please, I must go." And he rose from his seat and started down the long aisle to the front of the hall.

Perhaps twenty seconds passed, and suddenly the woman rose and awk-wardly crushed her way past my preacher friend out into the aisle. With a kind of pathetic, stumbling, half run, almost like one blind, she ran after her husband. As she came up with him she caught his hand with a little pleading motion like a child; and these two went hand in hand to declare their faith in Jesus Christ.

What lies behind that little incident I do not know; but one thing is quite clear—here were two people who in discovering Jesus Christ discovered each other; here were two people who, being reconciled to God through Christ were reconciled to each other, through Christ.

When the barriers between them and God went down the barriers between each other crashed down also.

Christianity is the one thing in this world which can mend our broken personal relationships.

UNEXPECTED LOVELINESS                                          January 29

Mark Rutherford has a novel in which he describes a second marriage. The woman had already been married and she had a teen-age daughter.

The second husband could make absolutely nothing of the girl. She seemed a sullen, boorish, unlovely character without one single redeeming feature.

Then one day her mother fell ill. Overnight that girl underwent a complete transformation. She became the perfect nurse. There was a new radiance in her. Nothing was a trouble. No service was too menial. She served and she shone in her service.

To have judged her by first appearances would have been completely to misjudge her.

They say that there is a certain kind of stone. When you take it first in your hand it looks like a dull and lustreless piece of stone. It has no life, no sparkle, no brilliance. But if you keep turning it over, you will finally get it into a certain position when the rays of light strike it in a certain way, and it will begin to shine and sparkle like a diamond.

The sparkle is there if you will only look for it long enough.

People are like this. Everyone has some gift. Everyone does something well. Everyone has some redeeming feature.

It would make a vast difference in this world if instead of always looking for faults, we began to look for talents.

If we did so, we would most certainly get some surprises—and pleasant surprises too, for we would often find loveliness where we never expected loveliness to be.

THE HIDDEN STRENGTH                                          January 30

Jesus had the ability to see the real person.

Not many people would have seen pillars of the Church in an impetuous soul like Peter, or a pair of blusterers like James and John with a nickname like "sons of thunder".

But Jesus did.

Not many people would have picked a dour pessimist like Thomas to be a right-hand man.

But Jesus did.

Not many people would have wished to pay a visit to a quisling tax-gatherer like Zacchaeus or to have had a traitor like Matthew among his closest friends.

But Jesus did.

Jesus had the power to see the hidden strength and beauty in every life, and to waken the sleeping hero in the soul of every man.

THE GIFT OF RECEIVING                                        January 31

It is more blessed to give than to receive, but there is no virtue in refusing to receive at all.

*There is a certain amount of pride in refusing to receive.*

One of the things that the Church at Laodicea said was: "I don't want your gifts. I need nothing" (Rev. 3:17), and that was counted to it, not for righteousness, but for error. It wasn't a compliment; it was a condemnation.

It is a fine thing to give; but it can be the mark of pride to refuse to receive.

*There is a certain amount of self-conceit in refusing to receive.*

If we refuse to receive, what we in fact say is: "I want to have the pleasure of feeling that I have done you a favour, but I am not going to let you do anything for me."

The person who does this would like to think that he has a mind above reward, but his reward is his glow of inner satisfaction. He is in danger of basking in his own approval.

It is an excellent thing to be able to confer favours on others, and to be ready to do so, but again there is no virtue at all in wholly removing from others the opportunity to do some favour to us. The curious and the dangerous paradox of the Christian life is that zeal for service, and even willingness to sacrifice, may have in them some unconscious tinge of self-conceit.

*One of the characteristics of truly great people is that they can receive graciously.*

I know a very famous man in the academic world who by no means always dresses like an academic. In a London railway station he saw an old lady in difficulties and offered to carry her bag. When he had put it in her carriage for her, she gave him sixpence—which he gravely and courteously received rather than embarrass the old lady who offered it.

Jesus could receive.

He could take a boy's picnic lunch because it was all that the boy could offer and with it he could work a miracle (John 6:1–14).

He could take a room in the home of some anonymous friend in Jerusalem and use it to institute a sacrament which has come down through the centuries since.

Perhaps we should not be so sure that we are acting the noble character when we refuse to receive.

There is a courtesy in receiving as well as in giving.

It is sometimes more blessed to receive than to give.

# *February*

Let us think, one by one, about the Seven Deadly Sins.
At the head of the list is pride.

Pride is, in a sense, the *only* sin. Pride is the ground in which all the other sins grow, and the parent from which all the other sins come.

Basically, *pride is the exaltation of self*. It is the setting of too high a value on oneself.

One of the useful things that I have learned from being in the doctor's hands is that no one is indispensable!

A man is always in a dangerous condition when he begins to think that the universe is revolving round him.

Self-importance *is* pride. The trouble is that, if we allow ourselves to begin to think that we are indispensable in all sorts of things, we can, in the end, render ourselves unable to do the things in which we really are indispensable!

A mother is indispensable to her children; but, if she gets entangled in all sorts of public things—even Church things—and, if she begins to think that the outside world cannot get on without her, she may well fail in her duty to her home, that duty in which she *is* indispensable.

A man may get himself so immersed in outside things that he does not even know his own children, and is a stranger even in his own home.

Very often the driving force of our lives is a kind of disguised and concealed pride which makes us subconsciously regard ourselves as indispensable.

It is not a bad thing to learn that the world gets on quite well without us.

The natural result of pride is contempt for other people. There is no sin quite so unchristian as contempt.

There is a pride in birth, which can become snobbery.

There is a pride in knowledge, which can become intellectual arrogance.

There is a pride in achievement, which can become self-conceit.

There is a pride in money, which can become the belief that we can buy anything.

All these different kinds of pride have only to be looked at honestly to be seen to be ridiculous. No one has any more ancestors than anyone else! The most learned man is learned only within a very narrow sphere.

The greater a man's achievement, the more he must see that there is still to do.

It does not take much experience of life to find out that the things which matter most are the very things which money will never buy. All that the sin of contempt, in its many aspects, needs to cure it, is an honest facing of the facts.

The real essence of pride is *rebellion against God*.

According to one of the oldest legends in the world the Devil was originally an angel of light, Lucifer, the Morning Star, and he tried to set his throne above the throne of God, and was cast out of heaven because of his pride.

The root of *all* sin is the idea that we know better than God. We could even put it in a less "religious" way than that. The mistake of pride is that it defines and neglects the whole mass and weight of human experience.

The lesson of human experience is that, if a man breaks the laws of God, he suffers for it.

If he breaks the laws of health, he suffers.

If he tampers with the natural and physical laws of the universe, he destroys himself.

If he transgresses the moral law, in the end he suffers for it.

The way to happiness and to peace of body, mind and spirit is to accept, humbly, the laws of God.

Pride is the sin of the man who is a moral and an intellectual fool.

WRATH                                                           February 3

Wrath is repeatedly condemned in the New Testament.

Twice in Paul's letters two kindred sins are mentioned and forbidden side by side, and it is interesting and illuminating to see the difference between them. Both in Ephesians 4:31 and Colossians 3:8 wrath and anger are mentioned side by side.

In these two passages "wrath" is *thumos* and "anger" is *orge*.

In Greek there is a clear distinction between these two words.

*Thumos* is from a Greek root which means "to boil", and it describes the anger which blazes up quickly and just as quickly subsides.

The Greeks themselves likened it to a fire kindled with straw, a fire which crackles and blazes for a moment and then dies. *Thumos*, is then a burst of temper, a blaze of anger, a momentary outbreak of uncontrollable passion.

*Orge*, on the other hand, is described as the anger which has become inveterate. It describes the anger which lasts for a long time, the frame of mind which nurses its wrath to keep it warm, the attitude of mind which cannot forget or forgive a wrong or an injury, and which maintains its anger sometimes even for a lifetime.

Sometimes we regard the anger of a quick temper as a forgivable thing and we reckon as less serious, the anger which blazes out and then quickly subsides.

The teaching of the New Testament is that the quick blaze of an inflammable temper and the long-lasting anger of a bitter heart are *both* to be condemned.

WRATH (2)                                                      February 4

In his correspondence with the Corinthians, Paul numbers *thumos* as one of the things which wrecks a Church (2 Cor. 12:20).

In his letter to the Galatians, he numbers it among the sins of the flesh which are opposed to the Spirit (Gal. 5:20).

In First Timothy it is insisted that when a man prays there must be no *orge* in his heart (1 Tim. 2:8); and James insists that the Christian must be slow to anger (*orge*), for the anger of man can never work the will of God (Jas. 1:19, 20).

The Greeks were not far wrong when they defined anger as "a brief madness". When a man is angry, he is not in full control of himself. When that happens he does things and says things, to others and about others, which, in his calmer moments, he knows to be wrong.

Even if he does not actually do them or say them, he thinks them, or he wishes to do and say them. Jesus taught that the sin of thought is every bit as serious as the sin of action.

He laid it down: "He that is angry with his brother shall be in danger of the judgment" (Matt. 5:22). The *Authorised Version* adds the words "without a cause", but they are in none of the best manuscripts and are omitted by all the modern versions from the *Standard Revised Version* onwards.

Here is something to think about. There are many people who justify bursts of temper and blazes of anger by saying that it is "their nature", and "they cannot help it". If the New Testament is right, they cannot be, at one and the same time Christian and bad—or quick-tempered.

Let such people learn to think before they speak.

Let them think of the hurt and the harm their words cause, and of their own sorrow after the anger is over.

Let them take the old Quaker remedy of counting ten before they speak!

Above all, let them ask for the help of Jesus Christ.

ENVY                                                                    February 5

Envy is repeatedly forbidden in the New Testament.

In the New Testament there are two words for "envy", and there is an interesting distinction between them.

The first and the commoner is the word *phthonos*, together with its kindred verb *phthonein*. This word is altogether bad. It is a word which could not conceivably be used in a good sense. It describes an ugly thing.

It was this *phthonos* on the part of the Jewish orthodox religious authorities which brought about the crucifixion of Jesus (Matt. 27:18; Mark 15:10). This *phthonos* is the sin of the false teacher (1 Tim. 6:4); it is the sin of the unregenerate and the Christless world (Rom. 1:29; Titus 3:3); the Christian must strip it off and lay it aside for ever (1 Pet. 2:1).

The second word is the word *zelos*. It is the word which is used when it is said that "love knows no envy" (1 Cor. 13:4).

It is the sin which Paul fears may wreck the fellowship of the Corinthian Church (1 Cor. 3:3; 2 Cor. 12:20).

It is the sin which must have no part in the Christian character (Jas. 3:14, 16).

But in this word *zelos*, there is one of the tragedies of the human spirit. *Zelos* is not by any means always a bad word. It can in fact be a noble word. It is the word "zeal" in its Greek dress. It can describe the noble aspiration after the highest, the splendid emulation of a great example, the longing to rise to the heights which have been set before us.

*The tragedy is that noble aspiration can so easily become ignoble envy, that fine emulation can so easily become evil jealousy.*

There is such a narrow dividing line between striving to reach the example someone has set us and envying the person because he is better than we are.

Of all sins there is none so subtle as envy. There is none against which we need to be so continually on our guard.

The tragedy is that even admiration and respect can turn into envy, unless we are for ever watchful.

ENVY (2)                                                    February 6

There are three things about *envy* which we ought to note.

*How much of our criticism of others is due to unconscious envy?*

Sometimes we criticise or belittle or even jeer at someone who is successful. We may criticise the methods of such a man, the theology of such a man, even the character of such a man.

Let a man examine himself, and let him be very sure that his criticism is not born of envy. If he discovers the faintest taint of envy in his heart, let him be silent and let him hold his peace.

*Envy comes from failing to count our own blessings, and failing to realise that there is something which we can do and do supremely well.*

Foch said that the whole secret of war is "to do the best one can with the resources one has".

That is also the secret of life.

Remember what the little squirrel said to the great mountain: "*I* cannot carry forests on my back, but *you* cannot crack a nut."

If we count our blessings, and get on with what we can do, there will be no danger of envy.

*The root cause of envy is the exaltation of the self.*

So long as we think of our own prestige, our own importance, our own reputation, our own rights, we will necessarily be envious.

When we learn to think in terms of responsibilities and not of privileges, when we can learn to live in terms of duties and not of rights, envy will die a natural death.

When we forget ourselves and think of others, then we will think, not of what others have and have not, but of what we have and what others have not.

The desire to share and to serve will put an end to envy.

It is important that we should be clear about the meaning of the word "lust".

In the minds of most people "lust" tends to be almost exclusively identified with bodily and physical sin, with sexual indulgence and immorality. But the word "lust" has a far wider meaning than that.

Lust is the desire for anything which a man has no right to desire. It is the desire for a legitimate thing in an illegitimate way.

Lust is a right desire wrongly used.

*There is a physical lust.*

The basic fault in physical lust and in sexual immorality is that it deliberately uses other persons as a means towards gratifying an entirely selfish desire.

Any relationship between two people, if it is to be a Christian relationship, must be a partnership. Any relationship in which one person does all the taking and another all the giving is essentially wrong.

Any relationship in which one person simply makes use of another person is necessarily wrong.

It is *that* lust seeks to do.

There has been almost from the beginning in Christian thought, a dangerous tendency to think that the body is an evil thing, and to think that, therefore, anything to do with sex is evil.

We see that in the glorification of celibacy, for which there is no real support in the mature teaching of the New Testament.

We see it in the teaching of a heretic like Marcion who said bluntly that marriage is fornication.

We see it in the whole glorification of the monastic and the celibate life in the Roman Catholic Church.

Christopher Hollis, himself a devout Roman Catholic, tells how he heard of an Irish bishop who preached a sermon inveighing against the "damnable passion of love".

There is no justification for that in the teaching of Jesus, for Jesus held that there was no higher and no more binding relationship than marriage and true love (Matt. 19:3-9).

LUST (2)                                            February 8

When does love become *lust*?

Love becomes lust when one person wishes to use another person simply for the gratification of desire. If two people love each other, that love must beget a partnership of body, mind and spirit. It must be a total partnership, in which each partner finds a new completeness in life.

When a person uses another person for no other reason than to gratify one purely physical instinct, then love becomes lust.

*There is spiritual lust.*

Spiritual lust can be seen in what we commonly call ambition, the desire "to get to the top", the desire for power over other people, the desire to use other people for our own personal private ends and purposes.

Here again the fault is exactly the same. In all things our relationship with other people must be partnership. Whenever we wish to make use of them; whenever we try to use them as means towards an end; whenever our aim is to get things out of them rather than to share things with them, then spiritual lust, the desire for the forbidden thing, has entered it.

A man must want to make the best of his gifts. He must want to make the biggest contribution to life that he possibly can. But the basis of that desire must be not selfish, but selfless; not acquisitive but generous; not isolation from men but identity with men.

So long as a man keeps before him the idea of partnership, of fellowship, of sharing, of identifying himself with others, he will be in no danger of either physical or spiritual lust.

GLUTTONY                                           February 9

It was Aristotle who described every virtue as the mean between two extremes. On the one hand there is the extreme of "excess", on the other there is the extreme of "defect", and in between there is "the golden mean", or as we would rather call it, "the happy medium".

The extreme of excess, for example, would be recklessness. The extreme of defect would be cowardice, and the golden mean between would be courage.

The fifth of the deadly sins is gluttony. We can consider gluttony best in relation to Aristotle's golden mean.

In regard to things which satisfy the body, there are three possible attitudes. There is *asceticism*.

Asceticism is the attitude of mind which believes that the body should be deliberately starved and ill-treated, that to eat at all is a bad thing, and that the perfect ideal would be to eliminate food altogether!

This was the attitude of the monks and the hermits of the early Church, when they left the company of men and went out to live in the desert.

H. B. Workman in *The Evolution of the Monastic Ideal* quotes some examples of the way in which the monks and hermits in the Egyptian deserts lived.

Some passed days without food—the trial fast of Paul the Simple, when applying to Anthony that he might join the hermits, lasted four days—while others never partook of food until sunset. In the week before Easter some kept an almost unbroken fast ... Some never drank except upon rare occasions. Adolius, a Syrian monk of Jerusalem, only broke his fast during Lent one day in' five. A Cilician hermit named Conon for thirty years only had one meal a week.

There is a record of a certain Ptolemaeus, who for five years lived on the dew that he collected with a sponge from stones!

The New Testament gives no justification for this.

Jesus was happy to be at a wedding feast, and, when the multitude were hungry, his first thought was to give them food, and food in plenty.

GLUTTONY (2)                                                  February 10

*There is gluttony itself.*

Gluttony is greedy over-indulgence in material food.

In New Testament times a wave of refined gluttony swept over the Roman Empire. That was the time when men sat down to feasts of peacocks' brains and nightingales' tongues; when a certain Roman Emperor succeeded in spending a million and a half pounds on food in eighteen months; when the Romans practised the extraordinary custom of taking emetics between the courses of meals so that they might enjoy the next course better!

Gluttony is eating for eating's sake. It is "living to eat" instead of "eating to live".

The extreme of excess is just that.

*There is enjoyment.*

One of the great sayings in the Bible speaks of God "who giveth us richly all things to enjoy" (1 Tim. 6:17).

The Jews were not given to asceticism and to deliberate starvation. One Rabbi said to a would-be ascetic very wisely: "God will one day call us to account for all good things that we might have enjoyed, and did not enjoy."

Given this *principle of enjoyment* everything falls into place.

It will teach us how to use *all foods and drinks*.

No one can be said to enjoy a thing which has the consequence of making him ill afterwards, or if continual indulgence in it hurts and harms his body, and impairs his physical and mental efficiency.

Enjoyment involves a wise, temperate, disciplined use of all good gifts.

*It will mean that there is sound reason in occasionally abstaining even from good things.*

There is excellent sense in the use of a certain amount of fasting. If we are able to lay aside a pleasure for a time, it means that we have not become dependent on it.

It is always wise to be sure that we are the masters of our appetites and not allow our appetites to be our masters.

The Christian ethic avoids asceticism and gluttony alike, and remembers that God gave us all things richly to *enjoy*.

AVARICE                                                                February 11

There are some sins that have a certain attraction and fascination. A man to the end of the day might have lingering longings that he might indulge in them. But avarice is the least attractive of all sins.

No one would wish to be branded as a man of greed.

No man could possibly envy the life and the character and the mind of the miser.

Avarice, which is the sixth of the seven deadly sins, need not end in a man being a miser, however. Avarice is undue and illegitimate greed for money.

Avarice grows from certain wrong ideas about money and about what money can do.

*It grows from a wrong idea of the meaning of the word enough.*
Enough has been wisely, if cynically, defined as always being a little more than a man has!

The curious thing about money is that however much a man has, he would be perfectly happy and quite all right—so he thinks—if he only had a little more. Often he rises to the "little more", and still he wants a little more!

Epicurus, the Greek philosopher, said something, which shows an infinite knowledge of human nature; "If you wish to make a man happy, add not to his possessions, but take away from his desires." "To whom little is not enough," he said, "nothing is enough."

Let no one underrate the value of money. Poverty is no blessing. Even sorrow, as the proverb has it, is easier to bear when there is a loaf of bread.

But let a man remember that it is the truth of experience that, for him who thinks in terms of money, enough is never achievable.

AVARICE (2)                                                                February 12

*Avarice grows from a wrong idea of the source of happiness.*
However much material things help happiness when it already exists, they do not create happiness.

The Greeks had their famous story of Midas of Phrygia. He loved money, and he asked the gods to give him the gift of turning everything he touched to gold. They gave it to him. It was wonderful. He touched the flowers and they became gold; he touched the ordinary crockery and it became gold.

But then he tried to eat and drink, and no sooner did he touch the food and the drink than it became solid gold. His little daughter ran into the room; before he could stop her she ran and kissed him; and there she stood a little statue of solid gold.

In the end he besought the gods to take the gift away.

*Avarice grows from the idea that money is the source of security.*
People feel that to have plenty of money is to be able to enjoy life and to feel safe.

Jesus told the story of the man whose barns were bursting; who sat back saying to himself, "Eat, drink and be merry"; and whose soul was suddenly required of him, and who had to go on that journey on which none of these things could be taken.

Then Jesus said gently: "A man's life consisteth not in the abundance of the things that he possesses" (Luke 12:13–21).

The strange thing about the sin of avarice and the desire for money is that we think about it, and when we see what it means, we wonder how anyone could be such a fool as to be guilty of it!

Even the best and the wisest of us needs to remember that it is folly to lay up treasure on earth and not to seek to be rich towards God.

SLOTH                                                                    February 13

In modern lists of the seven deadly sins the seventh sin is listed as sloth; but, if we look at the older lists, we will find it described by another name, the name "accidie".

"Accidie" was once a commonly used English word. It was so, for instance, in the time of Chaucer. It has dropped almost completely out of modern usage, and there is no single word which in modern English will exactly give its meaning.

The sin which "accidie" describes may nowadays lack a definite name, but it is still easily recognised, and there are many who will have experienced it.

One of the classic expositions of it is by John Cassian, and he describes "accidie" as it affects the monk and the hermit and the man of God.

"Accidie", he says, describes the frame of mind in which a man comes to dislike the place where he is and to despise the people with whom he associates.

He feels that the place where he now is is a dull and arid place.

He feels that the society in which he now has to mix is without grace and spiritual perception.

He feels everything would be so much better, if he could get into a better place and move against more spiritual people.

He comes to feel that he is not getting anywhere; and he slips into a way of saying that he is no use to anyone and that he would never be missed.

In the end he becomes idle, unable to concentrate on anything. He wanders about looking for someone to talk to, unable to work himself and unwilling to let anyone else work. He grows "wraure", an old English word used by Chaucer which means peevish.

45

It is easy to see what the word "accidie" is describing. It is the attitude of boredom and of *ennui*.

It is the attitude of the man who would tell us that he is, in his own idiom, "fed-up".

It is the attitude of the man who can't be bothered with anything, who, in fact, "couldn't care less".

It is not an attractive attitude.

SLOTH (2)                                                                February 14

"Accidie", or sloth, is much, much worse than just plain laziness.

There *is* a streak of laziness in the most energetic of people. But "accidie" is the attitude of the man who has lost the joy of living and of working and of meeting people, who has even lost the joy of worship and of prayer, and who is bored with life in general so that he feels that there is nothing worth doing and nothing left to live for.

It is a very common and a very modern attitude.

A doctor has said that boredom is the modern illness, and that he believes that medicine will find a cure for cancer long before it will find a cure for boredom.

A Christian may fall into many sins, but it is incredible that a Christian should be bored.

The man who has fallen into this sin of "accidie", this weary hopelessness about life, has forgotten two things.

*He has forgotten why he ever came into this world.*

Every man who ever came into this world was sent into this world by God to do some special task. Every man is, as it has been put, a "dream of God".

That task need not be a task which is great as the world uses the word great. It may be to care for a child, to make someone else happy, to teach someone's mind, to cure someone's body, to bring sunshine into the lives of others across a counter or in an office, to make a home.

As Robert Burns had it:

> To make a happy friendship clime
>     For weans and wife—
> That's the true pathos and sublime
>     Of human life.

46

*He has forgotten where he is going to.*

He is going on. When life ends here, it will begin somewhere else; and all he has got to take with him to that other place is himself.

In this life a man is either fitting himself or unfitting himself for eternity. It is only by being faithful in little that he can one day be entrusted with much.

It may seem a strange thing that the seven deadly sins culminate in the sin of boredom.

It may be that it has never struck us that being bored is a sin at all.

But, when a man remembers his task in this world and his destination in the world to come, boredom can never enter his life.

DEATH IN THE CHURCH                                    February 15

A certain minister was called to a certain church in America. He was warned that the congregation was dead, but nevertheless he regarded the call as a challenge and he decided to accept it.

He soon discovered that the Church *was* dead. No planning, no toil, no exhortation, no urging could kindle a spark of life or waken any response.

He told the congregation that they were dead, and that he proposed to carry out the funeral of the Church.

A day was fixed.

Into the church there was brought a coffin; the church was decked with mourning wreaths.

The time of the "burial service" came.

The church was crowded as it had not been for years.

The minister carried out the "burial service". Then, at the end, as a last token of respect, he invited the congregation to file past the open coffin.

As they did so, they received a shock.

The coffin was open, and empty.

But the bottom of the coffin was not wood, it was glass. It was a mirror. As each man looked into the coffin of the dead Church he saw—his own face.

We often speak of the Church as if the Church was a kind of separate and independent entity, as if there was something called "The Church" which was quite different from ourselves.

But the fact is that *we* are the Church.

The Church is people.

It is its members.

If a congregation is dead, it is because its members are dead.

*Are we giving the Church tolerance or intolerance?*

The Church is full of people who think that there is no way of doing things but *their* way. To change a customary or traditional way of doing things is worse than heresy. But the way of doing things that annoys us may be the way of doing things which brings salvation to someone else's soul!

No one has a total monopoly of the truth or of doing things in the right way.

*Are we giving the Church our prayers or our forgetfulness?*

It is no small gift to uphold your minister's hands in prayer.

It is no small gift to come to the Church service after praying for the Spirit of God to dwell among his worshipping people.

A ministry which is wrapped around in prayer has every chance of being an effective ministry.

If we think our Church is dead, perhaps it is waiting for the life which we can bring to it.

Like most preachers I have in my time rolled out a lot of platitudes, true enough, but not the whole truth!

I have often said that we are never alone. "We have God."

It is only half true.

I have often told the story of the little girl who did not want to be left alone when she was put to bed and wanted someone to sit with her.

"You've got your doll," said her mother. "Your doll will keep you company."

"When I'm lonely," the child replied, "a doll is no good to me. I want someone with skin on her face."

We all do.

God comes to us, in our loneliness, in some human person.

There is a profound truth in the new theology when it says that God is neither up there, nor out there, but God is here in the person to person relationship with other people.

The Christian has therefore few more responsible tasks, and the Church few more fundamental duties, than the task and the duty of seeing that the old and the stranger are not left alone.

For to them, God can and does come in me and in you.

One of the most famous badges and coats of arms in the world is the badge of Achimoto College in West Africa. It was designed and conceived by that great man, Aggrey.

The badge of Achimoto is the picture of part of the keyboard of a piano with its black and its white notes. And the symbolism of it is this: You can extract some kind of tune by playing only on the black notes; and you can extract some kind of tune by playing only on the white notes; but if you are ever to produce a real tune and real harmony, you must use both black and white notes.

Therein lies the truth. But the truth is not easy; and even when the broad principle is accepted, there still remain many problems—such as inter-marriage—which are very far from any real solution.

It is not easy for people who were the leaders of the world and who were conscious of their superiority to learn a new gospel of equality.

There is, in human nature, as there always has been, a suspicion of the stranger. The Greeks considered it part of the very structure of nature that they should hate the "barbarians", that is the non-Greeks.

Homer tells of the wars of the Greeks and the barbarians and Socrates insisted that all Greek boys should read Homer so that enmity might be for ever perpetuated.

In the search for unity, ancient claims and prejudices die hard. Only in Christ are all things and all men gathered into one; and, if the Church does not lead the way in the new crusade for one world in Christ, no one else can.

LOVING AS WELL AS LOVED                                      February 19

Most people don't really want to love; what they want is to be loved; and the two things are quite different.

It is just there that the trouble lies.

Let us look today and tomorrow at some areas where this is true.

*It is true in human relationships.*

We are always looking for someone to whom we can go and to whom we can tell our troubles, someone who will understand us, someone who will be a cloak to us against the cold winds of the world, someone to whom we can talk, someone who will protect us, and help us, and comfort us, and care for us.

We want to be loved.

But we are far less conscious of the duty of making ourselves into the kind of person we want others to be.

We like to go to other people; but when other people come to us do we find them something of a nuisance?

We like to talk to others about our troubles and our problems; but when other people talk to us about theirs, do we classify them as bores?

We like to be surrounded by every care and comfort, but is it a bother to do the things for others we want them to do for us?

If we are honest, most of us will have to admit that we like the privilege of being loved, but are very unwilling to accept the disturbing duty of loving others.

Yet this we must do.

THE RESPONSIBILITY OF LOVE                                    February 20

*It is much the same with us and God.*

Loving and being loved?

We are very anxious that God should love us, but we are very unwilling really to love God ourselves.

One of the most shameful things about most people's religion is that their one idea is to make use of God. They are very eager to get into touch with God when they are in trouble; but when things are going easily and smoothly, God can take a very back seat in their lives.

John Wesley has an entry in his *Journal* which reads like this: "I had much satisfaction in conversing with a woman at Cowes, who was very ill, and very serious in mind. But in a few days she recovered from her sickness—and from her seriousness together."

Why bother about God and the serious things, when you don't need them?

Real love is a dangerous and a disturbing thing.

It awakens a sense of unworthiness.

It lays on us the obligation of selfless and unwearied service.

It brings responsibilities we never had to share before.

It brings its anxieties as well as its joys. And, when people want love, so often what they really want is not to love, but to be loved.

There is, in life, in nearly all of us, an innate selfishness in which we would wish to organise life for our own convenience and for our own comfort.

"God so loved the world that He *gave* . . ."

All true love involves giving as well as receiving. We must examine ourselves in our relationships with our fellow-men and in our relationships with God, lest we have drifted, all unconsciously, into a position in which we desire all the privileges of being loved and in which we refused all the responsibilities of loving.

NO ENTRY!                                                   February 21

It is good to be an adventurer. The world could not do without its adventurers.

But there are some roads which must be marked "No Entry".

It is tempting to play with fire. It is tempting to experiment with experience.

It is tempting to try the forbidden things, just to see what they are like.

But there are some adventures—conscience will tell us what they are— which must not be made. They may not ruin, but they will leave a mark.

Susannah Wesley was one of the great mothers in history.

One day one of her daughters wished to do something which was not altogether bad, but which was not right. When she was told not to do it, she obviously was not convinced.

It was late and she and her mother were sitting beside a dead fire. Her mother said to her: "Pick up that bit of coal." "I don't want to," said the girl. "Go on," said her mother. "The fire's out; it won't burn you." "I know that," said the girl. "I know it won't burn me, but it will blacken my hands." "Exactly," said Susannah Wesley. "That pleasure you want won't burn, but it will blacken. Leave it alone."

By all means let us be adventurers, but let us remember the roads which are marked "No Entry".

Let us listen when the voice of conscience unmistakably says: "Thus far and no farther."


FENCES                                                          February 22

There are fences between the different Churches, so that to this day we cannot come together in common to sit at the table of our Lord.

There are fences between the different theologies and the hatred of theologians for each other has become a byword.

There are fences which divide those who have different views of scripture, so that the so-called "fundamentalist" banishes the so-called "liberal" or "modernist" from the circle of salvation, and the so-called "liberal" or "modernist" regards the "fundamentalist" as a wilfully ignorant obscurantist.

There are fences which divide those who put their faith in different kinds of evangelism, so that the suggestion of any kind of evangelistic campaign is just as likely to split a community as it is to unite it.

We can never properly face the powers of evil when we are split and disintegrated among ourselves.

How shall we overcome these fences?

Let's look at this today, tomorrow and the next day.


*No matter what a man believes we should try to estimate that man at his true worth.*

Surely if a man holds a different kind of theology from that which I myself hold, I can still appreciate that man's intellectual worth, his moral greatness, and his spiritual devotion.


Lockhart in his *Life of Sir Walter Scott* tells how Thomas Campbell the poet and John Leyden had a quarrel and would not speak to each other. Lockhart himself went to Leyden and read to him Campbell's famous poem "Hohenlinden". When Leyden had heard it, he said: "Dash it, man, tell the fellow that I hate him; but, dash him, he has written the finest verses that have been published these fifty years."

Lockhart duly delivered the message to Campbell, and Campbell said: "Tell Leyden that I detest him, but I know the value of his critical approbation."


There is at least hope that the fences will come down, if, even when we differ from a man, we still appreciate his true worth.

*No matter what a man says he believes, we should try to judge the man not by his professed beliefs, but by what he is himself.*

Edwin Muir in his autobiography tells of his experience in Glasgow. He had stomach trouble. His life was a misery. He went to doctor after doctor, and their treatment was quite perfunctory and he was no better.

At last he was recommended to a certain doctor, with the warning that this doctor was a free-thinker. He went to him. He writes:

"He treated me with the utmost courtesy ... His patients were mostly very poor people, whom, I feel sure, he never charged for his advice; he worked in the slums out of pure goodness; he was never discourteous; he treated me as a fashionable practitioner in the West End might treat a rich patient, and in the end charged me some ridiculously small fee, refusing peremptorily to accept more ... He was an excellent doctor and a delightful man, and, in spite of his free-thinking, more like a Christian saint than any other being I have ever known."

If only we would stop sticking labels on people and take men as they are, the fences could come down.

*No matter how wise we are and how convinced we are, we do not possess the whole truth.*

No man has the right to assume that he is right in everything and everybody else is wrong in everything.

On August 3, 1650, Cromwell wrote a letter to the General Assembly of the Church of Scotland, and in it he said: "I beseech you, in the bowels of Christ, think it possible you may be mistaken."

This is not to plead that we should cease to be sure of things ourselves, but it is to plead that we should cease to believe that everyone else is wrong.

One of the greatest things that Paul ever said about Jesus Christ was written when he was thinking of the new unity of Gentile and of Jew in the Christian Church: "He hath broken down the middle wall of partition between us" (Eph. 2:14).

It is in destroying fences, not in erecting them, that true Christianity lies.

One of the great and epic feats of the war was in the breaching of the
Mohne Dam in 1943 by the squadron of eighteen aircraft under the command of Wing-Commander Gibson, who won the Victoria Cross for his
exploit.

This action put the Rhur valley out of commission and did much to hasten
the end of the war.

The aircraft had to dive 2,000 feet, and to fly at exactly 240 miles an hour
exactly sixty feet above the water. Mines had to be dropped so that they just
touched the wall of the dam. It was done; but it was done after two months
of night and day practice and preparation.

No fewer than 2,000 hours were spent in practice.

No fewer than 2,500 practice bombs were dropped.

Eric Linklater who tells this story in his book *The Art of Adventure*, goes
on to ask: "Is it, then, true to say that the art of adventure is a careful and
sufficient preparation for adventure?"

That which looked like a dramatic improvisation of a moment was in fact
the product of weeks of toil.

The great masters knew all about real effort.

Horace advised all authors to keep what they had written beside them for
nine years before they published it—advice which a journalist with a weekly
column can hardly take!

Plato's *Republic* begins with a simple sentence: "I went down to the Piraeus
yesterday with Glaucon, the son of Ariston, that I might offer up prayer to
the goddess." Yet on Plato's own manuscript, in his own handwriting, there
are thirteen different versions of that single sentence. He toiled at the sentence
until every cadence fell on the ear aright.

Thomas Gray's "Elegy" is one of the immortal poems. It was begun in
the summer of 1742; it was finally privately circulated on June 12, 1750.

It took no fewer than eight years to achieve these few immortal stanzas.

In any kind of life there is always the danger of a flabby kind of drifting.

It was A. J. Gossip who taught me practical training for the ministry when

I was a student at Trinity College in the very early 1930s. I have to my great loss forgotten much of what he told us, but one thing has stuck vividly to me. His advice to every minister was: "Put on your outdoor boots or shoes immediately after breakfast."

It was psychologically sound advice.

It is so fatally easy to adopt a slippered attitude to life, and to forget that, as the old Greek Hesiod put it, "In front of virtue the gods immortal have placed sweat."

MY SON, MY SON                                                    February 27

There are two ways in which a man can say, "My son".

Thomas Campbell was one of the greatest of the minor English poets. If he had never written anything else his poem "Ye Mariners of England" would assure him of immortality.

When Campbell's first volume of poems was published, he sent a copy to his father. The old man took it wonderingly and lovingly in his hand. "Who would have thought," he said, "that our Tom would ever have made the like of this?"

Proudly the old man could say, "My son!"

Neil Munro has his saga of stories about Erchie the beadle.*

Erchie and his wife had had a son, but the lad had run away from home to sea and they did not know where he was.

On a Saturday evening, Erchie and his wife would go out for a walk, and somehow their steps always took them down to the docks. And Erchie knew, although nothing was said, that his wife was always looking for the lad who had run away. And Erchie used to say to himself: "I wonder, if the laddie kent what a heartbreak he was to his mother, if he would bide away so long."

Sadly and with a broken heart, Erchie would say, "My son!"

There was a Son of whom God could speak with all joy. At the moment of his baptism the voice of God came to Jesus: "Thou art my beloved son; with thee I am well pleased" (Mark 1:11).

There was a son of whom God could say with pride and joy, "My Son!"

*In Scotland, the church officer who, in addition to looking after many "caretaking" responsibilities, was the man whose special duty was to look after the minister on Sundays particularly. The traditional beadle was often a real character, with great insight!—Ed.

There have, of course, been many attempts to define and to set down the essentials of belief. It so happens that certain things that I have been reading recently reminded me of three of them.

The word "fundamentalist" is a comparatively new word. It was coined in 1920 in an American Baptist periodical. A fundamentalist was, of course, a man who accepted and defended the fundamentals of the Christian faith, and these fundamentals were defined as five beliefs.

They were: (1) the inspiration and infallibility of Holy Scripture; (2) the personal deity of Jesus Christ, and the Virgin Birth as a witness to it; (3) the substitutionary atonement; (4) the physical resurrection of Jesus; (5) his personal coming again.

Ernest W. Bacon, in his biography of Spurgeon, tells how at the opening of the Metropolitan Tabernacle a special series of sermons was preached by eminent divines "in which the five points of Calvinism" were set forth.

The five points were: (1) election; (2) human depravity; (3) particular redemption; (4) effectual calling; (5) the final perseverance of believers in Christ Jesus.

Ernest Bacon himself, later in the book, distinguishes eleven main points in Calvin's preaching and theology.

They are: (1) the divine inspiration and authority of Scripture; (2) the sovereignty of God; (3) predestination and election; (4) the deity of Christ; (5) the substitutionary atonement of Christ; (6) justification by faith alone; (7) the work of the Holy Spirit; (8) holiness; (9) the loveliness of Christ; (10) the final perseverance of the saints; (11) the return of the Lord.

Here is what may be called the demand of strict orthodoxy; and one thing surely stands out with astonishing clarity. There is no mention of the Love of God as being the main foundation of all belief.

This must be wrong!

BACK TO SERENITY                              February 29

There is an old legend which tells that, when the people of Nazareth were hot and bothered and irritated and annoyed, they used to say, when Jesus was a baby: "Let us go and look at Mary's child." Somehow serenity came back.

When little things annoy us, the time has come to look at Jesus, to remember he looks at us.

In his presence is the secret of the quiet mind.

As an old evangelical chorus has it:

> Turn your eyes upon Jesus
> Look full on His wonderful face
> And the cares of earth will go
> strangely dim
> In the light of His glory and grace.

# *March*

"The Church is made up of those who, because they love Jesus, love God and love each other."

I do not think that I have ever heard a better definition of the Church.

*The Church is made up of those who love God.*

Do we really love God?

If we love anyone, that person is the centre of our thoughts and the centre of our lives.

Is God in the very centre of our lives?

Voltaire, as everyone knows, had little use for religion. He was one day walking with a friend when they passed a church.

Voltaire raised his hat as they passed.

"I thought," said the friend, "that you did not believe in God."

"Oh," said Voltaire, "we nod, but we do not speak."

Would it be true to say that very many of us have a nodding acquaintance with God, that God is on the circumference but not in the centre of our lives?

Can we honestly say that *we* love God?

*The Church is made up of those who love each other.*

How do we really feel towards our fellow-men?

Sometimes we despise them. Sometimes we even hate them. Sometimes we tolerate them. Sometimes we respect them and even admire them.

But do we really love them? Have we ever really made a sacrifice for them in all our lives? Would it be true to say that we sometimes even become a little irritated when someone tries to remind us of our responsibility to our fellow-men?

*The Church is made up of those who love God and who love their fellow-men, because they love Jesus.*

The tremendous thing about Jesus is that he does two things.

*He shows us what God is like.*

Before Jesus came, we might have thought that God was distant and remote and unknowable—but not now. Jesus said: "He who has seen me has seen the Father" (John 14:9). We have only to look at Jesus and to say: "God is like that."

*He shows us what a man should be like.*

In Jesus we see true manhood as it ought to be.

It is Jesus who shows us what man is like and what God is like.

Maybe the trouble is that we do not love God enough and we do not love men enough simply because we do not love Jesus enough.

"Man," said McNeile Dixon, "has an affair with the gods and an affair with the mortals." We can get neither of these affairs right until we get right with Jesus Christ.

GO ON! March 3

I was looking for a certain street in London. I had asked where it was and I had been given instructions as to how to get to it. To the best of my ability I followed the instructions, but the place I was looking for seemed very far away.

As I went along one street, I came to a place where the road branched, I went a little way along one fork, and then I decided that I had gone quite far enough and I turned back. At the junction of the roads I had noticed a policeman. He was still there when I came back, and I decided to ask him for instructions.

I told him where I wished to go and asked him where the street was. "Why, sir," he said, "I saw you pass; you were on the right way to it just now; but you turned back too soon."

*You were on the right way, but you turned back too soon.*

That is a good description of the reason for a great deal of failure in life.

The trouble about life is that we so often turn back too soon, that we so often put in one effort too few.

*It is that way with knowledge.*

There is a story about a famous man who was studying when he was a young man, and who was finding it pretty heavy going. He had almost made up his mind that it was all too much for him, and that he would quit. He was idly turning over the pages of his textbook and he was much dejected.

He came to the last leaf, and suddenly on the inside cover of the book he saw pasted a narrow strip of gummed paper. He was curious as to what might be below it, and he stripped it off. When the paper was removed he found himself looking at one short sentence: "Go on, young man, go on!"

He went on and the day came when he arrived at fame. He was on the very edge of turning back too soon—but he went on.

There is hardly anyone who could not make his life a richer thing, if he did not turn back too soon.

Keep thinking!

Go on!

THE CURE FOR DOUBT                                    March 4

*It is that way with thought.*

A certain lady who became a very famous scientist tells how she was started on the path that led to real knowledge.

She was out for a country walk with her father, himself a famous scientist, when she was very young. Quite suddenly he looked down at her, and apropos of nothing at all, said to her: "My dear, never believe anything anyone tells you."

He meant: "Don't accept things at second-hand; don't make your knowledge a carried story; think things out for yourself; and don't be satisfied until you have done so."

The reason why the faith of so many people collapses in the hour of trial is simply that it is not theirs. It is something that they have accepted because someone else said it, not because they have discovered it.

The one thing the Greek hated was the refusal to face the truth. He called it "the lie in the soul".

T. R. Glover wrote: "The Greek would agree with Plato that the lie in the soul was the worst of lies. It is doubtful if the Englishman would allow that; he insists on telling the truth, he has less passion for seeing the truth, he is described as "an adept at self-deception", he loves a dim religious light, cultivates fog and calls it reverence.

The cure for doubt is not to push a thing into the back of the mind and to refuse to think about it.

The cure for doubt is to think a way through the doubts.

We would have a faith that would be more secure if we did not turn back from thinking too soon.

## DON'T TURN BACK! March 5

*It is that way with goodness.*

The great example of this is the Rich Young Ruler. He wanted goodness. He came to Jesus and asked his guidance. Jesus quoted the commandments which are the basis of respectability.

The young man said that he had kept them all. "Well, then," said Jesus, "go and sell all your possessions and give them away." And the young man went away sorrowful, for he had great possessions. If he had honestly put his thoughts into words, he would have said: "I want goodness; but I don't want it as much as all that."

He turned back too soon.

In generosity to others, we so often turn back too soon.

In forgiving others, we so often turn back too soon.

In trying to break ourselves of this or that habit, we so often turn back too soon.

In trying to understand the other man, we so often turn back too soon.

We would be much better than we are but for this fatal habit of turning back too soon.

Jesus Christ wants men and women who will go all the way with him.

The tragedy is that the world is full of men and women who turn back too soon.

## IMMEDIATE RESULTS March 6

John Pollock, in his biography of Billy Graham, tells of an incident from his Harringay (London) Crusade.

At the time of the appeal two men who had been sitting side by side both rose to go forward. As it happened, one was a professional pickpocket. The pickpocket turned to the other man as they began to walk forward and said: "I must give you back your wallet which I took a few minutes ago!"

Here was conversion with immediate results!

When Zacchaeus really encountered Jesus, the first thing he did was to say: "The half of my goods I give to the poor; and, if I have defrauded anyone of anything, I restore it fourfold" (Luke 19:8).

Here again was conversion with immediate results.

When the Philippian gaoler was confronted with the action of God and when he believed, he and all his family were baptised. And then he took and washed the wounds of Paul and Silas, the weals on their back that the lash had left, and took them into his house, and set a meal before them (Acts 16:33, 34).

Here again was conversion with immediate results.

The significance of these stories is the practical character of the results of conversion. The people in question reacted not in a pious way but in a most practical way.

The real tests of conversion are not that a man should start attending prayer meetings and Bible study groups, although he may, of course, well do these things.

The real tests are in life itself.

TESTS OF CONVERSION                                    March 7

There are three obvious tests of conversion.

The first test is, *Does a man pay his debts?*
This is really what Zacchaeus did. He restored at once that which he had fraudulently taken.
It was a feature of the campaigns of both D. L. Moody and Billy Sunday that the first people to reap the practical benefit of the campaigns were the shopkeepers to whom the converts repaid many a long-standing debt.
It is a simple test but a good test that a man's conversion should make him honourably meet his obligations.
A man with a debt that he can pay and does not pay, denies his Christian profession.

The second test is, *Does a man mend all his quarrels?*
Nothing could be blunter than the First Letter of John. "If anyone says, 'I love God,' and hates his brother, he is a liar" (1 John 4:20).

No man is a converted man so long as he has in his life an unhealed quarrel with a fellow-man. Conversion does not relate a man only to God; it also must relate him to his fellow-men. No man is truly at peace with God until he is at peace with his fellow-men.

The teaching of Jesus is clear. A man cannot be forgiven until he forgives (Matt. 6:14, 15; 18:23-35).

If there is bitterness between a man and his fellow-men, that man is not converted.

The third test is, *Does it make a man a better workman?*

Human nature left to itself is both selfish and lazy. It is any man's tendency to do as little as possible and to demand as much as possible.

It is Paul's advice to Timothy: "Do your best to present yourself to God as one approved, a workman who has no need to be ashamed" (2 Tim. 2:15).

The converted man works in such a way that he could present his work to God. He is "ever in his great taskmaster's eye".

A man is not saved by works, but he is saved for works.

ENOUGH? March 8

A young minister I know well is a very good scholar. He told me about his university days when he was in the Arts Faculty. He had done well and he had come to a stage when he had to decide whether or not to take an honours degree in a particular group of subjects. Rightly or wrongly, he decided not to do so. He felt that the wider study of an ordinary degree might serve him better for the work of the ministry than the highly specialised work of an honours degree.

The student went to interview the professor in whose department he might have taken an honours degree and told him of his decision. The professor was clearly disappointed. He looked at the young man and said: "We do still need an educated ministry you know."

Here was a teacher who clearly felt that no qualification was too high for the ministry.

Contrast that with another story which Lewis Cameron tells us in his fascinating autobiography, *Opportunity My Ally*.

In Cameron's time Charles Niven was professor of Natural Philosophy in Aberdeen.

There was a certain student who had done so badly in his class that he was refused the class certificate which a man must have before he can sit his degree examination.

The professor said that he could not give the student the certificate, because he was quite sure that the student did not and would not ever know enough Natural Philosophy to teach it.

"But, sir," said the student, "I am not going to be a teacher."

"And, pray, what are you going to be?" said the professor.

"A minister, sir," said the lad.

The professor took his pen and promptly wrote a certificate. "Take it, boy," he said, "you know quite enough Natural Philosophy to preach the everlasting Gospel!"

In these two stories you have two ideas of education for the ministry.

In the first there is the idea that no educational training can be too high.

In the second you have the idea that, if a man is to preach the gospel, his general education is of secondary importance.

Which is the right view?

There is no doubt that the first view is right.

It is impossible to equip a man too highly for the work of the ministry.

KNOWLEDGE OF FIRE                                      March 9

*The preacher is of necessity a teacher; and the teacher must be equipped to teach.*

If anyone asks him: "What do you mean by that?" he must be able to tell them. The Bible is his textbook, and the Bible was written in foreign languages and in a foreign land many centuries ago.

He who would expound it truly must know something of the situation in which it was first written.

The Holy Spirit helps him who helps himself; and it is when a man brings to the Bible all the intensity of study of which he is capable that the Spirit co-operates with him and opens scripture to him.

*The preacher is a teacher who must teach the same people twice a Sunday over many years.*

Unless he is going to be dully repetitive he must have a wide knowledge of many things.

*It is likely nowadays that the minister will have to teach in a school sometimes not as a member of staff but as the parish minister.*

A dangerous and even disastrous situation arises when he has to confront a group of young people who are far better educated than he is, for no one can teach people unless the people respect him.

The task of the minister was never more difficult than it is today. A complete equipment for it was never more necessary.

Knowledge will not do everything, but when that knowledge becomes what a great evangelist called "Knowledge on Fire", then things really begin to happen.

God's Spirit is looking for minds to use.

The finer the instrument, the more the Spirit can use it.

THE BOAT HOME                                                                    March 10

A Scottish lady who emigrated with her family to America, and who has been very happy in the land of her adoption, has told me of a phrase which has become almost a catch-phrase in her family.

In the early days, when she had first come to America, and before she had settled down, she used to do a good bit of grumbling and regretting. And when she got into one of these moods her husband used always to say to her: "Well, there's a boat home!"

That phrase became a kind of catch-word in that household. The lady herself and her husband in due time had a family; and the children, though never allowed to forget their Scots ancestry, grew up as Americans.

When the daughter of the family was still only a little girl, a British visitor came to the house. This particular visitor was very discourteously criticising American politics in general and President Eisenhower in particular. The small girl could in the end stand it no longer, and she turned to the critical visitor and spoke the family watchword: "Well, if you don't like it, there's a boat home!"

The small girl was ordered at once in disgrace from the table. Later her father told her that he quite agreed with her, but that children did not talk that way to grown-ups. But the child's remark was effective, for the critical visitor criticised no more!

"There's a boat home." In that family what that phrase really meant was: "If you don't like it, leave it!" This is sound advice.

Admittedly, it is not always possible and there are times when we have to stick things out whether we like them or not; but there are equally times when we can, if we wish, take the boat home any time.

If we are for ever grumbling about our job, we would be well advised to get out and get another.

If we are for ever grumbling about our neighbours and the place where we stay, we would be well advised to get out and to stay somewhere else.

If we are for ever criticising some association or club to which we belong, we would be much better to leave it.

## THE HAPPY MARTYRS March 11

There is one area in which I believe what I said yesterday to be specially true.

If we are unhappy in any congregation, then the sooner we leave it the better for everyone concerned.

There are people who criticise the minister and his preaching; who find fault with the worship of the Church; who criticise the choir and the organist; who tell everyone that the minister never visits, that the office-bearers are a poor lot, and that the congregation is stand-offish and unfriendly.

If they feel like that, the remedy is in their own hands. They can leave!

An unhappy and dissatisfied Church member is a bad Church member. He can be a focus of discontent, infecting others with his own dissatisfaction.

It is not a question of being right or wrong about any particular situation. It is not a question of whether the criticism is justified or unjustified. The fact is that, if a man can not worship happily in one congregation, then he is far better to go and find one in which he can find satisfaction.

There are some people who get a good deal of pleasure out of being martyrs. There are some people who would not be happy without a grumble.

That will not do in the Church.

The Church offers us a wide choice. Somewhere within it, we can find the place where we are happy.

## KEEP OUT OF THE KITCHEN! March 12

Some time ago a friend of mine quoted to me a saying which I had not heard before.

We were talking about a mutual friend who not infrequently gets into controversy, but who is himself not very able to stand criticism. In talking of him my friend said: "Well, if you can't stand the heat, you should keep out of the kitchen."

If we can't stand the conditions of anything, we should not undertake to do it.

If we are not prepared to accept the conditions of any kind of work, we should not start that kind of work.

This set me thinking about the conditions we must accept if we are to work with people at all, and especially if we are to enter the ministry of the Church.

*If a man can't keep his temper, he should stay out of the ministry.*

A bad-tempered minister of Jesus Christ is clearly a contradiction in terms. The person presiding over any community or committee will set the tone of it.

If the man at the top is liable to fly into a temper then the whole atmosphere is vitiated. This certainly cannot be Christian.

*If a man can't stand criticism, he should keep out of the ministry.*

All leadership is open to criticism; and any man who proposes to make any kind of performance in public will certainly be criticised.

Of all professions the ministry is most liable to criticism, for the simple reason that people expect a standard from the ministry that they do not expect from any other profession.

It is a compliment to the ministry that such a standard is expected. A big man can accept criticism; he does not want to be surrounded by yes-men. He will realise that very often sensible criticism will save him from many a fault and mistake.

As for the other kind of criticism, the criticism that is malicious, niggling, trouble-making, prejudiced and unjustified, let a man learn to bear it in the confidence that, in the last analysis, the only criticism he need really fear is the criticism which finds an echo in his own conscience.

YOUR OWN MASTER                                                        March 13

There are some more areas in which we should "keep out of the kitchen".

*If a man cannot do routine work, he should keep out of the ministry.*

This may be put in another way. If a man has no self-discipline, the ministry is no job for him.

Most people have to work for a master, an employer, a superior. The minister is his own master. There is no one to make him work but himself.

There is no job in the world in which it is so easy to put things off and to leave things undone and to waste time as it is in the ministry. To be an efficient minister a man has to have the gift of doing the routine work as it comes with complete self-discipline.

If he does not do his work under his own orders, there is no one else to make him do it.

*If a man is looking for quick and visible results, he should keep out of the ministry.*

There are sure to be times when the visible result will come. But for the most part the minister must sow in patience beside the waters of hope and leave the harvest to God. And often it will only be after long years that he has the blessedness of seeing the effect of what he has done.

*If a man is looking for personal prominence, he should keep out of the ministry.*

Too often the attraction of the ministry is the pulpit. The young man's vision is the vision of himself holding some congregation spellbound. In any event by far the most important part of the work of the ministry is done out of the pulpit, and often no one ever hears of it or knows it except the person who is helped. As for the pulpit, the more a man draws attention to himself, the less he draws attention to Jesus Christ.

To make these demands seems almost to demand the impossible, but it has to be remembered that, if God gives a man a task to do, he also gives him the strength to do it.

THE MARKS OF THE CHURCH                                    March 14

Geoffrey Nuttall finds in John Bunyan's thought about the Church four things.

The Church "is (i) *separated from the world* (ii) *as a fellowship of believers which was* (iii) *gathered together in freedom* (iv) *to live a life of holiness*".

*The Church is separated from the world.*

Bunyan writes in his commentary on Genesis: "The work of the Church of God is not to fall in with any sinful fellowship, or to receive into their communion the ungodly world, but to show forth the praises and virtues of him who hath called them out from among such communicants into his marvellous light."

But let it be noted, this separation is not the separation of detachment; it is the separation of involvement. It does not mean that the Church is disengaged from the world, and leaves the world.

Jesus did not pray that God would take his people out of the world, but that God would keep them from the evil of the world (John 17:15).

The difference of the Christian life is to be shown, not by withdrawing from the world, but by living the Christian life in the world.

*The Church is a fellowship of believers.*

In the Bedford church where Bunyan was minister the members, when they became members, "determined to walk together in the fellowship of the Gospel". They jointly first gave themselves to God and then to one another.

In the fellowship of the Church a man commits himself both to God and to his fellow-men.

In the Church we meet God and we meet men.

In the Church it ought to be always possible to find both human and divine friendship, to find the friendship of God and the friendship of men.

*The fellowship of the Church is gathered in freedom.*

It is a voluntary association of men in faith and in holiness. So far did Bunyan go in this direction that he would not even say that Baptism was necessary for entry to the Church.

Nothing which belongs to outward circumstances, nothing "circumstantial", makes any difference.

The only limit of this freedom is the welfare of the fellowship. Professor Greaves quotes Lewis Bayley in *The Practise of Pietie*:

"If justice requireth that one rather unitie must perish, and that a rotten member must be cut off, to save the whole body from putrifying, *fiat Iustitia*, let justice be done."

Freedom there is, but it is freedom within a fellowship.

*Those within the Church are to live a life of holiness.*

Here we are back to the separation idea. The Greek word for "separate" and the Greek word for "holy" are the same. Separation, "difference" is holiness.

Richard Baxter said that the necessary qualification for Church membership is that Christians must be visible saints. And to be a visible saint is to live by "the right and Gospel-pattern".

As Bunyan put it the Church is a fellowship "gathered or constituted by, and walking after the Rule of the Word of God".

There is the ideal of the Church.

Teaching does not consist so much in telling people the right things as it does in asking people the right questions.

"A teacher", J. F. McFadyen once said, "should be an animated question-mark."

Socrates was one of the world's great teachers, and he was one of the world's most famous questioners. He used questions for two purposes. He used them to demonstrate to a man how much the man actually knew without knowing that he knew it.

In the famous dialogue, by question and answer he drew from the slave, who knew no geometry at all, the solution and the proof of the theorem of Pythagoras, that the square on the hypotenuse of a right-angled triangle equals the sum of the squares on the other two sides.

By question after question, the proof was extracted from a person who had no idea that he knew it.

Socrates also used questions to confront a man with himself, to drive the man into a position in which he would be compelled to see his own inconsistency and his own folly.

It was through questions that Socrates taught.

So did Jesus. The great characteristic of the teaching of Jesus, that by which as a teacher he will always be known, is the parable.

The parable is a story which invites a question. At the end of a parable, there always comes the question, spoken or implied: "Well, what do *you* think?"

C. S. Lewis, in *The Great Divorce*, has an odd scene.

A busload of people from the Grey City of Hell are taken to the entrance of heaven. They are offered admission to heaven, but with one exception, they all refuse it.

The people in heaven are the Solid Persons, so radiant and so solid that they make the visitors from hell look like insubstantial shadows. One of the pale ghosts from hell is met by one of the Solid People from heaven. The pale ghost from hell had at one time been the employer of the Solid Person on earth, and the Solid Person had in his time on earth actually committed a murder.

The pale ghost was astonished that he was in hell while the man who had once been his employee and a murderer was in heaven.

"Look at me now," he says. "I gone straight all my life. I don't say I was a religious man and I don't say I had not faults, far from it. But I done my best all my life, see? I done my best by everyone, that's the sort of chap I was.

I never asked for anything that wasn't mine by rights. If I wanted a drink I paid for it and if I took my wages I done my job, see? ... I'm asking for nothing but my rights ... I'm not asking for anyone's bleeding charity." The Solid Person answered: "Then do. At once. Ask for the Bleeding Charity."

Hell is full of people who believe that they never needed anyone or anything, that they were able to live life by themselves.

Heaven is the place for the man who knows his need and who is willing to ask.

## THE SENSE OF NEED                                    March 18

The lack of a sense of need is a strange thing, for life is designed to awaken in us the sense of need.

### We cannot cope with things alone.

The responsibilities of life threaten to crush us; the sorrows of life threaten to submerge us; the anxieties of life bring the failure of nerve; the tasks of life leave us weary and exhausted.

We are, as Abraham Lincoln once said, driven to God because we have nowhere else to go. The very difficulty of life should awaken the sense of need in us.

### We cannot find the way alone.

We have problems to which we can see no solution; we stand at crossroads; we do not know which way to take. We have not the necessary wisdom to take the decision which life demands from us.

We are meant to ask: "Lord, what do you want me to do?"

### We cannot stand the scrutiny of God alone.

No man can stand in the presence of the living God, unashamed and unafraid. We may put up a respectable front to the world. We may be free of the sins for which the law of man can touch us. But it is a different thing to stand in the presence of the God who is "of purer eyes than to behold iniquity."

We have to say: "God be merciful to me, a sinner."

We have to know our need.

Where are you going? That could be the most important question in life.

Where are you going, if you are young? Where are you going in your studies? Are you studying in such a way that you will make yourself the kind of person for whom life will be a series of open doors: or are you studying in such a way that life cannot be anything other than a series of dead-end jobs?

Where are you going in your interests and your hobbies? Are you giving your interest to things which are such that they will last for a lifetime, or are you giving it entirely to things that you are bound to grow out of, and in which there is necessarily a diminishing satisfaction?

Where are you going in your friendships? Are they such as to enrich life, or are they such as to surround life with risk?

It is important to start out in the right direction. When you are young, the question, "Where are you going?" is very important indeed.

IN THE PRIME OF LIFE          March 20

Where are you going, if you are in the middle years?

It is in the middle years that life becomes most strenuous. Before we know what life is like, we are under the delusion that the higher up we get, the easier it is. The opposite is true. The higher up we get, the harder we have to work. It is one of the paradoxical dangers of modern life that a man reaches a maximum position of responsibility when he is slightly past his physical peak, and is therefore not quite so able to support it.

In the middle years the question is whether we are going to go on to kill ourselves, or whether we are going to be wise enough to know when to slacken the tension and lay down the task, at least in part.

Where are you going if you are near the end?

The Christian faith has never any doubt of that. "Good night," wrote F. B. Meyer in one of his last letters, when he knew that the end was near, "I'll see you in the morning."

*Quo vadis?*

C. S. Lewis in his book *The Four Loves* identified three attitudes in love.
There is need-love.
There is gift-love.
There is appreciative love.

In terms of human love, the love of a man for a maid, need-love would say:
"I cannot live without you."
Gift-love would say: "The most important thing in the world for me is to
make her happy."
Appreciative love would rejoice in the existence of the person, and give
thanks for the beauty and the loveliness and the goodness of the person, even
if it was well aware that the person was not for it, and could never be for it.

In terms of God, need-love is driven to God by a sense that it cannot deal
with life without God.
Gift-love finds its joy and its happiness in serving God.
Appreciative love gives thanks and glory to God for his very existence and
for his handiwork in his creation.

NEED-LOVE March 22

Let us look at the three kinds of love we described yesterday.

It is with need-love that most people start.
The cry of the human heart is indeed "I need thee every hour".
"Whom have I in heaven but thee?" says the Psalmist, "there is nothing
on earth that I desire besides thee" (Ps. 73:25).
Lincoln frankly confessed: "I have often been driven to my knees in
prayer, because I had nowhere else to go."

It is characteristic of human beings that they have to be dependent on
someone. The man who is self-sufficient is a very rare creature, and hardly
a normal creature.
Dependence on God is of the very essence of religion.
Dependence on some person is of the very essence of humanity.

GIFT-LOVE March 23

Gift-love is an essential part of love.
The love which thinks only in terms of taking is not true love; love instinctively thinks in terms of giving. It seems to express itself in the gift.

In human love, there is a certain danger in this. There is a kind of human love which is so anxious to give and to protect, that it may in the end create in the person loved an almost complete dependence. It can smother instead of develop the personality of the other.

Love gives in order to strengthen and not to weaken.

Gift-love is love which is well aware that, in God's service, we find our perfect freedom, and, in doing his will, our peace.

For the only gift that any man can bring to God is the gift of himself.

APPRECIATIVE LOVE                                          March 24

There is appreciative love.

In a sense, this is the love which has to be cultivated. Need-love is instinctive; gift-love arises naturally in the heart of any man who has any idea of love at all. But appreciative love is different.

The difference lies in one direction. There is, in human nature, an almost universal tendency to take things for granted.

In human relationships we take the love and the care and the continual service we receive for granted. In divine relationships likewise we take the world and all the gifts of nature for granted.

We take as rights, in our relationships with both men and God, those things which are in fact gifts of grace.

We would do well to think again until we reawaken the sense of debt within our hearts.

The need-love which takes because it must; the gift-love which gives because it can do no other; the appreciative love which consciously remembers and gives thanks—yes, we need them all.

GOOD LOVELINESS                                           March 25

Ibsen makes Julian utter a criticism of the Christians.

Julian was the Roman Emperor who wished to put the clock back and to bring back the pagan gods. "Have you looked at those Christians closely? Hollow-eyed, pale-cheeked, flat-breasted all; they brood their lives away, unspurred by ambition; the sun shines for them but they do not see it; the earth offers them its fullness but they desire it not; all their desire is to renounce and suffer, that they may come to die."

There are Christians who are morally without a fault, but they are curiously unlovely. You could never put your head on their shoulders and sob out a sorry story. If you did, you would freeze to death.

In the Greek of the New Testament, there are two words for "good". There is *agathos*, and *agathos* simply describes the moral quality of a thing as good.

There is *kalos*, and *kalos* means not only "good" but also "winsome" and "attractive".

In *kalos* there is always *loveliness*, and it is *kalos* which the New Testament uses again and again to describe the Christian goodness.

In real Christianity there is always a winsome attractiveness.

This is a lovely thing.

J. P. Struthers of Greenock used to insist that it would do the Church more good than anything else if only Christians every now and again would do "a bonnie thing".

Struthers lived in a manse which was at the end of a road which led up to the hills behind Greenock, a road which in the evening lovers used to walk. Struthers used to pick the flowers from his garden and make them into little posies, which he laid along the wall in front of his house; and the lads knew that he had left them there for them to pick up and to give to their girls as they passed.

That is why all men loved Struthers, because he was always doing things like that.


It is told that once a woman came to Henry Drummond to ask him to visit her husband who was dying. Drummond said that of course he would come.

But he asked the woman why she had asked him when he had never even seen the husband and did not know the dying man at all.

"O, sir," she said, "I would like him to have a breath of you about him before he died."

Drummond was not much of a scientist and maybe he was still less of a theologian, but Drummond had a sheen and radiance on him that made men want him with them.


Jesus loved the world.

He played with children when he was on the way to Jerusalem to die.

He was happy at a wedding feast.

76

The outcast men and women who were sinners did not cross the street to avoid him; he was their friend.

Someone has defined a saint as "someone in whom Christ lives again".

And we never show men Christ until we make goodness a winsome and a lovely thing.

## SLEEP TALKING March 27

It is very difficult to define just what is a work of genius.

One of the queerest and the best of definitions of great poetry was that of the great classical scholar and poet, A. E. Housman. He said that his criterion of first-rate poetry was that it caused a contraction in the pit of the stomach.

In his commentary on Hebrews, James Moffatt, speaking of the appeal of Jesus, uses the phrase "the grip in the throat".

Most people have at one time or another had the experience of listening to some great piece of music which gave them a queer shiver up and down their spine, or reading a story, or listening to a sermon and suddenly finding a mist before their eyes, or listening to some great performance in such a way that they literally drew their breath and relaxed when it was over.

There is a truth in all this. It is the truth that we get at man much more deeply and much more really through their hearts and their emotions than through their minds and their intellects.

This is just one of the notes that are missing in so much modern preaching and so much modern theology.

Rhadakrishnan, the great Indian thinker, once said: "Your theologians seem to me like men who are talking in their sleep."

J. S. Whale talks about running round the burning bush taking photographs from suitable angles instead of taking off our shoes from our feet because the place whereon we stand is holy ground.

He talks of theologians who put their pipes in their mouths and stick their feet up on the mantelpiece and talk about theories of the atonement instead of bowing down before the wounds of Christ.

## REAL URGENT JOY March 28

If we are to win men there are certain notes that we must regain.

*We must regain the note of reality.*

The preaching and the teaching that matter are the preaching and teaching which come from a man to whom his subject obviously matters.

A great philosopher once said that no man need try to teach unless he has a philosophy of his own or of someone else's which with all the intensity of his being he wishes to propagate.

Have we been too apologetic, too polite in our presentation of the truth?

*We must regain the note of urgency.*

Richard Baxter wrote:

> I preach'd as never sure to preach again,
> And as a dying man to dying men!

It was Bunyan who heard the voice: "Wilt thou leave thy sins and go to heaven or wilt thou have thy sins and go to hell?" After all, it is not only something desirable with which we are presenting men; it is something essential, something which is a choice between life and death.

*We must regain the note of joy.*

Bunyan's conversion was begun when he heard the old women sitting in the sun talking about what God had done for their souls, and "Methinks that it was joy that made them speak."

It was the joy of the Moravians which showed Wesley what he lacked.

The man who would bring others to Christ must offer men Christ with the reality of utter conviction, with the urgency of one who insists that men should choose between life and death, and with the joy of one who has made the greatest discovery in all the world.

OUR TOMORROW                                                    March 29

I once saw by the roadside an advertisement for a well-known and well-tried patent medicine. It ran like this:

*"How you feel tomorrow depends a lot on today."*

That is one of the great practical rules of life with a threat and a challenge in it at one and the same time.

Our tomorrows must of necessity depend a great deal on our todays.

*Our future depends on how we use our memories today.*

The psychologists tell us that the golden age of memory is from the years seven to eleven.

Ignatius Loyola well knew that when he uttered his famous dictum that if you gave him a child for seven years he did not care who got him afterwards.

The psychologists dauntingly go the length of telling us that it is impossible to learn anything new after we are forty.

It may or may not be impossible; it is certainly difficult.

We should be storing our memories as early and as soon as we can. And we should be storing them with the right things.

But on the other side, Bishop Hans Lilje tells how in the days of the war he was imprisoned in solitary confinement by the Hitler government. Everything was taken from him, and in those days he found his strength and retained his sanity by going over and over the psalms and hymns that he had memorised when he was a boy.

There was a time quite recently—fortunately we are emerging from it—when it was considered bad educational practice to press the claims of memory work at all.

If we store our memories in time, we shall have treasures to draw on when we need them most, and we shall have defence to call on in the day of temptation.

THE OPEN MIND                                                            March 30

*Our future depends on how we use our minds today.*

In this world there is nothing easier to acquire than a shut mind.

I was standing in the entrance hall of our College one day talking to two theologians. The one was a young man with a questing and a seeking mind; the other was an old man of the most rigid conservatism, some might say, obscurantism.

The older man asked the younger man what he was lecturing on at the time; and the younger man replied that he was in the midst of a course on the modern theologians, Barth and Brunner, Buber and all the rest of them.

The older man looked down from his great height and said with a certain contempt for all things new: "The old is better."

Many a young minister's heart has been near to broken by the battle cry of so many churches: "We never did that here before."

A man must keep his mind open. That is not to say that he should change his principles like a theological weather-cock; but it is to say that we should be learning to the end of the day.

Sclerosis of the arteries can kill a man's body and sclerosis of the mind can kill his intellect and atrophy his soul.

NO MAN IS AN ISLAND                                                      March 31

Somewhere Bryan Green tells of an incident in America. He had conducted a campaign there over a period; and at the end of the campaign there was a meeting where people were asked to say in one or two sentences what that campaign had done for them. One by one they bore their witness and their testimony.

Then a Negro girl rose; she was not much of a speaker; she could hardly put the words together to make a sentence of public speech; and she said: "Through this campaign I found Jesus Christ and Jesus Christ made me able to forgive the man who murdered my father."

*Jesus Christ made me able to forgive.*

John Donne said in his "Devotions": "No man is an Island, entire of itself."

But life can so easily become a sea in which we live as islands separated by the gulfs of our misunderstandings.

It is only Jesus Christ who can reconcile us to God—and in the end to one another.

# *April*

It is often said that it is impossible to bear something for someone else.
Is that true?

In Jocelyn Gibb's *Light on C. S. Lewis*, Nevill Coghill tells a story C. S.
Lewis once told him.

Lewis married late in life. In his marriage he found the very perfection of
love, but too soon the wife he loved so much died of cancer.

Once when Lewis was with Coghill he looked across the quadrangle at
his wife. "I never expected," he said, "to have in my sixties the happiness
that passed me by in my twenties."

"It was then," writes Nevill Coghill, "that he told me of having been
allowed to accept her pain."

"You mean," said Coghill, "that the pain left her, and that you felt it for
her in your body?"

"Yes," said C. S. Lewis, "in my legs. It was crippling. But it relieved hers."

The Beatitude says: "Blessed are the merciful." The Hebrew word for
mercy is *chesedh*.

In his commentary on Matthew, T. H. Robinson writes of this word:
"*Chesedh* is the perfection of that mystical relation of one personality to
another which is the highest of all possible grades of friendship. It means a
systematic appreciation of other persons, the power, not merely to concentrate
blindly on them, but to feel deliberately with them, to see life from their
point of view."

It is involvement so complete that it issues in self-identification with the
other person.

It was this involvement and this self-identification that God accepted in Jesus Christ in the Incarnation. Matthew (8:17) quotes Isaiah 53:4: "This was to fulfil what was spoken by the prophet Isaiah: 'He took our infirmities and bore our diseases.'"

There is a real sense in which Jesus Christ bore and endured the sin and the suffering of the human situation; and those who are his followers must be like him.

THE SPIRITUAL LIFE                                                     April 2

The discipline of the working life will be nothing without the discipline of the spiritual life.

W. B. Yeats spoke of "the exhausting contemplation. No man can face the tasks of life without a background of the discipline of the life of the spirit".

This sounds difficult and demanding—and so it is. But we do well to remember David.

David wished for ground on which to erect an altar. He went to Araunah the Jebusite to buy the ground, and Araunah offered him it for nothing.

David answered: "I will surely buy it of thee at a price; neither will I offer burnt-offerings unto the Lord my God of that which cost me nothing" (2 Sam. 24:18–25).

Not a little of our failure comes from the fact that we seek to offer to men and to God that which cost us, either nothing, or far too little.

OPEN THE WINDOW!                                                     April 3

In Jane Austen's novel *Emma*, there is a sentence which may well serve as a text.

Mr. Churchill has just suggested that a window should be opened and the polite Mr. Woodhouse objects. "Open the windows!" he expostulates. "But, surely Mr. Churchill, nobody would think of opening the window at Randalls. Nobody could be so imprudent."

There are quite a lot of places in which people don't want the windows opened.

One of them is the Church!

The late W. M. Macgregor quotes the saying of the good bishop in Victor Hugo's *Les Miserables*: "I always bothered some of them, for through me the outside air came at them; my presence in their company made them feel as if a door had been left open, and there was a draught."

There are many things in the Church which could do with a breath of fresh air.

*We should let the wind blow on our Church services.*
We retain the ancient pattern which may be all right for the person who is brought up in the Church but is largely irrelevant for anyone who comes in for the first time.

The lack of adventure in the presentation of the gospel is one of the causes of the falling numbers who go to Church.

*We should let the wind blow on the Scriptures.*
It is time that the *Authorised Version* was laid honourably aside for the unparalleled work of literature that it is, and the new versions brought in for all teaching purposes and for all the public services of the Church.

We listen to Scripture, not for the beauty of the sound of it and not for its English style, but for what it says.

Unless Scripture is contemporary, it is nothing.

LET THE FRESH AIR IN!                                                    April 4

Open the window and let the fresh air in, we said yesterday.

*We should let the wind blow on our liturgy.*
There are few things which do more to remove reality from the services of the Church than the archaic irrelevance of so much of the liturgy. If a form of worship has been used for centuries, that is one very likely reason why it is irrelevant for today.

The true liturgist is not the man who worships the past, but the man who never forgets the pattern of worship, and who insists that he must offer to God the best language of today.

Prayer in the twentieth century is a twentieth-century man talking to God. The twentieth-century man does not normally speak Elizabethan English.

*We should let the wind blow on our sacraments.*
One of the most distressing facts in my own Church, the Church of Scotland, is that the sacrament of the Lord's Supper is attended by more members of the Church than any other service is, and that, at the same time, hardly anyone knows what is going on. The devaluation of this sacrament has been very sad.

God preserve us from a Church where it is imprudent to open the windows.

The Church ought to be a body of people living eagerly and vividly in the present and not a holy and antiquarian huddle of people whose spiritual home is in some centuries ago.

BY MANY ...                                                                       April 5

There are two interesting and significant incidents in Lewis Cameron's autobiography, *Opportunity My Ally*.

While Lewis Cameron was still a lecturer in Agriculture in Leeds, he was on holiday in Aberdeen. Friends invited him and the lady who was to be his wife to come to the evening service in Holborn United Free Church at which Dr. A. W. Scuddamore Forbes of the West Parish Church of St. Nicholas was to preach.

In a church which could seat a thousand people there were about forty people present.

Dr. Forbes preached on the text: "Jonah rose up to flee unto Tarshish from the presence of the Lord" (Jonah 1:3). Suddenly Dr. Forbes laid aside his manuscript and said: "Why are all these pews empty? The people like Jonah have fled from the presence of the Lord refusing to face his challenge. Why are our Divinity Halls empty? Young men are more concerned about their own material advantages and selfish pleasures than with the advancement of the Kingdom of God!"

In that moment something happened to Lewis Cameron, and he decided to enter the ministry.

A congregation of forty in a church seating a thousand—but at that service one man's life was changed.

OR BY FEW                                                                         April 6

One Sunday evening in January 1946 Lewis Cameron whom I mentioned yesterday set off from Edinburgh for St. Luke's Church, Milngavie. It was snowing hard. It was doubtful if he would get through and he only did get through by following a snow plough.

When he did get to the church it was to discover that the heating system had broken down and that there was only a handful of people in a building that was only a few degrees above freezing-point. He was to speak on the Social Service of his Church, and it seemed hardly worthwhile.

The next morning he received a phone call from a Glasgow lawyer who was one of the trustees in charge of a certain trust; and the upshot was that as a consequence of a sermon to a handful of people in a freezing church on a snowy January night the Church of Scotland received £104,226 for its social work.

A handful of people—but a tremendous result.

Numbers are not everything. It can be in the smallest congregation that the biggest things happen.

If that is so, a man should do his utmost and his best no matter whether his audience or congregation be a dozen or a thousand or ten thousand.

As Jonathan said: "Nothing can hinder the Lord from saving by many or by few" (1 Sam. 14:6).

The action of the Spirit of God is not dictated by numbers.

Few or many, God is there and God can act.

IT WORKS! April 7

I have just been hearing about a small boy whose father is a minister, and who is also exceedingly interested—as indeed all sensible people are—in railway engines (I am!).

It so happened that where he lived a new church was being built. He and his father were train-spotting one day, and a magnificent new engine appeared.

The father pointed out to the boy—I am not quite sure that the figures are accurate but that does not affect the point—that the engine had cost about £60,000 to build. And said his father: "That's as much as the new church cost."

The boy thought for a minute and said: "Well, I would rather have the engine. I think that it's worth the money far more than the church."

"How do you make that out?" his father asked him.

"Well," said the boy, "the engine works!"

The acid test of anything is "Does it work?" Or, as Jesus put it: "You will know them by their fruits" (Matt. 7:20).

DO THESE WORK? April 8

*The test of a theology is "Does it work?"*

Does a theology teach men what to believe or, as it has been put, does it teach them what to disbelieve?

Does it send men out to the market-place to live and to serve, or does it lock them up in a study or a class-room, interested more in theories than in people?

Is it involved in life, or is it divorced from life?

Is it communicable to the ordinary man, or is it the esoteric mystery of the intellectual élite?

### The test of a Church is "Does it work?"

Does a Church send its members out into the community to live for God and to live for men, or does it gather them in an isolated community of unworldly so-called holiness?

Does it raise barriers, or does it destroy barriers?

Does it unite Christians, or does it separate Christians?

Does it send out people whose lives are like lights in a dark place (Phil. 2:15), or does it send out people whose lives repel rather than attract either by their careless laxity or their self-righteous rigidity?

### The test of a profession is "Does it work?"

One of the best and the most notable things in modern evangelism—it has, in fact, always been a characteristic of evangelism rather than of the Church—is the opportunity for decision. But the test of a man's profession is not his willingness to stand up and declare for Jesus Christ in a meeting.

If we really want to know whether a man has made a true decision and a true profession, then the people to ask (as I am never tired of saying) are his wife, his children, his employer, or the community in which he lives.

PLAYING SAFE                                                    April 9

Thales, the Greek wise man, once said: "Suretyship is the fore-runner of ruin."

That is to say, it is always dangerous to go bail for a man; it is also a risk to sponsor a man; it is always perilous to stand guarantor for someone in some time of need.

Strangely enough, this is a saying which finds a close parallel in the Old Testament. In Proverbs, we read: "He that is surety for a stranger shall smart for it; and he that hateth suretyship is sure" (Prov. 11:15).

This is a saying which advises a very cautious and prudential approach to life. It advises against standing guarantor for any man, for to do so is to court nothing but trouble.

There is a sense in which this can be true. It is far from being necessarily true; but it *can* be true.

Shakespeare has it:

> Neither a borrower nor a lender be;
> For loan oft loses both itself and friend,
> And borrowing dulls the edge of husbandry.

To stand surety for a man is much the same as to lend him what he needs, and it is quite true that such an action often splits rather than cements friendship.

No one likes anyone to whom he is always conscious of being under an obligation, especially if that obligation is, as it were, for ever held over his head.

The art of giving is a difficult and delicate art.

In such a matter it is utterly essential not to let the right hand know what the left hand has done.

It is always necessary to be "giving and to forget the gift".

BE GENEROUS!                                                                April 10

But what I said in our last entry, is not what Thales meant. Thales simply meant that to stand surety for any man, to stand sponsor for any man, to guarantee any man's honour and honesty is, in nine cases out of ten, to be let down.

Even if this were true—and thank God it is not true—this would be very far from the Christian view of life.

In the Old Testament the duty of generosity is laid upon men.

In the fifteenth chapter of Deuteronomy, it is laid down that every seventh year in Israel should be a year of release, when debts are cancelled and wiped out.

It is quite obvious that, as the seventh year drew near, many a prudent and cautious man would be very unwilling to lend anything to anyone, in case the borrower took advantage of the year of release and deliberately never paid the debt. But even then the law is that, if at such a time a poor man in need comes and asks for help, the heart must not be hardened and the hand must not be shut, but the hand must be opened and he must be given sufficient for his need (Deut. 15:1-11).

The Christian ideal is a generosity which does not count the cost. Jesus said: "Give to him that asketh thee, and from him that would borrow of thee turn not thou away" (Matt. 5:42).

The cautious man of the world, as Thales advised, would only give, and only stand surety, if he was quite certain that he would lose nothing and would get his money back in full, and, if possible, with interest.

The Christian duty is to give generously, even when there is every chance that there will be no return.

### THE RISK OF THE OPEN HAND                                    April 11

Christian teaching is that it is better to be generous than cautious, that it is better to take the chance of being swindled than to risk turning away empty one who is genuinely and honestly in need.

Why should that be so?

It is the reverse of what the world reckons as wisdom and sense.

It is so because that is precisely what Jesus does for us.

On one occasion the very word "surety" is used of Jesus (Heb. 7:22). When Jesus came to this world, and when he died for me, he took the risk of whether or not the hearts of men would respond to this colossal act of love.

When God so loved the world that he gave his Son for men, he risked everything on the response of men.

The love of God did not forbear to give lest it should be the loser.

God gave and God did not count the cost; Jesus loved and kept nothing back.

Let the world stick to its prudential maxims.

The Christian must accept the risk of the generous heart and the open hand, even as God in Christ accepted it.

### THREE LAWS                                                   April 12

To the Athenians, Solon was the supreme lawgiver.

He was to the Athenians what Moses was to the Jews.

He came to power when the state of Athens was steadily degenerating, and by drastic measures he reconstituted the city. The rich had become richer and more powerful, because by lending money they had succeeded in concentrating all wealth in the hands of the few, and had reduced the ordinary people to a state not far from serfdom.

Solon took the bold step of cancelling all debts. He made it illegal for any man to give his own body as surety for his debt.

Many poor Athenians had given themselves as security for their debts; when the time for payment came, and they were not able to pay, this meant that they themselves passed into the hands of the money-lender, and so were sold as slaves.

This practice Solon forbade.

Solon laid down three unique laws.

He enacted that, *in any time of dispute within the nation, the man who took neither side should be disfranchised and should lose his rights as a citizen.*

When great issues were at stake, Solon regarded neutrality as a crime.

Solon declared that *men must speak no evil of the dead.*

He laid it down that, *if a father did not teach his son a trade, then the father had no right to claim support from his son in his old age.*

There is no doubt that Solon was one of the great creative lawgivers of the world.

Solon's experience of life, and Solon's wisdom were crystallised in the wisest of all sayings: "Know thyself."

To Solon the most important thing of all was self knowledge.

Solon was profoundly right.

Nothing is more necessary than that a man should know himself.

OUR WEAKNESS AND OUR STRENGTH                                   April 13

*We must know our own weakness.*

If we know our own weakness, we will go far to being saved from two things.

*We will be saved from temptation.*

If a man knows his own weakness, he will know the situations which he must avoid.

If a man has a weakness for too much liquor, he will be a very foolish man if he frequents inns and taverns.

If a man has a passion for gambling, he will be most ill-advised to frequent places and company where he will be tempted to gamble.

If a man knows that certain things make him lose his temper, he will do well to avoid them.

If we know our own weakness, and wisely remember it, half the battle with temptation will be won.

*We will be saved from frustration.*

To know our own weakness will protect us from desiring or undertaking that which is not for us.

Many a man would have been much happier in life, if he had been satisfied with a job he could do, and had not attempted a job that was beyond his powers, and which could bring nothing but worry and defeat.

*We must also know our own strength.*

Too much self-distrust is quite as bad as too much self-confidence. What the world loses because people will not accept responsibilities of which they are quite capable is incalculable.

The municipalities, the state, the trade unions, and above all the Church all lose services which would be invaluable, because those who are well able to render such services refuse to do so.

Often the refusal to accept office springs from a genuine feeling of unworthiness, but far too often it springs from laziness and from unwillingness to make the effort.

GROW! April 14

*We must find a way to know ourselves.*

The only way to know ourselves is to have a standard with which to compare ourselves, and thus to see our own weakness.

We have that standard in Jesus Christ.

To see ourselves and to see life in the light of Christ is to see ourselves as we are, however painful that experience may be.

*It is a duty to know ourselves but it is equally necessary to realise that no man need stay as he is.*

When we know ourselves, we will realise our own weakness and inadequacy; but for our inadequacy there remains the strength that is made perfect in our weakness (2 Cor. 12:9).

The Christian can know himself through Christ, and through Christ he can also know how that self of his can be made new.

He can grow in grace and in the likeness of Christ.

MY FATHER'S SON April 15

I received a letter from America. It was from a man who had read something which I had written, and who had noticed my name. He wrote to ask if I was the son of W. D. Barclay of Motherwell in Lanarkshire, Scotland, who had been a bank manager in Motherwell, and who had preached the gospel in many churches there.

It so happens that I am. For seventeen years we lived in Motherwell when I was a boy. My father was a banker by profession, but at heart he was a preacher, and his name was known as a preacher all over Lanarkshire.

It is a quarter of a century since he died, but there are many places, especially in Lanarkshire, and indeed all over Scotland, where I am still my father's son.

I thank God for this, for to few lads can there ever have been granted to have had a father and mother such as I had.

"Let us now praise famous men," sang the Son of Sirach, "and the fathers that begat us" (Ecclesiasticus 44:1).

GOOD PARENTS                                                    April 16

There are few greater gifts in this world than the gift of godly parents.

Heine, the German philosopher, once said that a man could not be too careful in the choice of his parents!

It is not given to us to choose them, but, when God has blessed us with them, he has given us a gift for which no gratitude can be too much.

J. M. Barrie said that when you looked into his mother's eyes you knew why God had sent her into the world—to open the eyes of others to all lovely things.

G. K. Chesterton used to tell how, when he was a boy, he had a toy theatre with cardboard characters. One of the characters was the figure of a man with a golden key. He had long since forgotten what character the cardboard figure actually stood for, but always he connected the man with the golden key with his father, because his father unlocked all kinds of wonderful things to him.

We should be grateful for our parents.

A GOOD FATHER                                                  April 17

There is a double duty laid upon us in relation to our parents.

*There is the duty of honouring our parents while we still have them.*
Barrie wrote after his mother's death: "Everything I could do for her in

this life I have done since I was a boy; I look back through the years and I cannot see the smallest thing left undone."

There are few—very few—who would venture to make a claim like that. But to be able to make it is something that all should aim at.

*There is also the duty of seeking to be parents on whom our own children will look back with gratitude and with joy.*

In our generation that is both easier and harder than it was for a previous generation.

The relationship between parent and child is very different from that which existed even thirty years ago. It is much easier, much less distant, much freer, much less restrained and much less constrained.

The advantage of this is that it makes friendship with our children much easier. The disadvantage is that it makes discipline, when it is necessary, much more difficult. But somehow the parent must solve the problem of being at one and the same time the partner and the guide of his child.

There is laid on the parent, too, a heavy responsibility. It is by the name "Father" that we address God; and the only way in which a child can put meaning and content into the word "father" is from what he learns of its meaning from his own father.

It is one of the grimmest commentaries on fatherhood that Luther could hardly bring himself to pray the Lord's Prayer and to say, "Our Father", because of the sternness, the strictness and even the cruelty of his own father.

Joseph of Nazareth, of whom we know so little, and who is so much in the background of the gospel story, must have been a wonderful father, when Jesus so naturally and so simply gave the name "Father" to God.

THE CURSE OF COLD WATER                                    April 18

An American professor called Ilion T. Jones quotes a saying of that great American preacher, Clovis G. Chappell: "No man has a right so to preach as to send his hearers away on flat tyres. Every discouraging sermon is a wicked sermon . . . A discouraged man is not an asset but a liability."

Professor Jones also quotes an entry from the diary of Robert Louis Stevenson.

After a visit to church, Stevenson wrote in his diary: "I have been to church today and am not depressed." A church service which was not depressing was to him such an unusual phenomenon that it deserved a special entry in his diary.

There could hardly be a more un-Christian way of living than to go about in such a way as to depress and to discourage other people.

In the Royal Navy there is a regulation that no officer shall speak discouragingly to any other officer in the discharge of his duties.

In the Senior Service discouragement is forbidden. Yet the world is full of discouragers.

*There are those who discourage every great plan and every great dream.*

There are the experts in the pouring of cold water on other people's visions. There are so many people, in the Church especially, whose favourite adjective is "hopeless" and whose watchword is "impossible".

It is far better to fail in some great attempt than not to try anything at all. If we do try to do something it is amazing what can happen.

No man knows what might happen in the Church and in the world, if people would only stop pouring so much cold water.

CRITICISE IN LOVE!                                              April 19

*There are those whose one ability in life is to find fault.*

They have eyes which are focused to find fault, and tongues which are tuned to criticise.

The strange thing is that they consistently concentrate on what a man has not done, and forget everything that he has done. If on any occasion he has made a mistake, they never forget it, and they never allow him to forget it either.

No one in his senses should resent criticism.

Professor Jones, whom I referred to yesterday, reminds us that "during his first few years in London, Spurgeon received a weekly letter from an anonymous critic, listing the young preacher's faults. In later years Spurgeon thanked God for his self-appointed critic, and regretted that he could not express appreciation to him in person. His criticisms were invaluable, and made a distinct contribution to Spurgeon's speaking effectiveness."

The aim of criticism should always be to encourage a man to do better. The last thing that criticism should ever do is so to discourage a man that he has not the heart to try again at all.

Criticise by all means—but criticise in love.

*There are those who hit a man when he is down.*

When I was a boy I had a personal experience. In those days I played cricket.

There was one season when nothing would go right. J. M. Barrie once said in one of his cricket speeches: "The first time I saw Bradman bat he made one; the next time I saw him he was not so successful."

I had had three successive weeks when I was not so successful, and I was discouraged. There was a wise and old cricketer in charge of the team. The next week I was surprised to see my name on the team list at all, because I had expected to be dropped.

The afternoon of the game came; the list of the batting order was put up. I went to look at it, fully expecting to see myself lowered in the batting order to the tail of the team, as a series of noughts deserved. Lo and behold I discovered from the list that that wise old captain had moved me up to number one to open the innings.

He *was* wise! I squared my shoulders and went out and made up for at least some of the noughts—and it was encouragement that did it.

When a man has been a failure, then is the time, not to discourage, but to encourage him.

"Be of good cheer," said Jesus (John 16:33).

Keep your heart up, said Jesus. That is what we should always say to our fellow-men.

DIFFERENT PARABLES April 21

If Jesus had lived and taught in the twentieth century he would have constructed and told very different parables.

They would have been about shop-assistants, and typists and secretaries and garage mechanics and engineers.

He started from the here and now in A.D. 28 and he would start from the here and now in 1969.

No translation can do anything about this.

It is not the words that are strange, it is the whole world in which the thing moves.

It is usually the case that, to understand a gospel parable properly, we need instruction in Palestinian manners and customs. I wonder if there should not be an attempt, not to rewrite the Bible, but to re-express the Bible in terms of 1969, especially with children.

I am quite sure Jesus would have remade his own stories. Should we not have such a vivid doctrine of the Holy Spirit that we should seek the guidance and the help of the Holy Spirit to enable us to re-express the eternal and the unchanging truth for the child of today?

And for the adult too.

LETTING THE SIDE DOWN                                           April 22

I had the privilege once of listening to an address on the evangelism which was being planned and carried out in a certain English diocese. The address was given by a man who clearly had a fire in his bones.

In his address he told us, with sorrow, a story which is tragic from the point of view of the Christian Church.

In a certain town, which is the main town of the diocese, the civic authorities decided to begin youth club work.

When this was known, the Christian Council of the town sent the diocesan missioner to interview the civic authorities to ask if the Churches might be allowed into these youth clubs to give a certain amount of Christian instruction or at least to hold epilogues in them at the end of the evenings.

The answer of the civic authorities was "No", but they were prepared to hand the whole business of the youth clubs over to the Church lock, stock and barrel to run. If the Churches would run the clubs, the civic authorities would give finance and accommodation and every possible backing.

The missioner returned to the Christian Council thrilled. As he said himself, the whole youth work of the area had been handed to the Church on a plate!

All that was wanted now was volunteers and leaders to come forward and to seize this magnificent opportunity. But when an appeal was made, not one person came forward to help.

The offer of the civic authorities had to be regretfully declined.

The Church had lost an opportunity which was never likely to recur.

Christians so often let the side down. Yet, strange as it may seem, God is helpless without us.

If God wants a child taught, he must get a man or woman to teach that child.

If God wants the youth of a town evangelised, he must get Christian people to carry out that evangelism.

God must have his tools, his instruments, his fellow-labourers.
God needs YOU!


A CHANCE LOST                                                    April 23

In his book *Then and Now*, John Foster tells of an amazing historical instance of this Christian failure.

In 1271 Pope Gregory the Tenth received a request from Kublai Khan, the ruler of the Mongols, the widest Empire in the East the world has ever seen. Kublai Khan sent Nicolo and Maffeo Polo as his ambassadors to the Pope.

His message ran: "You shall go to your High Priest and shall pray him on our behalf to send me a hundred men skilled in your religion ... and so I shall be baptised, and, when I shall be baptised, all my barons and great men will be baptised, and then their subjects will receive baptism, and so there will be more Christians here than in your parts."

The whole East was being offered to Christ. Yet the Pope did nothing. In 1289 Pope Nicholas the Fourth did send missionaries, but they were far too late and far too few and the chance was lost.

What a difference it would have made if all China and the East had been gathered in to Christ. How different history and world politics would be today.

But when God needed them, men let God down.

Paul said: "We are labourers together with God" (1 Cor. 3:9).
The question is: Are we?
Or are *we*, too, letting the side down?


IN THE SKY                                                      April 24

Wordsworth in the famous "Ode, Intimations of Immortality", wrote about the glory that has passed from the earth.

> Heaven lies around us in our infancy!
> Shades of the prison-house begin to close
> Upon the growing boy.

In youth the lad is attended by the vision splendid, but then:

> At length the man perceives it die away,
> And fade into the light of common day.

Why the change?

There are so many who never get past the childhood stage of when God is in the sky. But if God remains "in the sky" for ever, then we lose him, because he would not be much use there anyway.

The God "up there" is a pretty irrelevant God.

If we would keep the presence of God real and vital and living, God must come out of the sky into the world—which is just what he did in Jesus.

"The Word became flesh and lived amongst us" (John 1:14).

As Tennyson put it:

> Speak to Him thou for He hears, and Spirit with Spirit can meet—
> Closer is He than breathing, and nearer than hands and feet.

Yes, he is.

## TRENDS IN EDUCATION

There can be a certain pessimism about education.

One of George Bernard Shaw's characters says cynically: "He who can, does; he who cannot, teaches." He implies that the teaching profession is staffed by those who failed in every other.

That is not true today, for there are probably more dedicated people in the teaching profession than in any other.

That very famous teacher Thomas Arnold of Rugby once said: "My object will be if possible to form Christian men, for Christian boys I can hardly hope to make."

Just as the first saying was a slander on teachers, the second is a slander on pupils, for it is one of the facts about teaching today that young people are greatly interested in religion, if not committed to it.

But there are certain wrong trends in education.

*Education must never be indoctrination.*

With characteristic violence of expression, Shaw makes one of his characters say: "The vilest abortionist is he who attempts to mould a child's character."

It is true that the teacher's task is to teach the child to think, not to teach him what to think.

To stimulate the young person to do his own thinking is the task of the teacher—which, of course, is not to say that certain foundations have not still to be laid.


## MEMORY TESTS April 26

*Education can be over-factual.*

Mr. Brown tells us of Dickens's Mr. McChoakumchild in *Hard Times* whose one aim was to implant facts, facts, facts, and who put imagination high among the deadly sins.

Of course, there are basic facts which are needed for the business of life, but a fact does not become important until it is appropriated in a situation.

The vision must be trained as well as the memory.

*There is, too, a kind of education which is almost entirely memorisation.*

Shaw speaks with violence about this kind of education which, he says, can be acquired "by any blockhead who has a good memory, and who has been broken in to school drudgery". "These memory tests," he goes on to say, "only enable teachers and scholars to be certified as proficient when they should have been certified as mentally defective."

There is a kind of examination whose sole purpose is to provide an opportunity for the person taught to write down exactly what he has heard. But as Epictetus said: "Sheep do not vomit up the grass to show the shepherd how much they have eaten. They turn it into wool."

Real knowledge does not consist so much in remembering everything as in knowing where to find the right answer.


## HABIT April 27

A friend of mine told me recently about an experience one of his friends had in Canada. It happened in the far north, and it happened at that time of year when the whole country was covered in snow.

Some men had gone out for a walk. Their way took them through a wood which was carpeted in snow and where every tree was like a Christmas tree.

One of the company was smoking a cigarette. He finished it and then he threw it on to the ground, but with the greatest possible care he crushed it with his foot until every last and smallest spark was finally extinguished.

The visitor to Canada looked on in astonishment. "Look," he said, "why on earth did you go to such trouble to extinguish your cigarette? The whole place is covered in snow. It could not possibly set anything alight. Why all this care?"

The Canadian said: "It's like this. If I came out here in the summer-time and I dropped a lighted cigarette the chances are I would cause a disastrous forest fire. And therefore I have deliberately habituated myself never to drop a cigarette end anywhere without making quite certain that it is totally extinguished. And now," he said, "I do it completely automatically."

This man had taught himself a saving habit.

## MANY WAYS                                          April 28

Clyde S. Kilby in *The Christian World of C. S. Lewis* tells of the first stage in the conversion of C. S. Lewis.

"It seemed to Lewis that God was as surely after him as a cat searching for a mouse."

He then quotes Lewis's own words: "You must picture me alone in that room in Magdalen, night after night, feeling, whenever my mind lifted for even a second from my work, the steady, unrelenting approach of Him whom I so earnestly desired not to meet. That which I greatly feared had at last come upon me." As he knelt down in prayer and admitted that God was God he felt himself in his own words "the most dejected and reluctant convert in all England".

C. S. Lewis's experience did not end there, but that was certainly the beginning.

Sometimes conversion is unwilling submission by people fighting to the last ditch against it. In this case, it was a glorious liberation and emancipation, come all unexpectedly to one who was never thinking of it.

There is no "standard" way of being converted.

It is the fault of certain kinds of evangelism that it has in its mind a pattern which the conversion process ought to follow.

There is no such pattern.

It may come through the unwilling surrender of C. S. Lewis, or through the joyous splendour of revelation which came to Saul Kane.

We must not force the grace of God into one mould.
God works in many ways.

## LESSONS FROM ANOTHER GENERATION                    April 29

A book entitled *Richard Wilton, a forgotten Victorian*, was written by Mary Blamire Young, his great-grand-daughter, on the basis of family letters and memories.

Clergymen of the olden days can teach us something!

True, they had no insistent telephone calls, no constant committee meetings, no evening organisations. But in the day of these clergymen of a century ago three things stand out.

*They did not forget to study.*

Richard Wilton's day begins with his spell at his commentary—and by the time that letter was written he was an old man. Study was always an integral part of his day.

There runs through both letters *a great pastoral concern*. These men shared the simple lives and the simple needs of their people. The schoolchildren are taught, the gardener's allotment is admired, the woman who coughed in church must be helped. The minister is the pastor.

And maybe most significant of all, these old men of God had time for their own families, to teach their own children and to have time for their own wife. They were not so busy keeping the vineyards of others that they neglected their own.

Whatever progress there had been, that pattern of the ministry, now more than a century old, still stands for good.

NO DESPAIR                                                                April 30

The Church must surely be the one institution which *cannot* know despair.

*In the Christian faith there is hope for the world.*

It is possible to look at the world and to feel that men are possessed by a kind of suicidal insanity which cannot end in anything other than a disintegrated chaos. But as Bengt Sundkler tells us in his new biography of Nathan Soderblom, Soderblom used to say often: "The only remedy is to give the commonwealth of nations a Christian soul, because without that soul it is a dead body and with a non-Christian soul it is a beast or a devil."

Christ has the remedy for the human situation.

The application of that remedy is the business of the Church.

*In the Christian faith there is hope for men.*

Time and again I have quoted that sermon title in one of Fosdick's volumes: *No man need stay the way he is.* Often a person will defend himself or herself by saying: "I can't help it. I'm made that way. That's my nature. I can't change myself." That is the final heresy.

True, a man can't change himself. But if Christ cannot change him, then the whole claim of Christianity is a lie.

*But if the Church is to change the world and to change men and women, it must be changed itself.*

The more one sees of the Church, the more one senses a deep-down attitude of defeat. There are so many people in the Church who have simply accepted the situation. Diminishing and ageing congregations, an increasing irrelevance in the eyes of the common man—there are many who are well aware of these things, but they have simply accepted them as things about which there is nothing to be done.

Of course, the situation will not change without blood and sweat and tears on our part. But a Church which has accepted the situation is a Church which is on the way to death.

God give us, not the defeatism which accepts things as they are, but the divine discontent which in the life and the strength of Jesus Christ will battle to change them.

EVERYMAN'S EASTER                                    Easter Day

John Masefield in "The Everlasting Mercy" tells of the conversion of the drunken reprobate, Saul Kane. The moment came when Saul Kane was a changed man with one life behind him and another in front of him. He has just left the drinking-place in which he had so often been drunk; but something has happened.

> The bolted door had broken in
> I knew that I had done with sin.

Then he goes on to speak of what the world was like in that moment of change:

> The station brook, to my new eyes,
> Was babbling out of Paradise;
> The waters rushing from the rain
> Were singing Christ has risen again
> I thought all earthly creatures knelt
> From rapture of the joy I felt.

The narrow station-wall's brick ledge
The wild hop withering in the hedge,
The lights in huntsman's upper storey
Were parts of an eternal glory,
Were God's eternal garden flowers.
I stood in bliss at this for hours.

It is a description of the sheer joy of the finding of the life which is new.

It is the meaning of resurrection.
It is everyman's Easter.

# *May*

I have by chance discovered the origin of a well-known phrase.

In Cambridge the name "Hobson" recurs.

There is a Hobson Street.

There is a Hobson's Conduit, which used to stand in the centre of the market-place and which is now in Trumpington Street.

This Hobson kept a livery stable in Cambridge in the seventeenth century. If you came to him to hire a horse, it was his unbreakable rule that you took the one next to the door—or you got none at all.

It is from this Hobson and his insistence that, without choice, you took the horse next to the door that there comes the phrase "Hobson's choice".

When we are confronted with Hobson's choice, it simply means that we are confronted with a situation in which there are no alternatives, and when we have to accept what is there.


Life quite often confronts us with a choice which is Hobson's choice.

It may happen that through force of circumstances we are left with no alternative.

Illness may leave us with no choice as to the kind of work that we have to do.

It may be that misfortune and lack of money leave us with no choice as to what it is possible for us to have.

It may be that a disappointment leaves us with no choice as to what we must go on doing.

It may be that the action of others closes doors that might have been open to us.

In such a situation—and it comes to everyone—the great secret and the great virtue is to accept what we have and to get on with the job.

The world is full of people who, because they did not get what they want, have become soured and embittered and querulous and sometimes even obstructive of others who have what they think *they* should have.

The Stoics had a saying which sounds merciless but which is true. "If you can't get what you want, want what you can get."

It is a good rule for life.

## "HERE I STAND!" May 2

It sometimes happens that a man has no choice from the point of view of principle. In this case the compulsion does not come from outside him, but from inside him. It is not, so to speak, physically impossible for him to do anything else, but it is morally impossible.

He is in the situation of Martin Luther who was compelled by inner compulsion to say: "Here I stand; I can do no other; so help me God."

The world and society and politics and the Church need men who feel that moral compulsion and who will abide by it, because they find it impossible to do anything else. We need men who cannot be bought, and who will prove that it is a lie to say that "every man has his price". We need men who cannot be seduced. We need men who cannot be frightened out of doing the thing which the moral imperative demands.

We must of course avoid confusing stubbornness with principle. It is true that this compelling principle does not operate very often in life. But when it does come, then the real man is the man who realises that he has no moral alternative. He must obey.

Hobson's choice!

When circumstances force it upon us, we must accept it, not doubting that there is opportunity and challenge in what is left as much as there was in what is taken away.

When a moral issue confronts us with it, we must choose the way of conscience and of principle and refuse to leave it.

## GRASP THAT OPPORTUNITY! May 3

I have re-read a book which was once immensely popular, but which has begun to be considered out of date. I am quite sure that it deserves to be widely rediscovered. The book is T. R. Glover's *The Jesus of History*.

Glover has some very interesting things to say about the parables of Jesus, and, in particular, about the twin parables of the treasure hidden in the field and the pearl of great price (Matt. 13:44–46).

In these two parables Glover sees four things which are of the very essence of achievement in the Christian life.

They begin with the recognition of an opportunity.

The men who found the treasure and the pearl saw at once that this was literally the opportunity of a lifetime.

There are few greater gifts than the ability to see the opportunity when it comes. The same situation can come to two men. One will see it as a disaster and the other as an opportunity; one will see it as something about which nothing can be done, the other will see it as an inspiring challenge to action.

There is the famous story about the army which suddenly fell into an ambush set by its enemies. One commander said to the General: "Alas, we have fallen into the hands of the enemy." The General answered: "Why not say that they have fallen into ours?"

The Christian sees every situation as an opportunity and a challenge.

THE PRICE                                                                      May 4

The two parables go on to a resolution. Immediately the opportunity presented itself, the men involved took their decision to grasp it. There was no delay and no dither.

The opportunity emerged; the opportunity was grasped.

Both men were prepared to pay the price of grasping the opportunity. They sold all that they had to buy the field and the pearl. They were prepared to pay the price of turning the opportunity into reality.

Life gives nothing for nothing. There are still many who turn sadly away (Matt. 19:22), because they will not pay the price the opportunity demands.

The price will always be toil; the price may sometimes be sacrifice; but the price has to be paid.

But when the opportunity is recognised, when the decision is taken, when the price is paid, then the end is joy.

The treasure and the pearl were possessed.

In the parables, the end was success. But even if, in the end, there is no success, there is more joy in attempting something great and failing in it than in not attempting it at all.

To try and to fail is better than not to try at all.

In *The Jesus of History*, T. R. Glover discusses the triumph of Christianity in the ancient world.

It was a highly improbable triumph. How did it happen that a small group of simple and unlettered men could go out into the world with the story of a crucified Jewish criminal and persuade men and women to take that Jesus as saviour and Lord?

Glover's answer is that the Christians were enabled by the grace of God to do three things—they out-lived, they out-died, and they out-thought the pagan world.

*They out-lived the world.*

Why were they able to do this? Because they could say of Jesus: "He loved me and he gave himself for me" (Gal. 2:20). Every man had acquired a new dignity and a new worth because he could say that for him, as a person, the Son of God had died.

Further, he believed that the Son of God had loved and given himself for all men. He had therefore a motive for service that no one else had.

He was eager to help the man for whom Christ died. He had a motive of forgiveness such as no one else had. However unpleasant that other man might be, Jesus Christ had died for him.

He had a motive for purity such as no one else had. He could look at a prostitute—"the victim of the common lust" as Tertullian called her—and he could know that even for her Christ had died. And therefore he must treat her as the daughter of God and the beloved of Jesus Christ.

Once a man could say "he loved me and gave himself for me", and once he knew that that was true of everyone including himself, life could become a "new creation".

*The Christians out-died the world.*

It was this that won Tertullian, the famous Roman lawyer. He saw the Christians die, and it shook him to the depths of his being. "Every man," he said, "who sees it is moved with some misgiving, and is set on fire to learn the reason; he enquires and he is taught; and when he has learned the truth he instantly follows it himself."

When simple men and women could choose to die like that, and to die in agony, there must be something in that for which they died.

### The Christians out-thought the world.

The ancient world was credulous and superstitious. The Christian was clear-sighted and fearless.

Lucian tells how he saw on heathen shrines the notice: "Christians keep out." The Christian saw too clearly through the mumbo-jumbo.

In the ancient world the way to destroy your enemy was to attach his name to a demon and the demon would kill him. "Go on," said the Christian, "attach my name to a demon. I don't care. I have a name which is above every name to keep me safe."

The Christian thought fearlessly and clearly. The number of heresies shows the freedom and the vigour with which the Christian thought. He had a freedom of thought and speech that no one else had ever had.

If we are to persuade the world that Christianity is worthwhile, the way of the early Christians is the only way. We have to out-live the world in service, in charity, in purity and in joy.

We have to out-die the world in that we show the world that we are still prepared to pay the price of being a Christian.

We have to out-think the world, not clinging to the old ways and the old words, but ever ready for the adventure of thought in whatever age we live.

CONTINUING THE STORY                                                    May 7

The gauge of railway lines in Britain, that is the distance between the lines, is four feet eight and a half inches.

The old Great Western Railway tried to break away from this and to use a seven-feet gauge, but it was in the end, in spite of the struggle of Brunel, its great engineer, compelled to come 'into line'.

Four feet eight and a half inches seems a very odd distance indeed. How did it come about?

There is more than one explanation of it, but I have just come across an explanation which is very interesting.

The first railway lines were laid, not for steam engines to run on, but for carts to be hauled over them by horses. A horse could haul a much heavier load if the cart or waggon ran on rails rather than on a road.

The first rails were therefore laid on wooden boards which had themselves been laid on the top of the ruts which waggons and cart-wheels had already made on the roads.

The rails were laid to fit the ruts which were already there.

But this only pushes the question one step farther back. Why were the cart ruts four feet eight and a half inches in gauge?

It is to explain this that a very interesting suggestion has been made. It has been said that the gauge, the distance between the wheels, of a Roman chariot was four feet eight and a half inches, and that it was that which started the whole thing.

Centuries ago the Roman chariots left their ruts on the roads; carts and waggons were built to the same gauge. In due time the rails were laid to that gauge too.

If that is so, there is a direct connection between the Roman chariot and the great modern trains thundering to London sometimes at a hundred miles an hour.

There is a direct continuity between them.

This is true in all spheres.

There is a direct connection between the first coracle to float on the water and those great historic ships like the Queen Mary and the Queen Elizabeth, the Cunarder Queens.

There is a direct connection between the first tree trunk that was flung across a stream to make a bridge and the new Tay Bridge.

It is all a continuing story.

A DEBT TO THE PAST                                                    May 8

The "continuing story" has certain implications.

*We must remember the fact of continuity.*

The present necessarily grows out of the past. No age stands isolated and alone. It stands upon the foundation of all that went before.

That is why the Christian Church can never jettison the Old Testament. Without the Old Testament to go before, there could not have been a New Testament at all.

The continuity must be remembered.

*This puts us in debt to the past.*

We are where we are today in the ladder of progress because of those who went before. No age has to start from scratch. It starts from where previous ages have brought the world and it starts with what they have handed down and handed on.

There is an inevitable debt to the past that has to be recognised.

But this also puts us in obligation to the future. To the future we will be in the past, and the future will be helped or harmed by what we hand down. Each generation is a link in a chain, inseparably attached to what has gone before and to what will come after.

"Others have laboured, and you have entered into their labour," Jesus said to his disciples (John 4:38).

We have entered into the labours of others.

Some day, others will enter into our labours.

THE GOLFER                                                          May 9

Where we holiday there are two golf courses. One is a good course, the kind of course that you could play a championship on. The other is a course for the very young and the very old and the very inefficient.

Needless to say, nowadays I play on the second of the two courses!

The great feature of the second course is that it hasn't got an inch of rough on it all the way round. Everywhere the grass is cut and short and smooth. So what happens is that you stand on the tee and you hit the ball something like two hundred yards into the middle distance. But, if the ball goes off in the direction of mid-off or mid-on, if it is sliced or pulled or hooked, you don't worry. You know that it will be sitting pretty on the nice, short, green grass, and that you will have no difficulty finding it and no difficulty with your second shot.

You do not, therefore, ever have any real bother getting your four or, at worst, your five, and you get the impression that you are pretty good!

I had been playing all my holiday on the course with no rough, the course on which I could belt the ball without worrying where it landed and I was saying to myself when it was time to go home: "I'm not so bad yet. I can still play." But very soon after we came home, I had a job to do in a town where there are some first-class golf courses. I decided to take my clubs and to have a game when I had finished my work.

I hadn't played three holes when I discovered that on a course, a real course, where there was a fairway flanked by two stretches of deep rough, you couldn't belt the ball two hundred yards away in the direction of mid-off or mid-on (to use cricket terms again!) without getting into serious trouble. If you weren't straight, you were in trouble all the time. And I wasn't straight.

So, as a golfer I was found out.

This goes for life too!

If things are too easy, you won't cope with the real test when it comes.

It is never wise to make things too easy for anyone. If you make things too easy for a person, you just unfit him to face the real test. It is never wise to make the task of a child or of a student too easy. It only leads to trouble in the long run.

This is one reason why the standards of any profession or craft should remain as high as they can be kept. This is one reason why any kind of dilution should be most carefully controlled. Make things too easy and there is certainly trouble ahead.

It is never wise to encourage the idea that you can make mistakes and escape punishment. My easy golf course made me forget that on a real course mistakes are punished. I had to learn all over again that you can't make mistakes and get away with it.

It is no kindness to people, especially when they are in training, to encourage them to think that they can get away with anything. Failure to apply the necessary discipline simply unfits a man for the necessary tests of real life.

If we are wise, we will be constantly on our guard against the peril of wanting things too easy or of making things too easy.

After all, Scripture has it: "Blessed is the man whom thou dost chasten, O Lord" (Ps. 94:12), and, "The Lord disciplines him whom he loves" (Heb. 12:6).

## THE WAY OF FAITH May 11

I want to look at some of the things that Bunyan said about faith.

*Faith, said Bunyan "cannot sit still; faith is forcible".*

Faith, he said, "is a principle of life by which a Christian lives . . . a principle of motion by which the soul walks forward towards heaven in the way of holiness. It is also a principle of strength, by which the soul opposeth its lust, the Devil and this world, and overcomes them."

Faith is far more than mere intellectual assent to something. Faith is that which drives a man to action; it is that which compels a man to believe so intensely in something that he has to do something about it.

*Faith is that which makes the gospel message "contemporaneous".*

For the man who has faith, the story of Jesus is not something which happened in the past; it is something which is happening now.

"Faith," said Luther, "taketh hold of Christ, and hath him present, and holdeth him enclosed, as the ring doth the precious stone."

Through faith Jesus Christ lives in the here and now.

*Faith is fixed on Jesus Christ.*

Luther called faith "a certaine stedfast beholding, which looketh upon nothing else but Christ".

Thomas Goodwin said that faith is the resting of the heart on Christ "nakedly and alone, for life and salvation".

As the Westminster Confession put it, it is "accepting, receiving and resting upon Christ alone".

Our knowledge of God, and our trust in God, come from the fact that we believe that what Jesus says about God is true.

A "PRACTICAL AFFIANCE"                                         May 12

Faith, as defined by Richard Baxter, includes three things.

*Faith is the assent of the intellect.*

There is an intellectual element in faith. If we cannot in honesty and with conviction and with reason believe in the existence of God and in the historical reality of Jesus, there can be no such thing as faith.

The mind and the intelligence do enter into faith.

*Faith is the consent of the will.*

Faith must go beyond the mere assent to certain facts.

The devils, as James says (2:19), believe in God but they still remain devils.

Faith must proceed to action in light of the facts. Faith believes, and then turns belief into action.

*Faith, as Baxter says, is a "practical affiance", trusting Christ as Saviour.*

By a "practical affiance", Baxter means a trust which is not theoretical, but which has its effect upon life. Faith is taking Jesus at his word, and believing that he meant what he said, and that his promises are true and his commands binding.

The more we study faith, the greater it becomes.

Here are two areas in which trust may fail—according to the Bible.

The biblical writers saw *the futility of force and power.* "Not in my bow do I trust," says the Psalmist, "nor can my sword save me" (Ps. 44:6).

The prophet warns the people that the fortified cities in which they trust will be destroyed (Jer. 5:17); and one of the main lines of the prophets is the futility of foreign alliances to beget any real security.

The biblical writers insist on the futility of any human trust. "Cursed is the man who trusts in man," says Jeremiah, "and makes flesh his arm" (Jer. 17:5). "Put not your trust in princes," says the Psalmist, "in a son of man in whom there is no help" (Ps. 146:3).

Human help in any event can go thus far and no farther.

On the other hand the whole Bible is full of the joyful voices of men who trusted in God and who were not confounded. "To thee they cried, and were saved," says the Psalmist, "in thee they trusted and were not disappointed" (Ps. 22:5). The trust that will never be disappointed is the trust in God.

This is not to say that the man who trusts in God will live a protected, trouble-free, sorrow-free life; but it is to say that the man who trusts in God will find the strength to meet any situation, however tragic and however terrible, and to come through it still erect and still master of his fate.

Trust in God, not simply for protection, but for that unconquerable strength to meet all that life can do to us.

FRIEND

May 14

I myself was an only child, but my wife is one of five sisters. I therefore have a charming assortment of nephews and nieces and grand-nephews and grand-nieces!

In 1968 my wife was across in Canada with Jane, our daughter, to visit a sister of hers who lives and works there. Naturally many photographs were taken. In 1969 my wife's sister was across in Scotland visiting her own family and us. Naturally, the photographs were on show.

They were being shown to Julie, one of our grand-nieces, then just about three years old, who lives very near us and who knows Jane well. When Julie saw the photograph of Jane and my wife, she said: "Look! That's Jane and her friend!"

Mother and daughter—mother and friend.
How wonderful!


THE GAP                                          May 15

It would be wonderful if parents could indeed always be called the friends
of their children. There is so often a strange and almost unbridgeable gap
between parents and children so that they are almost strangers to each other.

There are reasons for that gap.

*There is the inevitable gap between the generations.*
I repeat here the story of May Sinclair, the author, who, as I told in the
last book of this kind,* said to her little girl that, when she was a little girl,
there were certain things that she was not allowed to do. "But you must
remember, Mummie," the little girl said, "you were then and I'm now."

Of course, there is the gap between the then and the now. Parents do not
bridge that gap by being determinedly "with it".
There is, in fact, nothing more embarrassing than, in the old phrase—
"mutton trying to look like lamb!"
Gap there is, but each generation must be itself.

Age trying to behave like youth is worse than youth aping age.

We must begin by being ourselves.


A FRIEND INDEED!                                 May 16

There is, so far as the so-called generation gap is concerned, the gap
produced by the whole concept of authority.
No one likes the feeling of being subject to authority. There was a time
when a child had to obey, and, if he asked why, he was told by the parent,
"because I said so".
Nothing but trouble can emerge from an attitude like that. There must
always be sympathy; there must always be a genuine attempt to understand
the other point of view, and there must always be communication.
A person is much more likely to obey, if he knows the reason why he is
being asked to do a thing.

*Through the Year with William Barclay* (Hodder and Stoughton, London, 1971).

The parent who is a dictator is simply insulting his child's intelligence and personality by demanding a blind and unreasoning obedience.

The parent who is a guide and a counsellor in the business of life is at least treating the child as a person—and that is the first essential.

If a parent is to be a friend to his child, there must be communication.

The tragedy of modern family life is that so very often parents and children drift so far apart from each other that in the end they cannot even make conversation. They have nothing to say to each other.

This is the situation which must not arise; and that it should not arise is the responsibility of the parent.

Happy is the child whose parents are not only his parents, but also his friends.

THE LANGUAGE OF DOUBT                                    May 17

I remember some years ago speaking to a man who stands very high in international Y.M.C.A. affairs. He is not English, but he speaks English so well that he would pass for an Englishman anywhere.

In the course of our talk, I asked him how many languages he spoke. He told me that he spoke Swedish—his native language—English, French, German and Spanish.

He not only spoke these languages conversationally. He spoke them well enough to make public speeches in them.

We may never acquire a grasp of foreign languages like that, but, if we are going to help people, there are certain languages which we need to be able to speak.

For example, the language of doubt.

It is very difficult for a man who has never experienced a twinge of doubt to talk to a man whose mind and heart are tortured by questions.

It was said of someone that he had "skirted the howling deserts of doubt". And a wise man, commenting on that, said that he would have been much better to go through them and come out at the other side.

A faith is not the highest kind of faith until it has been tested.

We should never be ashamed of having doubts. They are the way to real certainty. Only the man who has had them and faced them can help others.

Tennyson said, rightly, that there is often more faith in honest doubt than in the unthinking acceptance of a conventional creed.

A friend sent me some advice that John Wycliffe laid down for Bible study.

Wycliffe said: "It will greatly help ye to understand the Scripture, if thou shalt mark, not only what is written, but by whom, and to whom, with what words, at what time, where, to what intent, with what circumstances, considering what goeth before and what followeth."

Some centuries later F. J. A. Hort in his introduction to his unfinished commentary on First Peter was to write: "To understand a book rightly, we want to know who wrote it, for what readers it was written, for what purposes, and under what circumstances."

This is valuable advice.

It simply means that we can never fully understand a book unless we understand something of the circumstances in which it was written, and of the person who wrote it; and we can never fully interpret a passage unless we take it with what comes after, that is, within its context.

To realise this, begins to make the Bible understood.

It makes a difference to know *who* wrote particular words in the Bible.

"My grace is sufficient for you" (2 Cor. 12:9).

If someone had written that on whom the wind had never been allowed to blow; if it had been written by a man who had never known want or poverty or pain or toil, we might justly question its validity. But when we know that it was written by a man with a pain like a stake twisting in his body, and with a record of adventure that reads like an epic (2 Cor. 11:23–28), then it really means something.

It gains its value from the man who said it.

It makes a difference to know *to whom* particular words were written.

In 1 Cor. 6:9–11 Paul makes a list of all the most blatant sinners and then writes: "And such were some of you," but now they are as cleansed as they were once polluted, he goes on.

The people to whom that was written lived in Corinth, notoriously and admittedly the most immoral city in the ancient world, the city out of bounds to Roman soldiers on leave because it was so dangerous, the city with the Temple of Aphrodite whose thousand priestesses were sacred prostitutes and who every night plied their trade in the streets of Corinth.

If you were to say that the grace of God is operative in some respectable, god-fearing area, it would indeed be something. But if this can be said of a sink of iniquity like Corinth, then this is the trumpet call of moral victory.

WHERE AND WHEN                                                    May 20

It makes a difference to know *where* particular words have been written.

The John who writes the Revelation begins his vision, "I was on the isle called Patmos" (Rev. 1:9).

Patmos was a little island to which criminals were sent to work in chain gangs in the quarries. It was therefore in a convict settlement in a chain gang on a prison island that there came to John one of the greatest visions that ever came to the mind of any man.

Even in such a place as that, a man can see the glory of God.

It makes a difference to know *when* particular words were written.

"Fear God," Peter writes, "honour the Emperor" (1 Pet. 2:17). It might seem taken by itself an ordinary enough injunction. But who was the Emperor in question?

If we are right in believing that this letter is from the lips of the apostle Peter himself, then the Emperor in question is none other than Nero.

It is then the duty of a Christian to be a good citizen, not only at times when it is easy to be so, and when everything is in his favour, but also at a time when it is difficult for anyone to be a good citizen and when the state is hostile and cruel.

The more we know about Scripture, the greater the message of Scripture becomes.

SYMPATHY                                                          May 21

There is more than one reaction to pain and anguish.

*Some people run away from it.*

There are people who are frightened of sickness, who can hardly bear to enter a sick-room. In the presence of pain and illness and trouble, their one desire is to get away from it and to keep away from it.

They are not violently to be blamed for this. There is something in them that makes them act like this. But it is something they are bound to try to conquer.

*Some people have no sense of sympathy.*

They are themselves so healthy and so unaware of pain that they cannot understand, and make no effort to understand, the pain of others. They are themselves so sane and well balanced that they cannot understand the nerves or the shrinking of others. They regard the whole thing with complete incomprehension.

These people are almost worse than the first kind. They have an inability to put themselves in the other person's place.

Yet in the Incarnation, this is exactly what God did.

He entered into humanity's pain.

*There are the people for whom pain and suffering in others brings out the best.*

They have the instinct and the ability to help.

It is people like that for whom we all have reason to thank God.

A LIVING SACRIFICE                                             May 22

Jesus must have been physically fit.

In his days in Palestine, the carpenter did not buy his wood from the wholesaler.

He went out to the hillside, chose his sapling, swung his axe, cut it down and bore it home on his shoulder.

That is what Jesus did.

Think of the life he lived with never a roof over his head and on the road from morning to night.

He was no pale, anaemic figure but a tall, bronzed young man who could have walked any modern hiker off his feet, I suspect!

One of the tragedies of religion is that there are times when men have thought it almost a religious duty to neglect their bodies.

We may fitly talk of such a thing as the gospel of physical fitness.

If we are feeling depressed, let us remember it may be due not to neglect of our souls but to neglect of our bodies.

"Present your bodies a living sacrifice, holy, acceptable unto God, which is your reasonable service" (Rom. 12:1).

YOU HAVE A BODY                                               May 23

There is a very surprising young man who is a friend of mine. He would have liked to have been a minister, but life did not run that way for him. He actually works in a big chemist's shop which stays open all night. He works a shift that finishes at eleven o'clock at night.

He still studies as hard as he can. He still takes classes when he can; and he is the only person I know who has set himself to learn Coptic!

Last night I went into the shop where he works to get a tube of a certain preparation which promises to relieve aches and pains. We talked for a moment or two as we usually do, and he said to me: "When I was a boy I used to go to a little mission hall. One of the members was an old man who had lived a pretty wild life when he was young and who had been soundly converted. And one of the things he often used to say was: 'God will forgive you, but your body never does.'"

There is a whole world of truth in that.

John B. Gough, the great temperance orator, became a man of God. He glorified in God's forgiveness; he pleaded with others to accept it; and one of the things he used to say to young men was: "Watch what you are doing. God can forgive you, but the scars remain."

One of the faults of Christianity has often been that it has often spoken as if man was nothing but a soul.

The great Christians knew well that man has a body too.

The greatest of them knew how important that body was.

SPIRITUAL DRYNESS                                            May 24

One night Saint Francis was wakened by cries from the dormitory. When he went in he found a young brother who had practised such asceticism that he was literally dying of hunger. Francis ordered the table to be spread with all the food in the place. He bade the monks sit down, said grace and then he spoke to them.

"Dearest," he said, "we must look after Brother Body or he will turn melancholy and become a drag on us. After all, if we want him to serve us in work and in prayer, we must give him no reasonable cause to murmur."

Philip Doddridge has a sermon on "Spiritual Dryness". In it he says:

Here I would first advise you most carefully to enquire, whether your present distress does indeed arise from causes which are truly spiritual? Or whether it may not have its foundation in some disorder of body. . . .

When this is the case the help of the physician is to be sought rather than that of the divine, or, at least, by all means together with it; and medicine, diet, exercise and air may in a few weeks effect that which the strongest reasonings, the most pathetic exhortation or consolations, might for many months have attempted in vain.

In *On Praise and Meditation*, Richard Baxter writes:
"I advise thee as a further help to this heavenly life not to neglect the due care of thy bodily health. Thy body is a useful servant if thou give it its due and no more than is due; but it is a most devouring tyrant if thou suffer it to have what it unreasonably desires; and it is as a blunted knife if thou unjustly deny it what is necessary to its support."

HUMAN GOODNESS                                                                    May 25

As I walk up to Trinity College in the mornings I pass one of the busiest crossings in Glasgow. There is a newspaper seller who has his stance there. As often as not, when I pass, he is not there. His newspapers are there, and scattered on the top of them there is a collection of copper coins. People take a newspaper and drop their coins there.

I don't suppose that newspaper seller ever loses a coin or is swindled out of a newspaper.

Newspapers themselves are full of stories of thefts and swindles and robberies, but the more you think of it the more you see that life goes on on the assumption of the fundamental honesty of men.

Here is a tremendous truth. *We have to explain not only the mystery of human sin. We have to explain the still greater mystery of human goodness.*

The odd fact in life is that, though we are haunted by sin, we are haunted by goodness, too.

Robert Louis Stevenson spoke of people "clutching the remnants of virtue in the brothel or on the scaffold".

We cannot sin in peace.

Somehow that goodness is there.

Jesus knew that he had the gift of seeing the sleeping hero in the soul of every man, even when that man was a little quisling like Zacchaeus.

Once when Michelangelo was chiselling away at a great ugly shapeless block of marble, he was asked what he was doing.

His answer was: "I am releasing the angel that is imprisoned in this stone."

There is an angel and a hero in every man.

That is what Jesus knew, and that is the basis on which he acted.

Shakespeare knew men.

In the first act of *The Tempest*, he draws the picture of the storm at sea. When shipwreck is imminent, he has the grim stage direction: "Enter mariners, wet," and their first cry is: "All lost! to prayers, to prayers! All lost!"

It was only when all was lost that they turned to prayers.

In *King Henry V* Shakespeare has the immortal scene when the hostess of the tavern and Pistol, Nym and Bardolph talk of the death of Falstaff (King Henry V, ii, 3).

'A parted even just between twelve and one, even at the turning o' the tide; for after I saw him fumble with the sheets and play with the flowers and smile upon his fingers' ends, I knew that there was but one way; for his nose was as sharp as a pen, and a' babbled of green fields. "How now, Sir John?" quoth I: "what man! be a good cheer." So a' cried out "God, God, God!" three or four times: now I, to comfort him, bid him a' should not think of God; I hoped there was no need to trouble himself with any such thoughts yet.

No need to trouble himself yet with thoughts of God! So many people are like that.

*How do we know that we have plenty of time?*

I think it is Dr. Boreham who somewhere tells of meeting a doctor friend, and seeing that the doctor was much depressed.

Boreham asked what the matter was. The doctor said: "I have just come from a man for whom I can do nothing; and if he had come to me months ago, when he felt the first twinges of the thing that will kill him, I could have cured him quite easily. But he has let it go too far."

So many people connect religion with the ambulance corps and not the firing line of life. It is disastrously easy to put off too long the calling of the ambulance.

The Bible is full of the thought that things must be done while yet there is time.

Must we forget about God until we need him?
Is God someone of whom we only make use?
Is God a lifebelt or a friend?

There was an old saint who spent much time in prayer.
Someone asked why he spent so much.
He answered:
"I talk to God every day so that when the desperate moment comes he will know my voice."

## FOUR IDOLS

Bacon, in a famous passage, pictured the errors and the fallacies which attack the human mind under the picture of the four idols—*the idol of the tribe, the idol of the cave, the idol of the market-place, and the idol of the theatre*.

In the Bacon picture these four symbolic idols do not have quite the meaning that they would seem to have at first sight.

The errors which come from *the idol of the tribe* are the errors which arise just because man is man, just because he is a member of the general tribe of mankind, just because he is in fact a limited person, both in knowledge and in power.

We make our errors often simply because we forget that we are men; we forget that we are not the creator but the created. We forget that we do not know all, and that God knows best.

A man is a victim of the idol of the tribe when he thinks that he knows better than God, when he forgets that he is a man, and so fails to ask for or to accept the guidance of God.

## PROJECTION

The errors and the mistakes which come from *the idol of the cave* are the errors which come from trying to make our own idiosyncrasies and peculiarities into general laws and rules. The cave is the cave of self.

This mistake emerges specially in one direction. Man forgets that he is made in the image of God and tries to make God in his image.

A man may make his religion a kind of projection of himself. He thinks that all religion must be his religion.

The most serious example of this is the way in which so much missionary work to all intents and purposes identified Christianity and Western civilisation. Christianity was preached, but it was preached in terms of Western clothes, Western manners, Western Church structures, Western industry and economics.

When the Salvation Army went to India it rapidly saw that there never could be any real progress until they stopped identifying Christianity and Western civilisation and thought in terms of India. An Indian said to Tucker: "We will accept Christ when he takes off his hat, trousers and boots", in other words when he was de-Westernised, and so the Army became Indian to make India Christian.

It is a great lesson.

Christianity must never be identified with our private version of it, still less with the social and economic background we know.

The errors which come from *the idol of the market-place* are the errors which arise from the fact that we misunderstand each other's language. Words mean different things to different people. Words are the great coinage and communication of the market-place, and when we talk we misunderstand and are misunderstood.

We use words in different senses and meanings, so that, as we so often tragically find, we suddenly discover that we have been talking and arguing at cross purposes all the time.

It is a simple but essential rule that in any argument or discussion we should be sure that we understand each other, and know what the other says and means.

The errors which come from *the idol of the theatre* are the errors which come from false systems of thought which, as it were, follow each other on to the stage of history.

The great necessity is that we should remember that no human system of thought is final, that none has the whole truth, that there is more to God than ever any man has discovered.

If we remember this, it will save us from the mistake which has so often brought tragedy to the Church—the error of loving systems more than we love God.

*The idol of the tribe, the idol of the cave, the idol of the market-place, the idol of the theatre,* the mistakes which come from forgetting we are men, the mistakes which come from making ourselves the norm for everything, the mistakes which come from the elusiveness of the meaning of words, the mistakes which come from the undue exaltation of any system—avoid them all!

## THE SUBSTITUTE                                                         May 30

James Black, the famous preacher, was to preach at special services in a country place. After his arrival he went down with so bad a throat that he could not speak at all.

It was known that Frank Cairns was in the village, so a deputation went to him and asked him to stand in. He agreed, and he was specially requested to point out to the congregation—there was no time to advertise the change— he was not James Black.

More than once this request was made. And even in the vestry before the service, at the very last minute, the session clerk once again requested Frank to be sure to say that he was not James Black.

Frank Cairns entered the pulpit. "I must tell you," he said, "that I am not Dr. Black; I am Frank Cairns; *nevertheless*, let us worship God!"

Sometimes a man can be made to feel a substitute, but tremendous things have been done by second-choice men.

Once on a wild and snowy winter morning, Spurgeon when he was a lad, set out to go to church. The weather was so bad that he could not reach the church to which he intended to go. In the church he did find, the preacher had not arrived because he was storm-bound. It was in a substitute church and by a substitute preacher that Spurgeon was converted. What a gift of God's grace to the Church Spurgeon's conversion was to be!

## IT'S NEVER TOO LATE                                                    May 31

When that famous actress Marie Tempest was sixty-five she had a part in the play *Mr. Pim Passes By*. Although she gave a brilliant performance, the play was a failure.

When it was withdrawn there was a very gloomy luncheon party; and then Marie Tempest suddenly brightened up: "Everybody" she said, "at the beginning of their career must expect reverses."

At sixty-five she was thinking only in terms of beginning!

You remember these wonderful lines which Tennyson wrote, as he drew the picture of the aged Ulysses inviting his friends even in old age to set out from Ithaca upon some new adventure.

You and I are old:
  Old age hath yet his
  honour and his toil;
Death closes all: but
  something ere the end,
Some work of noble note
  may yet be done,
Not unbecoming men that
  strove with gods.
The lights begin to twinkle
  from the rocks:
The long day wanes: the slow
  moon climbs; the deep
Moans round with many voices.
  Come, my friends,
'Tis not too late to seek
  a newer world.

It is never too late to seek a newer world.

# June

I remember a ten-days' motoring holiday we once had. In that ten days we covered no less than 1,467 miles. We went first to Fort William, then to Mallaig, to Inverness, and then from there we went right up to the far north, to Wick and to Thurso.

You can see from that list of places that we travelled through some of the loneliest places in Scotland. And over some of the most difficult roads.

As we were travelling, one thing struck me particularly. Wherever we went, even in the loneliest parts of the country, we would pass a telephone box. In the middle of a moor, or on a lonely stretch of road, all of a sudden one of these little red boxes would come in sight.

That is very valuable because it means that no matter where you are, if you do get into trouble, somewhere not very far away there is one of these little red telephone boxes, from which you can call for help.

It means that even in the remote country places, if there is no telephone in the house, and if there is sudden illness or trouble, people can go to one of these little red boxes and send a message for help.

And you can do it twenty-four hours a day, at any time of the day, or at any time of the night, because there is always someone in the telephone exchange waiting to answer a call for help.

Life is like that. No matter where we are, we can send out a call to God for help.

All the great men have known that.

Abraham Lincoln was a man who spent a lot of time in prayer. One of his friends once asked him how he could afford to waste—as he said—so much time in prayer.

Lincoln's answer was this: "I would be the greatest fool on earth, if I thought that I could sustain the demands of this high office without the help of a strength which is far greater than my own."

CALLING GOD                                                              June 2

One of the very great generals of the 1914–18 war was the French general Marshal Foch. He was in command of all the Allied armies in Europe and of course that was a terrible responsibility.

On one occasion a staff meeting had been called, and all the officers and commanders turned up. Foch himself was not there.

One of his officers said, "I think I know where we can find him." He went round to a little ruined church which was near army headquarters and there was Foch kneeling in prayer before the altar.

These men knew that whenever they were in trouble and up against it, they could send a message to God, and God would hear it.

We don't have to do things all by ourselves.

God is always there to help.

These little red telephone boxes in the remote and the lonely parts of the country which I mentioned yesterday had another use.

If you lived somewhere in the wilds of Sutherlandshire, or Ross-shire, or Inverness-shire, you wouldn't see your friends very often. It wouldn't be a question of taking a 5p run in the bus or a 10p ticket on the train to see them —it would be a day's journey and more!

I am quite sure that when people who live in these far away and remote parts of the country feel lonely and want to speak to their friends, they just pick up the telephone and have a talk. They do it quite often, for everybody knows that if you don't keep in touch with your friends, friendship is so very apt to fade away.

That is the way we should be with God.

Some time every day we should, as it were, put a call through to God.

FIXED APPOINTMENT                                                        June 3

There was a noted bishop called Bertram Pollock.

A bishop is a very busy man, with all kinds of meetings and calls on his time. But Bertram Pollock had three times every day when he spoke to God.

Once, just as one of these times was about to begin, a visitor came to the door. His servant came to Bertram Pollock to tell him that a visitor had arrived. Bertram Pollock said, "Put him in an ante-room and tell him to wait for a minute or two. I've got an appointment with God."

Every day we should have our appointments with God, when we pray to him and speak to him and tell him of our needs.

Prayer is our way of asking God for help, and of talking to him. Like the telephone boxes, we can, as we said before, use prayer twenty-four hours a day, at any time in the day and the night, and God will be there to answer.

The Psalmist said: "This poor man cried, and the Lord heard him, and saved him out of all his troubles" (Ps. 34:6).

No one ever put through a call to God which was not answered in some way.

PICTURES THAT REMAIN                                          June 4

I was born in Wick. I had not seen it since 1912, but the extraordinary thing is that when we went back to Wick recently, I immediately and without hesitation recognised the street where we used to stay and could go straight to the house where I was born.

That set me thinking about memory.

Memory is a frightening thing. There are so many pictures which remain for ever unobliterated in our minds. In fact the psychologists tell us that we never forget anything. Everything we have ever done and seen is buried in our minds. It may not be there on the conscious level, but it is buried deep down in the unconscious, and even there it has its effect upon us.

Obviously if we never forget anything, we should be very careful indeed what we give ourselves to remember!

*We should be careful what we look at.*

Sir Joshua Reynolds, the great artist, used to refuse even to look at an inferior painting, because, he said, even to look at an inferior picture had an effect on his own art.

Somewhere the picture of everything that we have seen is buried in the unconscious depths of our memories. Whether we know it or not, that picture is affecting us.

If we allow ourselves to look at soiled and smutted things, there is defilement within our memories, even if we are unaware that it is there.

If memory retains everything, *we should be very careful what we listen to.*

Old Thomas Fuller once said: "Almost fifty years ago I heard a profane jest and still remember it. How many pious passages of a far later date have I forgotten!"

He listened to the soiled thing, and it stuck on the surface of his memory. We should be careful what we listen to, for every soiled and questionable thing is there somewhere in our memories.

*We should be careful what we read.*

The classical psychological example of the way in which a thing is never forgotten is the story of a certain servant girl. She fell ill, and in her illness she suffered from delirium. In her delirium she poured out a flood of language which no one could understand. Then someone who knew Hebrew happened one day to be visiting her during one of her fits of delirium, and discovered that this servant girl was actually reciting whole chapters of the Old Testament in Hebrew.

She, of course, had never studied Hebrew. What had happened was this. At one time she had been a serving maid in a manse. The minister who lived there had been in the habit, each morning, of reading aloud to himself a chapter of the Hebrew Bible as he walked up and down his study. While he read, this servant girl had been brushing and dusting and polishing the landing outside the study door.

She had heard this Hebrew, and, all unknown to her, it had lodged in her memory.

In her fits of delirium, it came up from her "unconscious", and she recited it.

In that, lies a warning!

Because something is buried in the depths of our unconscious, it does not mean that it is not having its effect upon us.

We should never willingly let our eyes rest on soiled and questionable things.

Certainly we should never let our eyes rest on them in order to get a mistaken pleasure out of them.

There is many a man still suffering from the hidden taint of the evil thing which he allowed himself to look at, to listen to or to read.

"Whatsoever things are true, whatsoever things are honest, whatsoever things are just, whatsoever things are pure, whatsoever things are lovely, whatsoever things are of good report; if there be any virtue, and if there be any praise, *think on these things*" (Phil. 4:8).

## THE ROAD TO HOLINESS June 7

It is curious how sanctification has become a kind of lost doctrine of the Christian faith.

The Greek word for sanctification is *hagiasmos*.

All Greek nouns which end in *-asmos* describe a continuing process, and *hagiasmos* could well be translated "the road to holiness".

Are we every day a little farther along the road to holiness, the road to loveliness, the road to beauty? Or are we pretty well stuck in the one place, no better than we were a day, a week, a month, a year ago?

If we are going to make any progress along the way to holiness and beauty, there are certain things we need.

*We need first a bit of self-examination.*

W. H. Davies said that there was something wrong with life, if we had no time to stand and stare. But we should not only take time to stand and stare at the world. Every now and again we should take a good look at ourselves.

Dr. Johnson used to say that that was one of the greatest uses of the Sunday. Sunday ought to be used for self-examination. We should always examine ourselves to see if we are a little farther on than we were the week previously.

No one wants a morbid self-examination, but there is undoubtedly a place in life for a periodical stock-taking of ourselves.

On the road to holiness *we need something to aim at.*

When we are going on a long journey in a motor car, we take out the map and look at the route, and we say: "We'll get to such and such a place by tonight, and we'll spend the night there." We are so determined to get there and so confident that we will get there that we book rooms in an hotel there before we even start!

When a lad is studying, he knows that he has got to get to a certain stage for the examination. He has got to get to that chapter, that theorem, that section in the book, that line in the text.

Even in games a man sets himself a certain standard. He sets himself a figure and makes up his mind to get his golf handicap down to that.

In every sphere of life we set ourselves an aim and a goal. Strangely enough we seldom do that in the business of life itself.

We would get on a great deal better and go a great deal farther, if we set ourselves deliberately to gain this new virtue and to lose that old fault.

*But we need someone to help.*

Harry Emerson Fosdick has a sermon somewhere—I have forgotten the sermon, but I can't forget the title!—entitled: "No man need stay the way he is." If Christianity means anything, that is exactly what it does mean. It is Jesus's power that he can enable us to get farther and farther along the road to holiness, if we will ask for and take the help which he continually offers to us.

"I press towards the mark," said Paul (Phil. 3:14).

It is not enough for a Christian to accept a life which is stuck in the one place.

Life for him should be this road to holiness, the upward and the onward way.

I got out of my car and I was sitting on a rock.

Two small girls appeared. They would not be any more than six or seven, and they were both pushing prams in which there were children younger than themselves.

One was another little girl of about three or four, and the other was a baby of about six or seven months old.

The three-year-old was duly disentangled from her pram, but the baby was left in his.

They played around for a bit, and then one of them said to me: "We're going along the shore and up another way, and back round by the sea-front. Will you look after the baby till we come back, mister?"

I said: "But what if he starts crying?" "O," said the other little girl, "just lift him and walk about with him and sing to him."

(If I started singing to him, this baby was going to have something to cry about indeed!)

Off they went. And they were away so long that I began to think that they had either abandoned the baby or forgotten about him or got lost. Then I began to get anxious about the time. If I wanted to get home at the right time, it was time that I moved. But I couldn't leave the baby.

I became more and more anxious, and more and more puzzled about what to do, but I still felt that I couldn't go away and leave the baby, who had mercifully—for his own sake—been placidly quiet all the time.

At last the little girls turned up again.

"Look," I said. "I thought you were lost. Aren't you frightened to go away and leave the baby like that?"

Back came the answer from one of them: "O no, mister, I knew you would take care of him." "Aye," said the other, "I knew he would be all right with you."

I was glad that I had waited, even if it had kept me late, because I hadn't let down the trust of these little girls.

THE GREAT OBLIGATION                                June 10

There is no obligation in this world like the obligation of being trusted.

It is impossible to fail or to let down someone who trusts you.

*God has trusted us.*

Surely that is what the fact of free will means. God could have made us automata who were compelled to be good whether we liked it or not, creatures who had no choice. But God gave us free will to obey or to disobey himself, to accept or to reject himself, to bring joy or sorrow to himself.

God put all his trust in men.

*Every day in life our loved ones trust us.*

A husband trusts his wife, and a wife trusts her husband. Our children trust us in the most absolute way.

All personal relationships are founded on trust.

*Jesus trusts us.*

That is really what Paul meant when he spoke about the Church being the body of Christ (1 Cor. 12:27; Eph. 1:23). Jesus is no longer in this world in the flesh, and therefore the plain truth is that if Jesus wants a task done, he has to get a man to do it for him.

In the most literal sense we have to be hands to do his work, feet to run upon his errands, a voice to speak for him.

Jesus has entrusted *his* work to *our* hands.

THE THRILL OF LEARNING                                         June 11

*There is nothing in this world worth learning that can be learned without a struggle.*

That is, in fact, the thrill of learning. If a thing was easy to learn, there would be no kick in mastering it. The thrill is to struggle away with some subject for a long time, and then quite suddenly to have the excitement of discovering that one understands what before was unintelligible.

Damon Runyon wrote to his son: "You will improve the more you write. Good writing is simply a matter of application, but I learned many years ago that the words will not put themselves down on paper in dreams or in conversations."

Writing is struggling to write—not dreaming about writing or talking about writing.

Paderewski, perhaps the greatest of the pianists, thought nothing of going over a bar of music as many as forty times until he was sure he was playing it exactly as it ought to be played. Before a concert he always played through his entire programme though no doubt he had already played the pieces of which it was composed times without number.

One day he played before Queen Victoria, and the Queen was deeply moved by his performance. "Mr. Paderewski," she said, "you are a genius." "That may be," answered Paderewski, "but before I was a genius, I was a drudge."

No one will ever acquire any kind of knowledge or any kind of greatness without a struggle. But in the struggle lies the thrill.

## AT LITTLE COST June 12

The most tragic example of indiscipline in English letters is the career of Coleridge. Never was a man blessed with so great a mind, and never did a man do so little with it.

He left Cambridge to join the army. He left the army because, with all his erudition, he could not rub down a horse. He came to Oxford and left without a degree.

He began a paper called the *Watchman* which ran for ten numbers and then died.

As has been said of him: "He had every gift save one—the gift of sustained and concentrated effort."

He himself said that he had all kinds of books ready for printing "except for transcription". He would never face the discipline of writing them down.

There are many ministers and laymen in pulpits today whose ministrations fail to be as effective as they might be, for the simple reason that they will not accept the discipline of writing out every word of their sermons, and of carefully preparing their prayers.

It is the tragedy of the Church that there are too many preachers who are seeking to render unto God that which costs them nothing, or at most, that which costs them very little.

## REAL LIFE June 13

It is real life that Jesus offers.

"I am come," he said, "that they might have life, and that they might have it more abundantly" (John 10:10).

What is it that Jesus does to life?

*He gives us a new view of the world.*

If all that Jesus said is true, this world is the training-ground of eternity. The value of any action is dependent on the end for which it is done.

Bernard Newman tells somewhere of being in a peasant house in the remote places of the Balkans.

The daughter of the house spent all her time sewing. Bernard Newman thought that she must be labouring away to earn a little more money at this sewing which never seemed to stop. "Don't you ever get tired, stitch, stitch, stitching away?" he said. "Oh no, sir," she said. "You see this is my wedding dress."

The object for which the dress was being made, made all the difference in the world to that which she had to do.

It made the difference between drudgery and glory.

A NEW VIEW                                                                   June 14

*Jesus gives us a new view of men.*

If Jesus was right, then every man has it in him to be nothing less than a son of God.

Oscar Browning (as H. E. Wortham tells of him in *Victorian Eton and Cambridge*) may not have been a first-class scholar, but he was a first-class teacher.

As a teacher, his one working-rule was that the stupid boy did not exist. If any seemed stupid, the fault lay in himself for "not having found the exact spot in which their minds were assailable".

One of Browning's fellow dons at King's said of him: "He saw as if by instinct a man's good qualities and weaknesses, intellectual and moral, and suppressed the one and developed the other with unremitting but unobtrusive skill. Again and again within my own knowledge he discerned latent gifts where the ordinary observer would see little or nothing, and having discovered the potential excellence had not rested until it became actual."

If Jesus is right, we can neither hate men nor despise men any more, for we move in a world of sons of God.

IN THE LIGHT OF ETERNITY                                                     June 15

*Jesus gives us a new view of life.*

If Jesus is right, life becomes a pilgrimage to eternity, and every act of service to our fellow-men is a mile-stone on it.

No teacher ever linked eternity to time as Jesus did. To other teachers the philosopher sitting in his study thinking his long, involved, abstruse thoughts was the man who was dealing with eternity.

To Jesus the man who was giving a cup of cold water to the thirsty, the man who was visiting the sick and those in prison, the man who was feeding the hungry and clothing the naked, and welcoming the stranger was the man who was dealing with eternity.

Jesus gives us life because he teaches us to see life *sub specie aeternitatis*, in the light of eternity. We see this world in the light of eternity and it becomes no longer a world of drudgery and unimportant tasks, but a world which is the training-school for the life which is beyond.

When we see our fellow-men in the light of eternity, they are no longer people whom we can despise and dislike, but they are sons of God, whether they know it or not.

When we see life in the light of eternity, it becomes no longer one thing after another in a petty succession, but it becomes the pilgrimage of the soul to God.

REMEMBER THE SUNDAY ...                                          June 16

As I was on my way to church, my eye caught a placard advertising a Sunday newspaper. The claim of this newspaper on this placard was that it was *An Essential Part of Sunday*.

I do not suppose that anyone would agree that any newspaper is an essential part of Sunday, if the word "essential" is being used in anything like its true meaning. But, suppose we were asked to draw up a list of the essential things about Sunday, what would that list include? I have said things like this before,* but want to add some comments to what I said then.

The commandment says: Remember the Sabbath day, to keep it holy. In the Bible this word "holy" has a very special meaning. "Holy" means different, separate from and other than ordinary things.

A temple is "holy" because it is different from other buildings; a victim for sacrifice is "holy" because he is different from other animals; a priest is "holy" because he is different from other men. God is supremely "holy" because God belongs to a quite different sphere of being from that to which men belong.

So we could say that the commandment means: *Remember the Sabbath day, to keep it differently from other days.*

I know that the Sabbath and the Sunday are different days, that the Sabbath is the last day of the week and the Sunday the first day of the week, that the Sabbath is a Jewish institution commemorating the rest of God on the seventh day when creation was complete, and that the

*In *Through the Year with William Barclay* (entries for September 8 and 9).

Sunday is a Christian institution commemorating the Resurrection of Jesus Christ.

So then let us alter the wording of the commandment very slightly and with complete justification:

*Remember the Lord's Day to keep it differently from other days.*

DAY OF REST June 17

Wherein then should this difference between Sabbath and Sunday lie?
*It is still true that the Lord's Day should be a day of rest.*

That is not only a *spiritual* necessity, it is a *physical* necessity.

Modern life moves at an ever faster and faster pace. The result is that people grow ever more and more tired.

A famous man was asked what he thought was the most characteristic feature of modern people, and he answered: "Tired eyes."

In the days of the French Revolution the Sunday was abolished by law, but it had to be brought back, because the health of the nation would not stand a week without a day of rest.

Everything needs its day of rest.

The old golf green-keeper was right. When he was asked his opinion of Sunday golf, his answer was: "If you don't need a rest, the greens do."

The Lord's Day is a day of rest, and, as such, it is a great social and humanitarian institution.

FAMILY DAY June 18

*The Lord's Day should be a day of family fellowship.*

It is the one day when the family have the opportunity to be together.

It is the one day when the father has the chance to be with his wife and with his children.

The family and the Sunday are very closely intertwined.

Edwin Muir in his autobiography tells of Sunday nights in his old home in the Orkney Islands: "Every Sunday night my father gathered us together to read a chapter of the Bible and kneel down in prayer. These Sunday nights are among my happiest memories; there was a feeling of complete security and union among us as we sat reading about David or Elijah."

The Sunday ought to be the day on which the unity of the family is re-discovered and confirmed.

STOCK-TAKING                                                    June 19

*The Lord's Day ought to be a day of self-examination.*

In this rushed and busy modern world we are apt to be so busy living that we have no time to think *how* we are living. Sunday is the day when we ought to take time to take stock.

We ought to examine ourselves to see if we have advanced or slipped back along the road to holiness. For Dr. Johnson that was an essential part of the Sunday. On every Sunday we should hear God's voice saying to us: "*Let a man examine himself.*"

*The Lord's Day should be a day of worship.*

Jesus went into the Synagogue in Nazareth on the Sabbath as his custom was (Luke 4:16).

The worship of God in the company of men was for Jesus an habitual and essential part of God's day.

In the rush and press of things it is easy to forget God.

It is easy to be too busy to pray.

It is easy to be so busy with the things of time that the things of eternity are forgotten.

On the Lord's Day a man should re-establish the bond that binds himself to his fellow-men and to his God.

TRUE PERSPECTIVE                                               June 20

One of the most staggering things about the human mind is how it can lose all sense of proportion. It can magnify trifles until they fill the whole horizon. It can set side by side things which are of no importance and things which are of eternal importance and feel no shattering incongruity in the juxtaposition.

Edmund Gosse tells how his father chronicled his birth in his diary. His father was a naturalist. It was a household in which the birth of a child was not really welcomed.

When Edmund was born his father entered in his diary: "E. delivered of a son. Received green swallow from Jamaica."

With an astonishing lack of perspective the birth of a man child into the world and the arrival of a green swallow from Jamaica are set down side by side.

Mrs. Belloc Lowndes in her book of memories, *A Passing World*, sets down a letter which she wrote to her mother in the autumn of 1914, in the early days of the First World War: "London has become very melancholy. The mourning worn by relatives of the soldiers who have been killed is beginning to show in the streets, and strikes a tragic note. Everything is going to be terribly dear. I got in a case of China tea this morning at the old price, and in the afternoon it went up twopence a pound, so now I wish I had got in two cases."

Here is a woman complaining that the price of China tea is going up twopence a pound when she was moving in a world of broken hearts.

The sheer insensitive blindness of a juxtaposition like that is appalling.

TRIVIALITIES                                                              June 21

Somewhere there is an incident told by Dr. Johnson—I quote from memory.

A man who worked in a paper factory came to see him. This man had taken from the factory two or three sheets of paper and some pieces of string to tie up certain parcels of his own. He had convinced himself that by so doing he had committed a deadly sin and he would not stop talking and lamenting about this trivial business.

At last Johnson burst out to him: "Stop bothering about paper and packthread when we are all living together in a world that is bursting with sin and sorrow."

We live in a world where people are for ever getting things out of true perspective, a world where one of the rarest of all things is a sense of proportion, a world where people so often seem quite incapable of distinguishing between the things which matter and the things which do not matter.

How often friendships are shattered by some trifle!

How often the peace of a congregation is wrecked on some completely unimportant detail!

How often people delude themselves that they are standing on principles when they are fussing about trifles!

How often someone whose heart is breaking is astonished and bewildered at the trivialities which fill other people's lives and talk!

There is only one way to get our perspectives right—and that is to see things in the light of eternity, and in the light of the Cross.

## PROPORTION                                         June 22

Alan Walker in *Everybody's Calvary* tells of a young minister in a little country village church. He had invited the congregation to wait after the service for a celebration of the sacrament. Only two people waited. He thought of cancelling the whole service; but he went on.

As he went through the ancient ritual he came to the passage: "Therefore with angels and archangels and all the company of heaven . . ."

He stopped. The wonder of it gripped him: "Angels and archangels and all the company of heaven . . ." "God forgive me," he said, "I did not know I was in that company."

If we could see this world against the background of eternity; if we could see it in the light of the Cross; if we could see it in the presence of God, or, if that is asking too much, if we could see it simply against the background of human tragedy and human sorrow and human broken hearts, we would get back the true perspective.

We would recover a sense of proportion.

Trifles would be seen as trifles.
God would come first.
Other things would take their proper place.

## THE OPEN DOOR                                       June 23

I was in a house which was a house of grief. In the room there was a humble soul who had come to express his sympathy in that hour of sorrow. Other people were shown in; and this man, although he had been there a very short time, rose to go.

The host of the house asked him to stay. "But," said the humble man, "I don't want to intrude." Back came the answer: "No one can intrude in this house."

It was a noble saying. Here was a man with a sore heart, but an open heart. Here was a house of mourning, but a house with an open door.

Long ago the writer of the Revelation set it down as the invitation of God: "Behold I have set before thee an open door, and no man can shut it" (Rev. 3:8).

*We can be sure that there is no such thing as social snobbery with God.*

Godfrey Winn, in one of his war books, tells of a thing that Ginger Bailey, a fighter pilot in the R.A.F., told him.

Ginger Bailey had won the D.F.M. and the D.F.C. He went to Buckingham Palace to be decorated by the king. When he was telling Godfrey Winn about it he said: "Do you know, Godfrey, after I had done my bow to the king as we were briefed, he bowed back at me."

The fighter pilot was astonished at the courtesy of the king.

Of one thing we can be sure—the humblest man is welcome to the presence of God.

ACCEPTED                                                    June 24

*God will never despise the poor efforts that we can bring to him.*

Alasdair Alpin Macgregor tells of a terrible thing in his book of memories, *The Troubled Years.*

He was a soldier in the 1914–18 war. It was the battle of the Menin Gate. His father was a martinet and a disciplinarian and a stickler that things should be done in the right way.

With hell behind and hell in front, Alasdair Alpin Macgregor sat for a moment and scribbled a note to say that he was still alive and put it into one of the green envelopes which soldiers were given to hold their letters.

Two weeks later the letter came back to him, and written across it in his father's handwriting was the sentence: "This sort of letter not wanted here."

Alasdair Alpin Macgregor never again wrote to his father.

True, as he lay in hospital later, his father apologised to him for that heartless action, but the wound was there.

That is the kind of thing that God would never do.

The prayer we may pray, the message we may send to God may be but a poor and a stammering and a halting thing, but God will never despise the prayer of the needy heart.

We are always accepted.

AN OPEN INVITATION                                         June 25

*We can be quite sure that we have an open invitation to the presence of God.*

There is a beautiful story of Alexander Whyte of Free St. George's, Edinburgh (as his church used to be known).

At one time A. B. Macaulay was his assistant, and there was a deep bond of affection between the old preacher and the young scholar.

The day came when Macaulay was leaving Free St. George's for a church of his own. He was paying his farewell visit to Whyte's study. Whyte said something like this: "I wanted to give you a present before you left us. I might have given you a book or a picture, but you have plenty of books and pictures."

Then he put his hand in his pocket and took something out. He held it out to Macaulay. "So," he said, "I decided to give you this. It's the key of my house. Whenever you're in Edinburgh, use it."

He was setting before Macaulay an ever-open door.

That is what God does to us.

This is the new thing about Christianity. No one had ever even dreamed of a God like that before. Men had always known of a God of might and majesty and power, a God of terror and of fear, but, until Jesus came, no one ever dreamed of a God whose heart and whose door were wide open to saint and to sinner alike.

He would be a foolish man who had the right to enter into the presence of someone who was very great and very kind, and who never used that right. God has set before us the open door which no one can ever shut.

He is a foolish man who refuses to accept the ever-open hospitality of the love of God.

THE WAY OF DUTY                                                    June 26

Charles Graves, in *Great Days*, tells of one of the heroic exploits of the Second World War.

It happened at the siege of Tobruk. The Coldstream Guards cut their way out of Tobruk. When they emerged they were mere shadows of men, and of two battalions only two hundred men were left.

The survivors were cared for by the R.A.F. A Coldstream Guards major was talking to the R.A.F. unit's medical officer. The R.A.F. man said: "After all, as Foot Guards, you had no option but to have a go."

Whereat another R.A.F. man said: "It must be pretty tough to be in the Brigade of Guards, because the tradition compels you to carry on irrespective of circumstances."

It was simply a sense of duty which turned men into heroes.

It has again and again happened that this sense of duty led a man to greatness.

Tennyson wrote in his "Ode on the Death of the Duke of Wellington":

> Not once or twice in our rough island-story
> The path of duty was the way to glory.

When Napoleon read Wellington's dispatches, he made the criticism that, in Wellington's accounts of his campaigns, the word "duty" occurred often and the word "glory" never.

Wellington's answer was this: "Does not the foolish fellow see, that even if my aim was glory, duty is the way to it?"

The way of duty may start with a certain stern grimness, but it has a way of ending in a splendour of glory.


## "I MUST . . ." June 27

Let no man think that this sense of duty is a low and an inadequate and an unworthy motive. It is a most interesting, and a most moving, thing to go through the gospels and again and again to hear Jesus saying: "I *must*."

"I *must* be about my Father's business" (Luke 2:49).

"I *must* preach the gospel" (Luke 4:43).

He tells his disciples that he "*must* go to Jerusalem" (Matt. 16:21).

"The Son of Man *must* suffer" (Mark 8:31).

"The Son of Man *must* be delivered up" (Luke 24:7).

"I *must* work the works of Him that sent me" (John 9:4).

"The Son of Man *must* be lifted up" (John 12:34).


There was never anyone in whom the sense of duty was stronger than it was in Jesus Christ.

He too went to his work saying: "I *must*."


There can come a day to every man when the foundations are shaken and the world is dark and there seems to be nothing left to live for. But when everything else is gone, the sense of duty remains.

That sense of duty can be the way to the dawn beyond the dark, for, although Jesus said that he *must* suffer, he also said that he *must* rise again.


## KEEP YOUR EYE ON IT! June 28

Alasdair Alpin Macgregor, in his volume of autobiography entitled *Vanished Waters*, quotes an old Irish belief and a very charming little poem from Kerry.

The belief is that you can hold a leprechaun so long as you keep your eye on him, but, if you glance aside for even the fraction of a second, the leprechaun is gone.

The poem runs like this:

> Oh! as I went out one winter's night,
>    A leprechaun I spied,
> With scarlet cap and coat of green,
>    A cruiskeen at his side.
> He hammered and sang with tiny voice,
>    And drank his mountain dew;
> Oh! I laughed to think he was caught at last,
>    But the Faery was laughing too,
> With eager grasp I caught the elf—
>    "Your faery purse!" I cried.
> "I've given it away," he said,
>    "To the lady at your side."
> I turned to look—the elf was gone;
>    And what was I to do?
> Oh! I laughed to think of the fool I'd been:
>    And the Faery was laughing too.

So long as you keep your eye on the leprechaun you had him! Take your eye off him for a split second and he was gone!

There are other things than a leprechaun that we must keep our eyes fixed upon.

I remember a friend telling me how he and his wife had gone for an evening walk across a Highland moor. It was a lovely evening when they left, but as dusk descended, it brought also mist. They began to find themselves confused in the hazy darkness, and, being strangers to the area, they found it increasingly difficult to keep their sense of direction. They came to a point where the pathway divided. "Which way is it?" said my friend anxiously. His wife didn't know.

The mist had thickened. They felt a sense of panic beginning to grow. Then for a moment, the mist cleared a little. Through the haze, they could just see a tiny light. It was the oil lamp burning in the shepherd's cottage. They had passed it on the way.

"Keep your eye on that light," said my friend to his wife. "So long as we keep our eyes fixed on that, we can't go wrong."

So they watched the light, sometimes clearer, sometimes more faint, sometimes all but disappearing. But, keeping their eye on that lamp in the window, they came safely through the darkness.

Keep *your* eye on the light!

*We must keep our eye fixed on the ideal.*

In life, we grow satisfied with less and less. We must keep our eye fixed on the ideal of ourselves, the ideal of Christian manhood, the ideal of what we ought to be.

W. B. Yeats tells us that Macgregor Mathers had what he called a medicinal phrase to repeat in moments of adversity: "There is no part of me that is not of the gods."

In life it is so fatally easy to accept ourselves, to feel that our faults have no cure, and our habits no power that can break them.

We must keep the ideal of ourselves ever before our eyes.

We must keep our eye fixed on the ideal of our job and our work.

Many a man sets out to be a minister, a doctor, a teacher, a Sunday school teacher, a Church member with the highest ideal of his task, but so often bit by bit the ideal dies, until he is satisfied with a standard far below his dreams.

We must keep our eye fixed on the ideal of whatever work we have chosen, or have been chosen, to do.

LOOKING UNTO JESUS                                              June 30

*We must keep our eye fixed on Jesus.*

The writer of the Hebrews tells us to walk looking unto Jesus (Heb. 12:2).

The word he uses is the Greek word *aphoran*. *Apo* means "away" and *horan* means "to look", so the meaning of the word is to withdraw the eyes from all other things to concentrate upon one.

The concentrated gaze of life must be on Jesus Christ.

I have quoted it often but want to look at it a little bit more deeply here.

In the letter to the Philippians, Paul uses a tremendous phrase. He says "*I press toward the mark*" (Phil. 3:14).

The word he uses for "pressing toward" is the very vivid *epekteinesthai*.

It is the word which is used of a runner making his most strenuous effort, his whole body stretched out at an angle as he runs, his head up and his eyes fixed on the tape, his whole being concentrated on that white finishing line in the distance.

It is going to make all the difference in the world to life if we keep our eyes fixed on the ideal and fixed on Christ.

# *July*

## MY BROTHER'S KEEPER

July 1

There were two brothers in a family who were very close to one another. In their school days the younger one was crippled and could not walk. Every day the older brother carried his little crippled brother on his back to school.

One day a stranger met the two of them, the older brother tramping along a little bent with the effort and the little lame lad on his back.

The stranger stopped.

"That's a heavy burden you've got on your back," he said. And like a shot back came the answer: "That's no burden; that's my brother."

Sometimes—God forgive us—we think the sick and the aged and the infirm a burden.

They are not a burden.

They are our brothers and sisters.

We *are* our brothers' keepers.

*I* am my brother's keeper.

## "LET US GO . . ."

July 2

One Sunday I was preaching in a church which has a very large congregation. The Sacrament was due to be observed two weeks later.

The minister made the intimations. Several were about the communion services. He said that there would be communion services at eleven a.m., at two p.m. and at three-thirty p.m.

He then said something more about the service at three-thirty p.m. That service would be a service specially for the aged and the weak and the infirm. He said that it would not last more than half an hour.

He went on to say that if there were any who were unable to walk to the church the elders who had cars would call at their houses and bring them.

They would be brought to a door of the church which would save them a long walk up the aisle to the pews. They would be helped, and indeed, if need be, carried every step of the way; and at the end of the service, they would be carefully and lovingly taken home again.

I thought that was lovely. There would be many on that coming Sunday who loved God's house and "the place where his honour dwells", and who would be enabled to share in the fellowship of the Church in a way that would not be possible had transport not been provided and all things arranged for them; who would be glad when someone came to say, "Let us go to the house of the Lord."

CUPS OF TEA! July 3

My minister friend had another intimation to make. He announced that on the Friday before the Communion Sunday the "Preparatory Service" would be held in the evening. At that service the new members from other congregations, and the new members who had professed their faith would be welcomed and received into the fellowship of the Church.

So far the intimation was normal. But then came the extra bit!

After the service there would be a cup of tea in the hall and all the office-bearers and all the congregation present were invited to come and to meet the new members to give them a greeting and to make them welcome.

It is always a bit difficult to make an entry into a new church. People coming from other churches always feel strange. But here indeed was the open hand, the open door and the open heart.

You can laugh at church cups of tea, but I wonder how many shy folk have been made to feel at home by them. I wonder how many lasting friendships have been made. I wonder how many strangers have been made to feel welcome by that simple custom in that church.

Perhaps we could do a little more to make the stranger feel at home. Even just through cups of tea.

I met a distinguished minister in a group of people. I asked him how things were going with him.

Most ministers with large congregations are feeling a little weary in the early spring before the busy time comes to an end. He said that it was tough going, but he said it very cheerfully.

I said: "Well, you're in good heart about it anyway."

"Yes," he said, "when I feel a bit under the weather, and when things are worse than usual, I always remember a Scot I served with in the First World War. Things were at their worst—mud and blood and wounds and general agony.

"This chap described it all with a wealth of unrepeatable and unprintable adjectives; and then at the end of it he used to say: 'Och well! We're having a rare time!'"

There was a wealth of philosophy and of Christianity in that Scottish phrase.

Even when things are at their blackest and their hardest and their sorest, you've just got to "kid yourself on" you're "having a rare time".

It is amazing how the gloom will lift, if you can see things in that way!

Try it!

It is amazing how two people can go through exactly the same experience and get almost precisely opposite things out of it.

The old rhyme has it:

> Two men looked out of the prison bars;
> The one saw mud; the other the stars.

There is an old story about two girls who went for a long walk in the country together.

When they got back home, they were asked how they had got on.

One talked about nothing but the dusty roads and the flies and the heat and the general discomfort.

The other talked about a drift of bluebells in a wood and a glimpse of the sea at a turn in the road that she would never forget.

Keep your eyes open.

There is much to see.

And keep open your hearts.

One of the astonishing things is how much of this world's work has been done by sick men. I've mentioned some of these facts elsewhere, but it is worth recalling them again.

Julius Caesar was an epileptic.

Augustus had a stomach ulcer.

Nelson was wretchedly sea-sick every time he put to sea.

Paul had a "thorn in his flesh" which twisted like a torturing stake in his body.

Just when things were at their toughest and when he thought that he could not go on any longer, Paul heard God saying to him: "My grace is sufficient for you, for my strength is made perfect in weakness" (2 Cor. 12:9).

At the end of the day, after more than three years in prison, after ship-wrecks and beatings and batterings and stonings and all kinds of things, this same Paul is singing out: "Rejoice in the Lord always; and again I say, Rejoice." He is telling the world: "I can do all things through Christ who strengthens me" (Phil. 4:4, 13).

The old soldier's advice that I mentioned two days ago was good advice. If you "kid yourself on your having a rare time" a rift in the clouds does come.

The sun starts shining again—even if it is shining through the rain.

A friend of mine met a woman in a hospital. She was waiting for treatment to help a condition which was a result of an accident that she had had at her work. It was the second time she had had an accident, and the second time that she had received a long course of treatment.

In both cases the accident was due to the conditions under which she had to work.

She worked in a factory where the conditions were bad, where the wages were shockingly small, and where the workers had no Trade Union to take up and to plead their case.

In neither accident had the woman received any compensation, and she was not likely to receive any unless she went to law, and then every effort would be made to fight the case against her. She went on to tell how the owner of that factory had the reputation of being a very religious man. Indeed he had the reputation of being an exceptionally able and brilliant preacher of the gospel.

The woman said: "Me and my husband went to hear him preach one night. He's terrific; he's a spell-binder. But I don't believe he means a word of it, for I know how he treats his workers."

Here is one man whose daily life is cancelling out his preaching.

There is a great deal more to Christian witness than rising in a meeting and telling other people that we are saved, and in professing our faith in our Lord Jesus Christ.

There is no such thing as a Christian witness which is over in a minute.

Christian witness is a whole-time job.

THE DIFFERENCE                                                                July 8

If I wanted to know if a man was really saved, I would ask his wife.

If I wanted to know if a woman was really saved, I would ask her husband.

If I wanted to know if a lad or a girl was saved, I would ask his or her father or mother.

If I wanted to know if an employer was saved, I would ask his workmen.

If I wanted to know if a man was saved, I would ask his boss.

No one knows better than I do how far I fall short of that standard myself. But we see young people caught up in some evangelistic movement and enthusiastic for Bible study circles and prayer groups and such things, yet never doing anything to make things easier for an overworked mother in the house.

Bible study is never an end in itself. Not even prayer is an end in itself.

When Jesus prayed, he prayed in order that he might come back from the solitary place better equipped with the peace and the power of God for the battle of daily life and living.

Our Christianity should make a difference in the way we order a meal from a waitress or treat the shop assistant behind the counter.

It should make a difference in the way a man dictates a letter to his typist, and even in the consideration for other people with which he drives and parks his car.

Christianity should make a difference in the conscientiousness of our work, and in the courtesy with which we serve the public and in the consideration with which we live within our own homes.

Christian witness is not one moment's profession of our faith, however brave that moment may be.

Christian witness is a whole-time job every day.

You never know what will happen when you set out on a journey.
In the Bible there is a vivid story that proves that.
It is told in 1 Samuel 9.

A young man, Saul, set out with a servant to look for his father's asses.
The asses had strayed away, and he had set out to find them; and at the end
of the journey he found, not the asses, but a kingdom; for before he came home
Samuel had anointed him as the king of Israel.

He set out to look for his father's asses, and he found a crown.

It is wonderful what the routine of a day's work will produce, if we go about
it faithfully and diligently.

Take the case of Johann Sebastian Bach, the great composer. For years
he was teacher and organist in St. Thomas's School in Leipzig. For one
hundred and twenty-five pounds a year he had to train the boys' choir, play
at services, weddings and funerals and—most amazing of all—to produce
new compositions every week to be sung and played each Sunday.

They were seldom published. They were simply produced, played or
sung, and then pushed into a cupboard to grow old and dusty, forgotten for
years. In the day's work in Leipzig, Bach produced 265 church cantatas, 263
chorales, fourteen larger works, twenty-four secular cantatas, six concertos,
four overtures, eighteen piano and violin concertos; 356 organ works; and
162 pieces for the piano.

*All in the day's work*, this torrent of masterpieces was pouring out.

Another of the great musicians was Franz Joseph Haydn. His output was
colossal. It included 125 symphonies, 417 orchestral pieces, 121 pieces of
piano music, 116 songs and many another production besides.

Once he was asked why in all this mass of production he had never
produced a quintette. His answer was: "Because no one ever ordered
one!"

His masterpieces were produced *all in the day's work*.

Jesus told a story about a man who found a tremendous treasure in a field
(Mat. 13:44). That man must have been ploughing or digging or weeding
that field, and it was in the day's work that he found the treasure.

A novelist tells of a game that two children used to play. One says to the other: "When you are going along the road, do you ever pretend that there is something terrific waiting for you round the next corner, and you've got to go and face it? It makes walking so exciting."

We never know what is waiting for us round the corner.

Every day in life brings its opportunities—the opportunity to practise the greatest of all heroisms, the heroism of carrying on when we are up against it; the greatest of all conquests, the conquest over our own selves; the greatest of all honours, the honour of serving and helping someone in need.

Emily Dickinson has a lovely and simple little poem:

> If I can stop one heart from breaking,
> I shall not live in vain;
> If I can ease one life the aching,
> Or cool one pain,
> Or help one fainting robin
> Unto his nest again
> I shall not live in vain.

For the man who walks with Christ, there is glory along every way and at every journey's end.

## LAUGHTER                                                                 July 11

It is good to laugh.

It was that supremely lovable soul, Haydn, who said: "God will forgive me, if I serve him cheerfully."

The doctors tell us that it is literally a medical fact that he who laughs most lives longest, for laughter expands the lungs and makes a man breathe deeply. I've said this before, but I like to emphasise it!

It is strange how often the Church has been suspicious of laughter. There was a time—not completely at an end yet—when it was a heresy to make a congregation smile.

Eric Linklater tells of a school report he received when he was a schoolboy: "On the whole he is doing fairly well, but he is handicapped by a sense of humour."

Jesus could teach with a smile.

What a picture he drew when he talked about the man with a plank in his own eye gravely trying to remove the speck of dust from someone else's eye! (Matt. 7:3-5).

How the disciples must have appreciated it when the nickname "Sons of Thunder" got itself attached to that tempestuous pair James and John!

It is indeed good to laugh!


THIS I KNOW                                                                    July 12

I heard one of our greatest theologians begin a paper on a very difficult subject in a very simple way. He depicted an imaginary conversation between a student and an examiner.

"I can do nothing with this paper," said the student. "It is quite hopeless."

"Why?" said the examiner.

"Because," said the student, "it is far too difficult for me."

"Then," said the examiner, "put down what you know."


Life can at times be very difficult, but even at its most difficult times a man can put down what he knows. It is surprising sometimes how much you know!


*When we cannot see all the way, we can at least take the next step.*

When we set out in a motor car for a place that is fairly far away, at first its name does not appear on the signposts at all.

We have to go on the journey stage by stage without even seeing the name of our destination. But if we have taken the first steps right, then soon or late for certain the desired name will appear and we will know that we are on the way to our goal.


*When we cannot see how we are to complete a task, we can at least begin it.*

Suppose a minister goes to a new Church "extension" parish in a new area where the Church is beginning for the first time. He may have three or four thousand houses to visit. It may seem a hopeless task with no end to it, but he won't get it done by sitting down and thinking how hopeless it is. He can at least start on the nearest street of houses.

Any writer of books or articles would tell you that the universal experience of the writer is that the hardest sentence to write in any book or in any article is the first. I know that! But nothing will be done if we sit for ever looking at a blank sheet of paper.

The end of the task may not even be in sight, but the first step in the task is waiting to be done. We can always take that step.

Do it *now*!

## WHEN THE WAY IS DARK

*When much is dark, we can always hang on to what we know.*

Life can be very bewildering at times.

Life can be very wounding at times.

It may be very hard to see any sense in it.

There may be many things which must remain wrapped in mystery.

There are many things which defy understanding and many things which seem to have no explanation.

But Browning wrote one sentence:

"God, Thou art love: I build my faith on that."

That is what Paul said too: "He that spared not His own Son, but delivered Him up for us all, how shall He not with Him also freely give us all things?" (Rom. 8:32).

There was a time when even Jesus had to cling on to what he knew. In Gethsemane Jesus did not wish to die. No one wishes to die at thirty-three, least of all to die in the agony of the Cross. Ahead of him the way was dark.

He only knew two things.

He knew that he must accept the will of God; and he knew that the name of the God whose will he must accept was Father.

There are times when it will be like that with us also.

There are times when the end is out of sight—but the next step is there. "One step enough for me."

## NO INTERRUPTION

Travel by air is now quite normal. An aeroplane is simply a common and convenient vehicle for getting quickly from place to place.

As far as I am concerned, a journey by air is something that is still a thrill, and something which, quite unreasonably, I still approach with a certain trepidation!

I remember some years ago being on my way by plane to Germany. BEA supply their passengers with an excellent little handbook of information and of maps. One sentence in that book seemed to me a great ideal. "We have a motto, 'Our passengers are the purpose of our business—not an interruption in our work', and we shall try in every way to live up to it."

Not long before, the booklet had already said: "The bell at the side of your seat will bring your steward or stewardess to you. You have only to ask. Their job is to make your flight comfortable and pleasant."

A request for help is not an interruption or a nuisance; it is something which their staff exist to serve and satisfy.

Big business is built on nothing else than the Christian ideal of service! The more it fulfils that ideal, the more successful it is.

Bruce Barton somewhere tells of a shoe firm whose advertisement read: "We are at your feet" and of an automobile service station whose only claim it was: "We are prepared to crawl under your car oftener and to get ourselves dirtier than any of our competitors." Their stock in trade was *service*.

It is so easy to regard people as a nuisance. It is so easy, when people come with some wearisome request, or some interminable problem to discuss, to regard them as an unwarrantable interruption.

But people matter.

As we all do.

To God.

KNOCK HERE! July 15

Kermit Eby, that great American teacher, tells how it is his deliberate principle always to be available and always accessible to his pupils and students. The door to his house and to his help is always open.

"I know," he says, "that research is important; yet I also know that a man is more important than a footnote."

Nobody is an interruption or a nuisance to him.

The Salvation Army people tell of a certain Mrs. Berwick who retired from active work with the Army in Liverpool, and who came to spend her old age in London. She had been engaged for years on social work. The war came with its terrible air raids. People somehow or other got the idea that her house was safe.

She was old but the experience of her Liverpool days had never left her, and her first instinct was to bind up wounds and do what she could for the sufferer. So she assembled a simple first-aid box, and she put a notice in her window: "If you need help, knock here."

Knock!
Help will come!

## NO TROUBLE!    July 16

William Corbett Roberts was the somewhat unconventional but greatly beloved Rector of St. George's, Bloomsbury.

A stranger was one day looking for some information and left a message with one of the church cleaners.

The stranger said: "I hardly like to trouble him." Back came the cleaner's answer: "Nothing's a trouble to our Rector."

That was indeed a compliment.

When we are in the middle of writing a sermon or an article or a lecture, when we are comfortably settled down in front of the wireless or the television set, when we have some plan of our own, it is so easy to think of the chance visitor, the one who comes appealing for our help as an interruption and a nuisance.

Jesus was not like that.

Luke tells how Jesus tried to get away, how he took his disciples into a desert place privately to be alone, and how the crowds with their unceasing demands chased after him. He might so easily have told them that he must have his quiet time, his rest, his prayer, his preparation; but he didn't. He received them.

"He received them and spake unto them of the Kingdom of Heaven, and healed them that had need of healing" (Luke 9:10, 11).

No man can be like Jesus Christ and find another man in need an interruption or a nuisance.

## IMPOSSIBLE INDEPENDENCE    July 17

A friend of mine has told of a wise thing that a saintly old minister once said to him.

My friend and the old minister were together in the vestry before the service. They were both preparing to robe for the service. The old man lifted up his robe, and began to put it on.

My friend, rather diffidently, asked if he might help, for there are many elderly people who resent any offer of help. The old man turned and smiled. "Certainly," he said, "I'll be very glad of your help. When you refuse help, it is a sign that you have grown old."

What he meant was that when you refuse help, it is a sign that you are struggling to retain an independence, for which in your heart of hearts you know that you are no longer fit.

One of the great errors in life is the error of trying to maintain an unreasonable and an impossible independence.

To do so is the surest way to end in disaster.

*There are some people who are too independent to take advice.*

It was in the snows and ice and the blizzards of Russia that Napoleon's Grand Army perished, and that the beginning of his ultimate destruction emerged.

He was warned not to invade Russia. He was told by the experts that in that particular year the birds had migrated far earlier than usual, and that that was a certain sign of a specially severe winter to come.

Napoleon laughed at advice.

Advice might be useful for lesser men, but not for him.

He refused advice.

His army perished.

It is one of the tragedies of life that so many errors and so much heartbreak could be saved, if people were only humble enough to accept advice.

BLOW THE HORN! July 18

*There are some people who are too independent to ask for guidance.*

Again and again I catch myself doing something which is significant and symbolic. When I am driving in a strange town or a strange part of the country, I hate to ask the way. I like to do it with maps. Even when I get totally lost, I still find myself refusing to ask and insisting on finding my own way!

I have lost a lot of time in my life that way!

That is a small thing, but in the greater things of life, there is many a man who has shipwrecked things because he would not accept the guidance which might have kept him right.

*There are some people who are too independent to ask for help.*

There is a famous legend of the death of Roland, the greatest of Charlemagne's paladins. Along with his friend, Oliver, he was the rearguard of

Charlemagne's army. All unexpectedly he and his little force were suddenly surrounded by the Moors.

Now Roland wore at his side the great horn whose blast could be heard miles and miles away. "Blow the horn," said Oliver, "and Charlemagne will come back and help." But Roland refused; he was too proud to ask for help.

The battle raged, and always Roland refused to sound the call for help. One by one his men were slain, till only he and Oliver were left. Oliver was slain and Roland was wounded unto death.

Then and then only did he send the call for help across the hills and valleys. Charlemagne came hastening back; but Oliver was dead and Roland was dead, and not a man was left alive.

Roland had sent the call for help too late.
Blow the horn when you need to do it!


## THE PRIDE THAT IS FOLLY                                           July 19

Sometimes, in our pride, we think that we can cope with life ourselves. We think that we can bear the burdens and conquer the temptations and face the sorrows alone.

There is a pride in life which will not ask for help. That pride is folly. If we would be safe, we must be humble enough to ask for advice and guidance and help before it is too late.

There are two texts which should be written on our hearts. The first is: "Without me ye can do nothing" (John 15:5); the other is: "With God nothing shall be impossible" (Luke 1:37). I can't quote either often enough.

A false independence is the way to disaster.
The humility to ask for help is the way to safety.
There is no man who can deal with life alone.
There is no man who *needs* to deal with life alone.


## THOU SHALT NOT . . .                                              July 20

It is true that the approach to religion must be positive, but it is equally true that it is not possible to eliminate from religion all the "thou shalt not's".

There was a time when religion was far too much built on "thou shalt not"; but in our permissive society the pendulum has swung so far the other way that there tend to be no "thou shalt not's" at all.

It is time that the Church said uncompromisingly that there are certain things which are wrong, and wrong under any circumstances.

It is true that the Christian object towards the wrong-doer must be the wrong-doer's reformation, but it is equally true that the element of punishment cannot be entirely eliminated.

It is, nowadays, almost to be labelled "unchristian" to speak of punishment at all. But it is not punishment in itself which is wrong. What matters is the spirit and the aim of punishment.

Punishment administered in vengeance and in retribution is wrong.

Punishment administered in pride or in the delight to hurt is wrong.

But punishment administered in the spirit of discipline which is part of true love may often be right.

It will always be true that some people have to be taught that wrong-doing has its inevitable consequence, and that some people have to be shocked out of evil into good.

LEARNING FROM THE UNLIKELY                                July 21

I remember talking to a minister friend whom I know very well indeed. He told me something which I had never suspected—that he was the possessor of a very fiery and violent temper. He also told me of a lesson that he had learnt a long time ago, one which had enabled him to control and to master that temper.

My friend had been other things before he was a minister. At one time he had worked out in the East.

One morning when he was shaving, his native servant came in and said or did something which annoyed him, and which made his temper blaze out.

My friend took the soapy shaving brush that he had in his hand and hurled it at the native boy. The brush missed its target and fell on the floor.

Without a word, the native boy stooped and picked up the brush, and with a courteous bow handed it back to him.

My friend told me that that incident taught him a lesson which he never forgot. Here was a so-called Christian, a member of a so-called more civilised race, losing his temper like that. Here was the boy, who was a heathen and not a Christian at all, showing a perfect example of courtesy and forbearance.

So my friend learned the lesson of courtesy and self-control from an Eastern native boy who was not a Christian.

## MORE LESSONS FROM THE UNLIKELY July 22

*The Christian can often learn a lesson from the Communist.*

There is never any doubt that a Communist knows what he believes. He knows exactly the creed of Communism and all that it means and all that it stands for.

How many Christians know and understand their creed and their faith as a Communist knows and understands his?

*The Christian can often learn a lesson from the atheist.*

It is very often a feature of discussion that the atheist knows the Bible far better than the Christian does. When it comes to an argument about what the Bible says, the atheist time and time again will know the Bible in far greater detail than most Church members do.

*The people in the Church can often learn a lesson from people like Jehovah's Witnesses.*

The members of that sect will go from door to door selling their literature and pleading their case, and arguing their case with the greatest enthusiasm and the greatest intelligence.

How many of our Church members could we persuade to go round the doors spreading propaganda for their Church?

## WHAT A DIFFERENCE! July 23

Jesus told a story about a steward who was a thorough-going rascal.

In the old days these stewards held most responsible positions. They had control of the whole estate. Often the master himself, though wealthy, might not be able to read and write and calculate. The steward had everything in his hands.

This steward had used his position to help himself to his master's money. In due time he was found out. Immediately he started out and began to rig the accounts outstanding to his master, and began to arrange things so that the debtors would get away with much less than they really owed. He was going to see to it that even when he was dismissed he would have friends who were under an obligation to him to see him right.

When the master found out about it, he appreciated the steward's cleverness. The steward might be a rascal, but he was a clever rascal whose cleverness had to be admired. And Jesus finished up: "The children of this world are in their generation wiser than the children of light" (Luke 16:1–8).

What Jesus is saying is this: "If the religious people were half as much in earnest about their religion as the business people are about their business, what a difference it would make!"

If a man would put the effort into his Church that he puts into his business, what a difference it would make!
If a man would put the effort into his Christianity that some men put into their hobbies—for instance, into getting their golf handicaps down a stroke—what a difference it would make!

KNOWING HOW TO DO IT                                   July 24

There was a certain firm which had installed in their works a very complicated machine. One day the machine went wrong. The firm's own mechanics were unable to deal with the fault, so they sent out an S.O.S. for help to the makers of the machine.

In due course a man arrived. He looked at the machine, and all he seemed to do was to give a certain part of it a slight tap with a hammer and the machine was going as well as ever again.

At the end of the month the account came in and the account read: "To repairing the machine—£5.12s.6d."

This seemed a very large sum to charge for effecting a repair with a single tap with a hammer.

So the firm wrote to the makers of the machine asking them to detail the account and to explain how this sum of £5.12s.6d. was arrived at. Soon an answer to this demand arrived and now the detailed account read: "To mechanic's time in repairing machine—12s.6d; to knowing how to do it—£5."

The crucial part is to know *how* to do it.

SELF-DISCIPLINE                                             July 25

There is nothing more pathetic in this world than the sight of a man who drifts from job to job because he has no real trade and no real skill, because he has never accepted the discipline, the training, the work involved in knowing how to do anything in this world.

"It is good for a man," said the old prophet, "that he bear the yoke in his youth" (Lam. 3:27).

There may be times when the yoke of discipline and the task of learning seems hard, and when it seems much more attractive to take an easier and a more immediately profitable way, but the rewards of life are for the man who has borne the yoke in his youth and who had learned how to do it.

The greatest of all knowledge is the knowledge of God. As the old preacher said: "Remember now thy Creator in the days of thy youth" (Eccles. 12:1).

Get that knowledge early!
And hold on to it!

## THE NAMELESS HOST July 26

I am told there are some 2,400 parts in a typewriter. It must take hundreds of people to make a typewriter, to prepare it and deliver it to the man who is going to use it.

When I thought of that I began to think of the hundreds and hundreds of people whose names I do not know and will never know, who helped me to write this book. I couldn't do my work without a typewriter. I couldn't have a typewriter without the work of hundreds of nameless people and, as I type, I can't help thinking of my army of nameless helpers.

We are dependent for the simplest and the most essential things, on a nameless army of helpers.

I wonder how many hundreds of people from how many different countries it takes to produce one breakfast table. The farmer and his workers who grow the grain from which the bread is made, the people in India or China or Ceylon who grew the tea from which the tea is made, the sugar, the milk, the bacon, the eggs, the oranges for the marmalade, the people who grew them, the sailors who carried them across the sea, the transport workers who brought them along the roads and the railways, the people in the factories who manufactured them, the shopkeepers who sold them—the list of people who give us our breakfast each morning is endless.

Our dependence on the nameless host of people is an amazing thing. "I am a debtor," said Paul (Rom. 1:14). "We are members one of another," he said (Rom. 12:5). Just as the body cannot do without its many parts, so we cannot do without each other. There is that strange, vivid phrase in the Old Testament which speaks of being "bound up in the bundle of life" (1 Sam. 25:29).

We are all dependent on the nameless hosts who help.

*We are all dependent on nameless workers.*

We know the names of the great statesmen and the great artists and the great musicians and the great writers and the great philosophers, but no man knows the name of the man who invented the wheel or the water tap, on which so much depends.

We should stop and remember those on the work of whose hands we are dependent. Sometimes there is a tendency to despise those who work with their hands. But they are the people whom we could not do without.

*We are dependent on nameless witnesses.*

We know the names of the great saints and martyrs, but there are thousands upon thousands of simple men and women, whose names are forgotten, but who chose to die rather than to deny their Lord.

It is on the nameless ones that the very fabric of the Church is built.

Alistair Maclean writes in *High Country*: "I read a tale set in jewels the other day. It was of Luther marching through the streets of Worms to that mighty conflict in which the fate of the Reformation was finally decided. The streets were crowded. The multitudes were silent. The leader of the new Faith pressed steadily, almost stonily, on. Suddenly a voice, clear as a bell, rang through the air. 'Play the man, play the man. Fear not death. It can but slay the body. There is a life beyond.' It was noticed thereafter that the face of Captain Greatheart shone."

Might it be possible that we owe the Reformation, our Church, to the cry of encouragement of a nameless witness, when Luther's heart was near to shrinking from its task?

The Church is built on the witness of the nameless host of faithful ones.

We enter into other men's labours; so they must enter into ours.

We are dependent on the work of the host of nameless ones, so we must work with diligence that others may reap the benefit of the work we do.

We are dependent on the witness of the nameless host, so we too must bear our witness so that we may make it easier for others to follow Christ.

In the army of Christ we may not be the leaders and the generals whose names are on every lip; but we can at least be the private soldiers, whose names are unknown, but on whose valour the outcome of the battle must depend.

WORKING AND WAITING                                                        July 29

The more one reads of the life and of the work of great men, the more one sees that they had a twin capacity—*the capacity to work* and *the capacity to wait*.

The capacity of the great writers to work is an extraordinary thing. It was said of Southey that "he was never happy unless he was reading or writing a book".

Perhaps the supreme example of a writer's industry was that of Anthony Trollope.

Trollope was an inspector with the Post Office, first in Ireland and then in England. His work made it necessary for him to be travelling constantly every day. He devised a certain kind of writing pad which he could hold upon his knee, and by far the greater part of his early novels was written during journeys in railway trains.

On one occasion he had to go on postal business to Egypt. He describes the voyage, and how not even its difficulties were allowed to interfere with his prescribed output. "As I journeyed across France to Marseilles, and made thence a terribly rough voyage to Alexandria, I wrote my allotted number of pages every day. On this occasion more than once I left my paper on the cabin table, rushing away to be sick in the privacy of my state room. It was February, and the weather was miserable; but still I did my work."

The man who has learned the secret of work knows that in everyday things perspiration has done more than inspiration has ever done.

It would not be a bad thing if preachers were chained to their desks at least four mornings a week, and forbidden to rise until they had produced something to show for their labours!

Equally the great men had the ability to wait.

There is a time for a wise inactivity, an inactivity which in a sense is creatively active.

Strangely enough, Anthony Trollope himself tells us of Thomas Carlyle's reaction to his writing in trains. "Carlyle," says Trollope, "has since told me that a man when travelling should not read, but 'sit still and label his thoughts'."

Dr. Johnson used to say that one of the great uses of the Sunday was that on it the ordinary affairs of life were laid aside, and it gave a man the chance and the obligation to sit quietly and to take stock of himself and of his life.

Guy Rogers quotes a scene from *They Come, They Go* by Winifred Peck in which "the fussy, busy, conscientiously effusive parson" is pilloried. Two widows of two former rectors are listening at the house-warming of a third to the story of his efficiency.

The comment of one is kindly: "I expect by the time Mr. Hole is sixty and has taken to spectacles instead of pince-nez and prayer instead of so many meetings, he'll be a much more attractive Christian."

But the other's farewell is devastating: "Well, Mr. Hole, it was kind of you to ask us all here, and I'm glad to know of all you are doing in St. Mary Luce. But you're young and I'm old, and I feel it my duty to say one thing before I leave . . . There's one thing you'll be in danger of forgetting and leaving out of your life from first to last."

"And that is?" said the rector, dropping his pince-nez and smiling tolerantly on the old lady. "Why, God," she answered briefly.

It is the tragedy when too much working eliminates quiet waiting for God.

"I must work the works of Him that sent me, while it is day," he said. "For the night cometh when no man can work" (John 9:4). Yet this same Jesus said: "Come ye apart yourselves into a desert place, and rest awhile" (Mark 6:31).

In the fully organised life there will be the work which drives ahead, in any circumstances, and without the foolish waiting for a vague inspiration; but there will also be the wise waiting, which is the very thing which makes the constant working possible.

There will be a rhythm in a life in which a man works for men and waits with God.

I see three characteristics of our present-day Church young people.

*They think.*

They are not content to be told. They want to discuss and to argue and to think this out for themselves.

They do not believe that reverence consists in a hushed acceptance of ancient creeds and dogmas. They believe with Plato that "the unexamined life is the life not worth living".

I believe that we are building up today a generation who have thought out the faith which they hold. They may abandon many things in the process, but what is left is really and truly theirs, at first hand.

*They speak.*

These young people can put their thoughts and beliefs into words in a way that would do credit to anyone. I believe that we are building up today a generation which is articulate and one which can tell the world what it believes.

*They criticise.*

But their criticism is the criticism of love.

They criticise the Church, not because they wish to destroy the Church, but because the Church as it stands does not come up to their ideal of what it should be. They have not yet reached the stage of accepting second bests and of writing off ideals as impossible—and thank God for that!

The future of any Church lies in its young people. As a teacher in a university and as one who sees much of the youth fellowship movement, it is my conviction that the future of the Church was never brighter than it is today—if judged by our young people.

# *August*

The mottoes of the Scottish clans are very intriguing. Let us look at some of these during August.

The Macmillans come from more than one particular part of the country. They come from Knapdale in Argyllshire and from Galloway as well.

Perhaps they began by being a family of holy men connected with the Church, for it may be that the name of Macmillan is connected with the Gaelic word *moal*, which means bald or tonsured, as a monk is tonsured.

The Macmillans have a very fine Latin motto—*Miseris succurrere disco*, which means, I learn to succour the wretched, or, as we might put it, "I learn to help the unhappy".

There could be few finer mottoes than that.

If we are to learn to help the unhappy, certain things have to be remembered.

It is perfectly possible to walk through the world and not even notice the pain and the sorrow that are there.

*We must learn to see the unhappiness of others.*

In the old days in America Dwight L. Morrow was a very influential man who had a great deal to do with decisions as to whom his party would run as President. He had a daughter called Anne Morrow, who, when she was a child, used to be present almost unnoticed at some very important gatherings.

At one meeting the question was whether or not Calvin Coolidge was a suitable candidate for the Presidency. Coolidge had been invited to be there. He had been interviewed, and sized up. He had left the meeting, and now they were discussing whether or not he would do. Suddenly Anne's voice interrupted the discussions of the statesmen. "Of course he'll do," she said. Her father asked her why she was so sure. She lifted up a rather grubby thumb decorated by an even more grubby bandage. "He is the only one of you," she said, "who noticed that I had a sore thumb, and who asked me how it was getting on."

It was a child's test, but a good test.

It is so easy to be so aloof, to be so wrapped up in one's own self, to be so blind and deaf and insensitive that we never even notice the unhappiness of others.

INTO ACTION                                                                    August 2

"I learn to help the unhappy."

*We must learn to feel the unhappiness of others.*

It is not enough simply to see. When we see, we must also feel.

It is quite possible to see the unhappiness of others and to think—perhaps even unconsciously—that it has nothing to do with us. It is quite possible to see the unhappiness of others and to accept it as part of the landscape, as just one of these things which are in the nature of things.

William Morris used to say that every time he passed a drunken man on the street he felt personally responsible for that man.

The sight of human need, human unhappiness, human misery should always make an answering sword of grief and pity pierce our hearts.

*We must learn to act for the help of others.*

To see is not enough; even to feel is not enough; the seeing and the feeling must be turned into action. And that is so for a very special reason.

Francis of Assisi began by being a wealthy young lover of pleasure, one of the gilded youth of his day. Then one day he was riding when he saw a leper, in rags, alone, hideously disfigured. Up to that time Francis had thought of nothing but pleasure, but something made him lean down from his horse and throw his arms in a sudden wave of sympathy around that tattered wreck of a human being. And, as he did so, the figure in his arms seemed to change to Jesus Christ himself.

"Inasmuch as ye have done it unto one of the least of these my brethren," said Jesus, "ye have done it unto me" (Matt. 25:40).

Help given to a brother man in trouble is help given to Jesus Christ. Therein is the reason for every Christian to take as his motto: "I learn to help the unhappy, I learn to succour the wretched."

## PRAY AND WORK August 3

Ramsay is the family name of the Earl of Dalhousie, who is the head of one of the most ancient and famous Scottish families. The motto of the Ramsays is the Latin phrase *Ora et Labora*, which means, "Pray and Work".

There are no two activities more closely connected than prayer and work. The one is always incomplete and often futile without the other.

*To prayer must always be added work and labour and toil.*

No man need think that all he has to do is to pray for something and that then that something will fall into his hands. It is always wrong to look on God as the easy way out, to look on God as the person who will do for us what we are too lazy to do for ourselves.

Long ago the ancient philosopher Epicurus, who talked so much sense, said: "It is vain to ask of the gods what a man is capable of supplying for himself."

Nowhere are we better taught this than in the Lord's Prayer Jesus taught us to pray: "Give us this day our daily bread." But we cannot thus pray and then sit back and wait for our daily bread to fall into our hands. We have to work and toil, to sow the seed, till the ground, harvest the crop, grind the corn, prepare the food, before we can have our daily bread.

## THE COMBINATION August 4

"Pray and work."

Dick Sheppard used to love a certain story.

There was a man who had an allotment. Once it had been rough, unsightly, weed-infested ground, but he had laboured and toiled until it bore the loveliest flowers and the largest vegetables.

A pious friend was being shown over the allotment. He naturally commented on the beauty of the flowers and the excellence of the vegetables.

Then he said: "Yes, it's wonderful what God can do with a piece of ground, isn't it?"

"Yes," said the man who had toiled in the sweat of his brow over the allotment, "but you should have seen this piece of ground when God had it to himself!"

All great things come from the combination of God's help and man's toil.

A Christian man must pray, and must then do everything possible to make his prayer come true.

NEVER ALONE!                                                                     August 5

"Pray and work."

One of the noblest of the unwritten sayings of Jesus, the sayings which are not in our gospels is: "Raise the stone and thou shalt find me; cleave the wood and I am there." Jesus Christ is there to help the mason as he dresses the stone and the carpenter as he handles the wood.

It is one of the basic rules of life that no man is ever left to do any task by himself. Whenever he sets his hand to any good and useful undertaking Jesus is with him to strengthen and to help.

That is why time and time again men have been enabled to do things which humanly speaking were impossible; and that is why men have been prepared to put their hands to tasks which are obviously beyond their powers.

Jesus said to his disciples: "Go ye and teach all nations" (Matt. 28:19). That was a command addressed to no more than one hundred and twenty men, and they were men without influence, without money, without learning, without prestige (Acts 1:15). Yet these men laid their hands to that impossible task because Jesus had made another promise to them: "Lo, I am with you always even unto the end of the world" (Matt. 28:20).

With the task there always comes the power to do it.

Prayer and work must always go together.

God's grace and Christ's presence added to our toil make all things possible.

The Robertsons came originally from the Atholl country. No family was ever more faithful to the Stuarts and to Prince Charlie. Later their home was in the Rannoch country, at Dunalastair in the shadow of Schiehallion.

Their motto is a Latin phrase: *Virutis gloria merces*, which means: "Glory is the reward of virtue."

Here is a great truth.
The only way to glory is the way of honour, of honesty and of virtue.

*Glory is a deceptive word. It is a word which sounds as if it was clothed in glamour and in romance. But glory is always the product of unremitting toil.*

Anyone who achieves glory in any sphere of life has to work for it.
The great musician or the great singer comes only to his glory by the way of ceaseless practice for many hours a day every day.
The great writer or the great orator comes only to his glory by constant toil and discipline. The great athlete comes only to his through unremitting discipline and training.

There is no easy way to glory. *Per ardua ad astra*; the way to the stars is always steep.
"The gods," said Hesiod, "have ordained sweat as the price of all things precious."

Not the dilettante, but the toiler reaches the glory.

ONE SENTENCE                                        August 7

"Glory is the reward of virtue."

*There is a group of words all closely related, but all with very different meanings. There is "fame", there is "notoriety", there is "glory".*
They all imply that there is something outstanding about the person to whom they are ascribed.

To be "notorious" is to be known for things which are discreditable.
To be "famous" is to be known for great things, good and bad alike.
To have "glory" is always to be known for good.

Sometimes the Bible has a way of summing up a man in one sentence. It dismisses Nadah, king of Israel, in little more than one sentence: "He did evil in the sight of the Lord" (1 Kgs. 15:26).

Life has a way of summing up in one sentence. When a man is gone from this earth, he always leaves a memory which is so often summarised in one sentence. Many will say of him that he was sarcastic, that he was unreliable, that he was kind. But always for good or for bad there is the one sentence verdict.

What will that sentence be about us?
Notoriety, fame, or the glory which comes from goodness?
Which shall *we* leave behind?

THE GLORY WORTH HAVING                                     August 8

"Glory is the reward of virtue."

*The only glory worth having is glory that can be taken with us when we leave this world.*
We cannot take money; we cannot take fame; we cannot take place and power over other people; we cannot take achievement; we cannot take prestige.
The only thing which we can take with us when we leave this world is our selves; and therefore the only glory which is worth having is the glory of excellence of character and of Christian and Christlike living.

The glory of the Christian is not in gaining but in giving; not in getting but in spending; not in ruling but in serving; not in being the master of many but in being the servant of all.

It is a life like that which brings to a man the glory that will last when time ends and when eternity begins. For it is he who humbles himself who will be exalted, and he who exalts himself who will be abased (Matt. 23:12).

The glory of Jesus was to bear the Cross.
It must be even so for the Christian.

174

The Macfies of Macphees originally came from Colonsay, and their motto is *Pro Rege*, which means "For the King".

Here is the motto of loyalty, the motto of men who will never betray their king.

One of the great stories of loyalty, a story that has often been told and that will be retold just as often, is the story of the eight men of Glenmoriston.

It was in 1746 after the Duke of Cumberland had annihilated the armies of Prince Charlie at the Battle of Culloden. The Prince had escaped; and he was wandering literally in rags with one companion. The government had put a price on his head, offering the sum of £30,000 for him dead or alive.

He came to Glenmoriston and was all but starving. He saw smoke coming from a hut and he determined to go there, although there might be enemies there, for anything was better than slow death by starvation.

In the hut there were eight men, two Macdonalds, three Chisholms, one Macgregor, one Grant and one Macmillan. They were all thieves and criminals and had taken to the hills to escape justice.

When the Prince entered the door one of them recognised him, but hid his recognition. But the others had to be told, and, when they were told, for weeks these eight Highland outlaws guarded and protected and cared for the Prince. There was £30,000 on his head, but not one of these men was prepared to play the Judas.

They even made a journey to Fort Augustus at the peril of their liberty and lives to buy the Prince a pennyworth of ginger-bread.

"For the King."

For weeks the Prince sheltered with the men in Glenmoriston. When in the end he left them, he shook hands with each of them.

The years passed by and the time came when men in Scotland forgot danger and looked back on the Jacobite rebellion as a romantic episode.

By that time one of the eight men was in Edinburgh; his name was Hugh Chisholm. People would ask him to tell the tale of the days when he and his friends had sheltered the Prince in Glenmoriston and he would willingly tell it.

But one thing Hugh Chisholm always did; he would always shake hands with his left hand, for he said that he would never give to any other man the hand that once he had given to his Prince.

There is loyalty.

Would that our loyalty to God our King were of that standard!

## NEVER BEHIND August 11

The Douglases take their name from the moorland country in Lanarkshire and their motto is *Jamais Arrière*, which means, "Never Behind".

There are indeed certain things in which the Christian should never be behind.

*The Christian should never be behind in generosity.*

His heart should be the first heart to be pierced with the sword of grief and pity for the pain, the sorrow and the want of others; and his hand should be the first hand stretched out to help.

Dr. A. Rendle Short in his book, *The Bible and Modern Medicine*, points out how the Christian Church has always been in the very forefront of all work to alleviate pain and suffering.

The first blind asylum was founded by a Christian monk, Thalasius, and the first free dispensary by Apollonius, a Christian merchant.

The first hospital of which there is any record was founded by a Christian lady, Fabiola.

During the great Decian persecution the Church in Rome had under its care a great crowd of widows, orphans, blind, lame and sick folk.

The heathen prefect broke into the Church and demanded that the congregation should hand over its treasures to the state.

Laurentius the deacon pointed at the crowd of poor and sick and maimed and lonely and said: "These are the treasures of the Church."

## THE FIRST STEP August 12

"Never behind!"

*What is true of the Church should be true of the individual Christian.*

There is a story which tells how a crowd was watching a disaster which had befallen a carter and which had wrecked his cart. Amongst them there was an old Quaker. Many were the expressions of sympathy for the carter in his loss.

Amidst all the words the old Quaker stepped forward: "I am sorry five pounds," he said, handing a note to the carter. Then he turned to the crowd: "Friend," he said to each, "how much art thou sorry?"

The Christian should never be behind in backing the sympathy of words with the sympathy of deeds.

*The Christian should never be behind in forgiveness.*
The Christian should always be ready to be the one who makes the first approach. Even if he feels that he has been wronged and insulted, even if he feels, and feels rightly, that the fault is all on the other side, the Christian should always be ready to take the first step towards reconciliation and towards healing where there is division.

Many and many a quarrel and a bitterness would long since have been healed, if someone had had the grace and the humility to take the first step towards healing it.

WELL DONE! August 13

"Never behind!"

*The Christian should never be behind in praise.*
The people who are ready to say to others "Well done!" are all too few.

I once heard a well-known minister say that he had been twenty-five years in a certain charge and no one had ever thanked him for a sermon or said that he had enjoyed or been helped by one.

Abraham Lincoln knew human nature, and Abraham Lincoln said: "Everyone likes a compliment."

We could sow a great deal of happiness in this world, if we were a little readier to praise, where praise is needed.

*The Christian should never be behind in gratitude.*
One of the commonest and the ugliest sins is the failure to say thanks for all the benefits we have received both from our fellow-men and from God. It is a graceless thing always to be taking and never to acknowledge with gratitude the debt which we owe.

"O give thanks unto the Lord, for he is good," said the Psalmist (Ps. 106:1).
There are ambitions which are selfish and unworthy but the ambition never to be behind in generosity, in forgiveness, in praise, and in thanks is a truly Christian ambition.

The Hamiltons are one of the greatest Scottish families. The Duke of Hamilton is the premier peer of Scotland, the hereditary keeper of Holyroodhouse, the royal palace of Scotland, the peer who had the first vote in the Scottish Parliament, and who had the privilege of leading the vanguard of the Scots in battle.

The Hamiltons, like the Cummings, have a motto of one word, "Through". It is a magnificent motto.

*It is a Christian duty to think things through.*

"Prove all things," said Paul, "and hold fast that which is good" (1 Thess. 5:21).

If a faith is only held with the surface of man's mind, if to him it is only a conventional thing, which he has learned at second-hand, if he has never made any attempt to think it out and to think it through, then, when it is put to the test, it will certainly collapse and fail.

Dr. J. S. Whale has said that "it is a moral duty to be intelligent".

E. F. Scott has said that the failure of Christianity to be effective in the individual life and in the world is more often than we know due to nothing other than intellectual sloth.

That is what Tennyson meant too when he said that there was more faith in honest doubt than in half the creeds.

It is not of doubts that a man should be ashamed. What he should hate is the failure to face his doubts.

Nothing is reliable until it is tested, and neither is our faith.

We can only acquire a faith which will stand the test when we think things through.

MESSAGE DELIVERED!                                  August 15

"Through!"

*It is a Christian duty to see things through.*

There are many more glamorous virtues in this world, but there is no virtue which is more valuable than the virtue of perseverance, the power to see things through.

During the war in Bristol there was a boy cyclist messenger called Derek Belfall. He was sent on his bicycle with a message when a raid was threatening. He was almost at the post to which he was to deliver his message when a bomb fell. He was blown from his bicycle and mortally wounded.

When they came to pick him up, he was barely conscious. With a last effort he held out the message he had been given to deliver. "Messenger Belfall reporting," he whispered, "I have delivered my message."

"I have finished the work which thou gavest me to do," said Jesus (John 17:4).

The deepest satisfaction in life is to see something through, and the tragedy is that the world is full of people whose lives are filled with uncompleted tasks and with things half done.

PASS THROUGH! August 16

"Through!"

*It is a Christian duty to pass through things.*

There is a phrase which occurs again and again in the Bible; it is the phrase, "It came to pass". It may not be a very good translation, but there is a symbolic truth in it.

The Christian should have a certain gift for passing through the experiences of life.

One of the tragedies in life is a life which is lingering for ever in the past.

There are people who live on past triumphs, on past moments of greatness, yet who fail completely in the duties of the present.

There are people who linger for ever in past disappointments, past griefs or sorrows, past failures, and who are resentful and bitter throughout their lives.

There is nothing which unfits a man for the present like the wrong kind of lingering in the past.

"Forgetting the things which are behind," said Paul, "and reaching out to the things that are before" (Phil. 3:13)—that is the Christian way to live life.

To think things through, to see things through, to pass through things, to go on—*this is life.*

The Cumming family trace their ancestry all the way back to Robert de Comyn who came to this country with William the Conqueror in 1066. Their motto consists of only one word: "Courage."

Courage is the one virtue which all men recognise and which all men admire.

Quinton Reynolds, a famous American journalist broadcaster, told, in a war book, of something that he saw in London during the days of the war.

He was walking down a London street. On the other side of the street a commissionaire was standing in a doorway. He was not very young; and in those war-time days of shabbiness, his uniform was not very resplendent.

As Quinton Reynolds watched, an army officer came down the road, and as he passed the old commissionaire, his arm swung to the salute and he passed on.

Why, thought Mr. Reynolds, should this officer salute this old commissionaire?

A moment afterwards a high-ranking R.A.F. officer passed, and, as he passed, he too swung to the salute as he passed the old commissionaire.

By this time Mr. Reynolds was watching in astonishment.

Then down the street there came nothing less than a major-general; and, as he passed the old commissionaire, he too gave him a sweeping salute.

Mr. Reynolds was astonished at all this. He crossed the road to have a closer look at the commissionaire. As he came closer to him he suddenly caught sight of something. On the left breast of the old man's tunic there was a ribbon, a dark red ribbon, the ribbon of the Victoria Cross, the highest of all awards for gallantry.

When any man wears that ribbon, the highest ranking officer in any of the services must salute it.

Courage demands the admiration of all.

"Courage!"

Every Christian needs courage, and, in these days in which we live, when the Church and the faith are under fire, the courage which we need most of all is the courage to witness to Jesus Christ, the courage never to be ashamed to show whose we are and whom we serve.

Hugh Redwood tells a story of a boy taken to a camp run by a Christian society. He came from a home where the name of Christ was never mentioned except as an oath.

At the camp for the first time in his life, he came across the custom of saying grace before meat. He had never seen this custom before, but when it was all explained to him this way of saying thanks appealed to him and he liked it.

At the end of the fortnight he came home. At the first meal he rose to say his grace. His eldest brother promptly knocked him down. "We want none of that stuff here," he said.

The next meal came; again the lad rose to say grace; and again he was promptly knocked down.

The next meal came; again the boy rose to say grace. His brother's fist was raised to knock him down again. The father, to whom Christianity was nothing, stopped him. "Stop it," he said. "You can think what you like about the boy, but he's got a sight more courage than you."

Tertullian was one of the greatest of the early Christian fathers. They say that, at one time, he may well have been the attorney general of the Roman Empire. He was certainly a lawyer, and he was so impressed with the dauntless courage of the Christians whom he prosecuted that he enquired what made men like that, and he became a Christian.

Courage!
It is a great motto.
It ought to be the Christian motto too.
"I am not ashamed of the gospel of Christ," said Paul (Rom. 1:16).

TRY!                                                        August 19

The Dundases originally came from the country south of the Forth around Dunbar. Their motto is one French word: *Essayez!* which means: "Try!"

This is surely one of the greatest of all mottoes. It is surely a word which Jesus Christ is speaking to everyone who desires to be his follower.

*Men are divided into two classes, when they are confronted with any demand, or task, or challenge. There are those who say, "It's hopeless"; and there are those who say, "I'll try".*

When we read the stories of the healing miracles which Jesus worked, again and again we see that it was the man who was prepared to try who received the miracle.

Jesus said to the paralysed man whose friends carried him into his presence: "Take up your bed and walk" (Mark 2:11). The man might well have answered: "That is precisely what it is hopeless for me to try to do."

But he tried and the miracle happened.

Jesus said to the man with the withered hand: "Stretch out your hand" (Mark 3:5). It would have been easy for the man to say: "Can't you see that it is hopeless for me to try to do that?"

But he tried and the miracle happened.

Jesus said to the woman taken in adultery: "Go and sin no more" (John 8:11). It seems on the face of it a hopeless command to give to a woman like that.

But Jesus clearly expected her to go out and to obey it.

There is nothing which so holds up all progress and which so much keeps us from being what we ought to be as the dull, pessimistic saying: "It's hopeless."

There are many things which, tackled by ourselves, are hopeless.

There is nothing that is hopeless with Jesus Christ.


NOTHING IS IMPOSSIBLE                                    August 20

"Try!"

*Men are divided into those who say, "It's impossible", and those who say, "If you tell me to, I'll try"* (as we have already said).

One of the most astonishing things that the risen Christ ever said to his men was: "Ye shall be witnesses unto me both in Jerusalem, and in all Judea, and in Samaria, and unto the uttermost parts of the earth" (Acts 1:8). "Go ye and teach all nations" (Matt. 28:19). There were about one hundred and twenty of them (Acts 1:15).

They went.

If ever men would have been justified in saying, "It's impossible", it would have been these men. A command to one hundred and twenty uneducated Jews to evangelise the world looks like insanity. But they tried.

They did.

Once when the disciples had toiled all night long and caught nothing, Jesus told them again to let down their nets. Peter's answer was that they had toiled without success, and he could not see how things could be any better now, "Nevertheless at Thy word I will let down the net" (Luke 5:1–11).

The miracle happened.

With Jesus Christ the Christian need never say: "It's impossible"; he can always say: "I'll try."

The miracle can happen.

CHRIST'S OFFER                                                    August 21

"Try!"

*The same kind of thinking keeps so many people from accepting the offer of the gospel. So many people say of the offer of the gospel: "It's too good to be true."*
*But the answer is: "Try it and see."*

It is not really possible to argue a man into accepting the offer and the way of Jesus Christ. Once a man has accepted it, it is possible to do a great deal to assist his doubts and to enable him to reach his certainty. But the only real answer to a man who feels that Christianity cannot possibly be true is to say to him: "I can't argue with you; I can only say, 'Try it and see'."

Jesus Christ is always saying to us: "When things seem hopeless, try it and see what happens. If you think that my offer is too good to be true, try it and see what happens."

There is no better motto for a Christian than the Dundas motto: *Essayez!* "Try!"

Is there?

DREAD GOD                                                        August 22

The Carnegies are one of the great Scottish families connected with Southesk and with Kinnaird. They take their origin from a man called Jocelyn de Ballinhard who lived as long ago as 1203.

Their family motto is "Dread God".

A great motto it is.

*This motto speaks to us of the need of reverence.*

The fear of God, said the Hebrew sage, is the beginning of wisdom (Prov. 1:7). By "beginning" he may well mean not the thing with which wisdom begins, but the chief thing in wisdom.

The philosophers speak to us of what they call "the numinous".

The numinous is the feeling of awe which comes to every man at some time or other.

It is the feeling that we are in the presence of something which comes from beyond this world, the eerie feeling that there is a presence which is mysterious and inexplicable in the world, a presence of something which is "wholly other" than ourselves.

This, the philosophers tell us, is the raw material of all religion.

It is true that, through Jesus Christ, there has come to us the friendship of God, and that we can come to him with childlike confidence and boldness without dread. But there is a familiarity which can breed contempt in a man with an insensitive heart.

When we are in God's house, we should behave with reverence, remembering that the place whereon we stand is holy ground.

When we are in God's world we should behave with reverence, remembering that the whole world is the Temple of the Spirit of God, and that in him we live and move and have our being.

God is Father; but God is also God.

The way to approach God is on our knees.

"Dread God!"

*This motto speaks to us of the need of obedience.*

One of the great troubles of life is that we do not take the commands and the demands of God sufficiently seriously. Somehow, although we know them so well, we are so often prepared just to ignore them or to forget them, as if they did not matter very much.

When we disobey God, when we take our own way, we are not so much breaking God's law as we are breaking God's heart.

One of the things which keeps us from doing many a wrong action, is simply the fear to hurt those we love. If we remembered how our thoughtlessness and our disobedience hurt the heart of God, then we would fear and dread to disobey him.

*This motto speaks to us of the secret of courage.*

If we really fear God, we will never fear any man.

When they laid John Knox to rest in his grave, the Earl of Morton looked down, "Here lies one," he said, "who feared God so much that he never feared the face of any man."

To fear God is to find for ever the secret of courage in the face of man.

There is a craven and a coward fear. There is an abject and a humiliating fear. There is fear of the consequences, fear of the things that men can do, fear of the things that life can do.
That kind of fear has no place in the Christian life.

There is a cleansing and an antiseptic fear, a fear which is awe, reverence, dread of God. It is not fashionable now to think much of "the fear of God". It is much more fashionable to think sentimentally that God is a good fellow and all will be well!

The fear of God is the beginning of wisdom.
The fear of God is the foundation of reverence, the mainspring of obedience and the secret of that courage which will be true to the end.


NEVER UNPREPARED                                              August 24

The Frasers come from the Buchan country in the north-east of Scotland and the Johnstons come from the Borders.
Their mottoes are almost the same, one in French and the other in Latin. The motto of the Frasers is *Je suis prest*, which is old French for, "I am ready".
The motto of the Johnstons is *Numquam non paratus* which is Latin for, "Never unprepared".

*No man will ever seize his opportunity unless he is prepared.*
Sometimes, as we have noted before, a reserve is pitchforked all unexpectedly into a team and seizes his opportunity and plays a wonderful game.
Sometimes an actor or actress who is an understudy has at a moment's notice to play the star's part, and scores a personal triumph. But the success would be quite impossible unless the reserve had trained himself to physical fitness and unless the understudy had memorised and studied the part, to be ready to seize the opportunity when it came.
That is why study, discipline and preparation are of such tremendous importance when we are young. It is only the man who has made himself ready for it who can be offered the bigger job when it comes along.

We must remember the example of Jesus. It was not until he was thirty years old that Jesus left Nazareth to begin upon his task (Luke 3:23).

All these years he had spent preparing himself for the great task which God was one day to give him to do.

## WATCH! August 25

"Never unprepared!"
*To preparation must be added watchfulness. A man must see his opportunity when it comes.*

The Romans always painted the picture of Opportunity as a figure with plenty of hair in front but quite bald behind. If you meet opportunity face to face and recognise her, you can grasp her by the forelock and hold on to her, but, if you let her past, she is gone for ever, because there is no way of catching and holding her.

*To watchfulness must be added obedience.*
Opportunity is always a challenge and a summons. Opportunity does not give a man some great thing ready-made, dropping it, as it were, into his lap. Opportunity gives him the chance to get it for himself.

A man must obey the call of opportunity when it comes; if he does not, he has no grounds of complaint, if for ever after his life is lost in shoals and shallows and amongst the little things which could have been so much greater.

*No man can grasp his opportunity without the spirit of adventure in his heart.*
One of the most fatally easy things in this life is to grow too settled, to come to a stage when we do not want to be disturbed, when we are comfortably content to go on doing something which is far less than we could do, if we were adventurous enough to try.

Sometimes there comes to a man a challenge to do something new or go somewhere strange. He may refuse it saying, half in jest and half in earnest: "Better the devil you know than the devil you don't know."

Jesus will come to everyone of us asking us to do something for him and for the men for whom he died. His grace can prepare us for his task, but, when his call comes, we will fail him and we will fail men, unless we have the obedience to answer: "Here am I, send me" (Isa. 6:8).

Like Abraham we must be prepared to go out not knowing where we go (Heb. 11:8).

The Campbells are one of the greatest Scots families. The Duke of Argyll, with his castle at Inverary, is the head of the clan. He is hereditary Master of Her Majesty's Household, hereditary Lord Justice General, and hereditary Admiral of the Western Coasts and Isles of Scotland, besides being Keeper of the Royal Castles of Dunoon, Carrick, Dunstaffnage and Tarbert.

The Grahams, too, coming from Dalkeith and Eskdale, have written their names on Scottish history, in which everyone knows the names of the Duke of Montrose and John Graham of Claverhouse, the great Jacobite general, who was killed at Killiecrankie.

The Campbells and the Grahams have the same motto, the former in Latin and the other in French. The motto of the Campbells is *Ne obliviscaris*, and the motto of the Grahams is, *N'oubliez*, both of which mean, "Don't forget".

That is indeed a fine motto, a motto which expresses a duty which falls on every man.

Sometimes a man claims to be a "self-made" man. There is no such thing in this world as a self-made man. As Ulysses said, a man is a part of everything that he has met.

*We should never forget our debt to the past.*

No generation starts from scratch; every generation enters into the heritage which the past has left it.

No scientist and no doctor and no scholar has to begin at the beginning; he begins where his predecessors left off.

Every man enters into a heritage of civilisation, of liberty, of freedom, a heritage which was bought at the cost of the agony and the toil and the death of those who went before him.

It is our duty to remember those who made life what it is for us.

It is our duty to hand on our heritage, not weakened and soiled and tarnished but enhanced.

"Don't Forget!"

Harry Emerson Fosdick, the great American preacher, tells somewhere of a lad who was living recklessly. He was studying biology.

One day he was shown under the microscope the life of little creatures which are born and breed and die all within a matter of minutes.

He literally saw the generations of these microscopic creatures rise and pass away before his eyes. It made him think of life, and he suddenly said: "I resolve, God helping me, never to be a weak link in the chain."

We must remember *our debt to the past* and *our duty to the future*. This will involve remembering our teachers, our parents, our Church, and all the great and the good and the sacrificial men and women who made us what we are.

*We should never forget Jesus Christ and all that he has done for us.*

Jesus knew how easily men forget, and he gave them his sacrament in which he said: "This do *in remembrance* of me" (Luke 22:19). There may be many views of the sacrament which are a dark mystery to us. We may know only dimly what theologians mean when they talk about "the real presence" and so on, but every man can know what the sacrament means as an act of remembering Jesus Christ.

When John Newton was an old man, his memory left him and he forgot many things. One day he met William Jay and said to him: "I have forgotten many things, but I have never forgotten that Jesus Christ is my Saviour."

There is nothing so ugly and so hurting as ingratitude.

As Shakespeare's Lear said, it is "sharper than a serpent's tooth to have a thankless child".

Our motto and our resolution could very profitably be: "I will not forget."

"I HELP THE BRAVE"                                                        August 28

The territory of the Buchanans is mainly in Stirlingshire, in Central Scotland. The motto of the family is *Audaces iuvo*, "I help the brave".

I suppose that we might put this in the form of the popular proverb: "Fortune favours the brave."

There is no doubt that every generation needs the brave. There is no doubt that God specially needs the brave, and has special duties and special gifts for them.

In the work of the Church there are certain directions in which the brave are specially needed.

*The Church needs those who are brave in action.*

The most difficult thing in life is to be different. The easy thing is to be a "yes-man", to go with the crowd.

Robert Louis Stevenson's advice to a young man was: "Stop saying 'Amen' to what the world says, and keep your soul alive."

The Church and the world needs those who are brave enough, when it is necessary, to defy public opinion, to swim against the stream, to be different from the crowd, to have the courage to follow the voice of conscience, the demand of principle and the summons of God, to be in fact non-conformist.

*The Church needs those who are brave in thought, and who are brave enough to express their thoughts.*

It needs courage to follow where the truth leads. It is very much easier to go on repeating outworn slogans, to go on reciting outworn creeds, to go on using conventional and pious language, to confound fossilised orthodoxy with living faith.

It is a paradox that, unless a man is prepared to run the risk of being a heretic, he has little chance of arriving at the truth.

THIS EARNS RESPECT                                             August 29

"Help the Brave!"

*The Church needs those who are brave enough in purpose.*

The Christian should never forget that he is a man who is bound to attempt great things for God and to expect great things from God. The basic fault of so many congregations today is that they are well content to keep things as they are. For so many the task of the Church has become a holding engagement rather than a campaign of advance.

Neither a person nor an institution can stand still. It must either advance or retreat. It must either progress or decay.

We need those who are brave enough to think and plan and purpose and act adventurously.

*The Church needs those who are brave in their Christian witness.*

A certain great preacher used to speak of the scandal of the ordinariness of the lives of so many who are claiming to be Christian. There is no sphere of life today which is not crying out for witnessing Christians, Christians who are prepared to take their Christianity into the arena of life along with them.

It is so in business and in commerce; in the world of the Trade Unions; on the field of sport; in the world of entertainment; in the life of politics; in the sphere of education.

This Christian witness will not be a matter of criticism or fault-finding or superiority, still less a matter of that unctuous piety which characterises the "unco' guid" whom no one loves. It will be a matter of Christian manliness, and Christian purity, and Christian brotherliness, and Christian courage, and Christian love.

The one virtue which every one recognises at sight, and the one virtue which commands the respect of every man is the virtue of courage.

Fortune favours the brave.

God needs and helps the brave.


UNITE! August 30

The Brodies are originally a north-east country family, who came from around Nairn; and their motto consists of just one word: "Unite!"

It is a magnificent motto for unity is always strength.

*There must be unity in the family.*

William Soutar, the Scottish poet I referred to earlier, had a gift for epigrams. He once said in one flashing sentence: "A ruined world is rebuilt with hearth-stones."

He meant that the only thing which can give a shaken civilisation stability is the home.

We are all appalled by the problem of juvenile delinquency. The cure for that problem is not in the law, and not in the educational system. It is in the home.

Where the home stands supreme, there will be no juvenile delinquency.

One of the great tasks of today is to build Christian homes in which old and young, parents and children, this generation and the previous generation, are not divided in misunderstanding but united in real fellowship; where old and young have not drifted apart but are together.

*There must be unity in the Church.*

At a time when Church union is so much in the air, one sometimes has to ask with shame: How can we expect union between different branches of the Church, when so many congregations in every Church are torn and rent in two, and when every one of the Churches is itself divided into differing sects and parties?

Where there is bitterness, strife, hatred, envy, dispeace, the work of Christ can never be done.

God's greatest gift to the Church on earth is those who sow peace.
The devil's greatest allies are those who sow strife.

"Unite!"

*There must be unity in the nation.*

Bit by bit the old class distinctions which divided men are being broken down. There are few places today where the old feudal distinctions between master and servant still obtain.

I have been at more than one function at which the Provost of the Burgh (or, as they say in England, the Mayor) who occupied the place of honour was an ordinary workman in a public works, and at which one or more of the guests was the managing director of the same works!

That is as it should be. But one of the great national problems today is the fact that time and again one section in the community, one trade in the community, one set of craftsmen in the community, demand for themselves rights and privileges at the expense of the whole community.

Too often, each section of the community is quite indifferent to the result of its demands upon other sections of the community.

*There must be unity in the world.*

One would have thought that in our own generation no sane man would have talked of the possibility of war any more than any sane man would talk about the possibility of suicide.

It is very difficult to see how any Christian can now be anything other than pledged against all war.

It is totally impossible to imagine any circumstances under which Jesus Christ would approve the use of nuclear weapons.

The world today faces the simple alternative of unity or destruction.

Unity in the home can only come when Jesus Christ is the unseen but ever remembered guest in every home.

Unity in the Church can only come when the Church ceases to be the Church of Scotland or the Church of England or any other Church and becomes the Church of Christ.

Unity in the nation can only come when men set Christian duty and Christian responsibility far above party interest.

Unity in the world can only come when the kingdoms of the world become the kingdoms of the Lord and of his Christ.

# *September*

Sometimes one is bound to ask: "What is left when everything else is gone?" When something happens which seems to make life no longer worth living, when we feel that we neither want to nor can go on, what is left then?

The answer to that is very simple—when everything else is gone, a sense of duty remains.

Again and again it has been simply that sense of duty which has kept men on their feet.

Edwin Muir in his autobiography tells how, when he was in Prague, he was very ill. He called in an Austrian doctor who lived near by.

"He had an extraordinary calm, disillusioned and yet pleasant manner. The war (1914–18) had killed his ambition; he did not think that the battle of life was worth waging; all that remained to him was a sense of honour."

The sense of the duty of being a good doctor remained, when everything else was gone.

W. B. Yeats, in his autobiography, tells of an amazing thing which Aubrey Beardsley once said to him. One would not have taken Beardsley for a religious man, but once he said to Yeats: "All my life I have been fascinated by the spiritual life. When a child I saw a vision of a Bleeding Christ over the mantelpiece—but after all to do one's work when there are other things one wants to do so much more is a kind of religion."

The compulsion to do one's work, like the driving sense of duty, is one of the great dynamics of life.

193

Canon A. C. Deane, in his autobiography *Times Remembered*, tells of his old English teacher, a Mr. Barkworth. When he corrected "he did not only score and underline; he rewrote and transformed. He always wrote encouraging comments.

"One of these I have never forgotten, a scribble at the foot of the page which read: 'Capital! Read all the good English you can, take pains, and presently you will do something worth doing.'"

You can imagine what the encouragement meant to a boy of twelve or thirteen who was anxious to become a writer. Anyone who has reached my age will, during his life, have received a prodigious quantity of advice, for which, as he looks back, he is still grateful. Yet his warmest gratitude will be felt for those who gave him little advice but real encouragement.

It was said of Francis Allshorn, the great teacher, that when she had to criticise, she did it with her arm round you, so that the very criticism was an encouragement.

It is a terrible thing to quench the light in someone's eyes.

Encourage!

On any grounds, William Tyndale is a prince of translators.
In the Preface to the reader in his 1534 translation he writes:

As concerning all that I have translated or otherwise written, I beseech all men to read it for that purpose I wrote it: even to bring them to the knowledge of the scripture . . . And where they find faults let them shew it to me, if they be nigh, or write to me if they be far off: or write openly against it and improve it, and I promise them, if I perceive that their reason conclude (i.e. are conclusive) I will confess mine ignorance openly.

Here is the great scholar and translator asking for criticism and promising to welcome it when it comes.

In almost the next year another man who has written his name on the English Bible published his translation, and in his address to the Christian reader Miles Coverdale wrote:

Lowly and faithfully I have followed my interpreters, and that under correction. And if I have failed anywhere (as there is no man but misseth in something) love shall construe all to the best without any perverse judgment . . . If thou (the reader) hast knowledge therefore to judge where any fault is made, I doubt not but thou wilt help to amend it, if love be joined with knowledge. However whereinsoever I can perceive by myself, or by the information of some one else, that I have failed (as it is no wonder), I shall now by the help of God overlooke it better (revise it), and amend it.

Here is the second great translator asking for criticism and welcoming it.

TOUCHINESS                                                      September 4

As a contrast to what Tyndale and Coverdale said in yesterday's entry— and remembering that he is writing in jest—Ronald Knox, one of the greatest of modern translators writes in the preface to his book *On Englishing the Bible*:

I have long since given up protesting when controversialists misquote me, or newspaper columnists credit me with authorship of limericks that are none of mine. But if you question a rendering of mine in the New Testament, you come up against a parental instinct hardly less ferocious than that of a mother-bear. I shall smile it off, no doubt, in conversation, but you have lost marks.

He goes on to speak of that "unreasonable streak of touchiness" which is in most people.

Knox is obviously a wise man who welcomes criticism, so long as the criticism is the criticism of knowledge and love combined.

No one likes the criticism of ignorance, or the criticism which is designed to hurt; but wise and kindly criticism is something of infinite value.

To accept such criticism we need three things.

*We need humility.*
The man who cannot conceive that he is ever wrong is a sorry case.

*We need to love truth more than we love self.*
When we resent criticism, we are in effect more concerned with the preservation of our self-esteem than we are with the truth—and that is the way to lose truth.

*We need to love progress more than a static immobility.*
To refuse to listen to criticism is never to move, never to advance, never to improve—and that is death in life.

The greatest men and the greatest scholars welcomed criticism.
That is why they were great.

A certain newspaper had an interesting article on those unfortunate people who suffer from kleptomania, that twist in a mind which drives a person to put out his hands and take what he should not take.

It appears that women suffer from this strange urge far more than men. A psychologist set down some useful advice to people so tempted and so afflicted.

Clasp your hands together as tightly as you can, interlocking the fingers. It symbolizes determination not to stretch out your hands to crime. As such it can be a powerful psychological aid. Then go to a quiet corner and think hard of your husband and children, of how they would feel if, in the week before Christmas, you appeared in a dock and shamed them before the world.

Best of all, get out of the store immediately and away from these tempting counters. A great man once said that he could resist anything—but temptation. That is true for many of us.

Here is a prescription for the defeat of temptation. In it it has three most valuable ingredients, but the greatest and most powerful ingredient of all is missing.

Let us look today and tomorrow at the three which are there.

The first is determination.

*Determination is a strong weapon wherewith to defeat temptation.*

There is a world of difference between having a vague desire to do something fine, or a lurking sense that we should not do something, and an utter and deliberate determination to do it or not to do it.

The cases in which we really and fully and finally make up our minds about anything are far too few.

Practise the art of making up your mind!

TEMPTATIONS                                              September 7

Here are the two other ingredients present in our prescription for temptation.

*The memory of those we love is a powerful aid wherewith to resist temptation.*

There is nothing which so delights those who love us as when we do well. There is nothing which so hurts them as when we do badly.

Even if a man has a certain right to do what he likes with his own life, he never has any right to break someone else's heart.

*Never flirt with temptation.*

It is an error of judgment to allow ourselves to think about the forbidden thing, to look at it, to cast longing eyes upon it. To avoid it, to stay as far from it as possible is neither weakness nor cowardice. It is common sense.

There are times when the business of life means that we cannot escape the tempting things but to linger needlessly in their presence is to court disaster.

THE DEFENCE AGAINST TEMPTATION                          September 8

The greatest of all the ingredients in this prescription is however missing. For prayer is the greatest of all defences against temptation.

Edgar N. Jackson, in an excellent book on preaching entitled *Preaching to People's Needs*, writes this: "One psychiatrist has reported that though he himself does not pretend to be a religious man, he cannot help being impressed by the fact that, in twenty-five years of active practice in New York City, he has never had a patient who really knew how to pray."

It was his experience that it was the people who did not know how to pray who got life all tangled and messed up.

When we are in difficulty there is no help like the help of God, and no safeguard like the memory of the living and ever-present Christ. The human will can prove weak. Even the thought of those who love us can fail to restrain our passions. There are times when escape seems impossible.

Then is the time to remember that we do not fight this battle in our own strength, and that we do not struggle alone.

He who knew temptation in the wilderness and in the garden is with us.

In that presence alone is the grace which can make us clean and keep us clean.

### THE WORKMAN September 9

Jesus was a man who worked with his hands. He was thirty-three when he died upon his Cross and for thirty of his thirty-three years he was connected with the carpenter's shop in Nazareth.

There is an old legend which tells how Jesus was the best maker of ox-yokes in the whole of Galilee, and how people from far and wide came to Nazareth to buy the ox-yokes that Jesus of Nazareth made, for they were best of all.

One of the most famous and beautiful things that Jesus ever said goes back to the days when he was a carpenter. "My yoke is easy," said Jesus, "and my burden is light" (Matt. 11:30).

The Greek word for "easy" is *chrestos*, and *chrestos* really means "well-fitting".

In Palestine ox-yokes were made of wood. The ox would be brought to the carpenter's shop and its measurements taken. The yoke would be blocked out, and then the ox would be brought back for a fit on. This curve would be deepened, that rough place would be smoothed until the yoke fitted so exactly that it would never gall the backs of the patient beasts.

That is the kind of work Jesus did.

In those days, shops had their signs over them just as they have now; and it has been suggested that the sign above the shop of Jesus was a wooden ox-yoke, with the words painted upon it: "My yokes fit well."

Jesus was not ashamed to work with his hands.

### SENSELESS SNOBBERY September 10

Thomas Carlyle was one of the most voluminous of authors. His father, a good and godly man and an elder of the kirk, was a stonemason in Scotland.

There are places in Dumfries-shire where the bridges which Carlyle's father built still stand.

Carlyle said that he would rather have built one of his father's bridges than have written all his own books.

Thomas Carlyle did not despise a man who worked with his hands.

Where would a home be without the hands of a mother to cook the meals and scrub the house and care for the children?

How could the dream of the thinker ever be worked out in fact without the hands of the labouring man?

God save us all from that false sense of values which issues in that senseless snobbery which looks down on the man who works with his hands.

It was the hands of a working-man that were nailed to the Cross on Calvary's hill.

WHEN YOU PRAY                                             September 11

There is much to be learned from the physical attitude of men when they pray.

There are at least four ways in which a man can pray to God.

I give you two of these today.

*Jesus told of a tax-gatherer who came to the Temple to pray.*

He would not even dare to lift up his eyes to heaven, but beat upon his breast, saying: "God be merciful to me a sinner" (Luke 18:13).

That is *the prayer of the downcast head*; that is *the prayer of the heart that is ashamed*. That is the prayer of the man who has sinned, and who is seeking only the mercy of God.

No man can even think of approaching God without thinking of how unworthy he is to enter into the presence of the God who is of purer eyes than to behold iniquity.

Once Abraham Lincoln said: "I have often been driven to my knees in prayer because I had nowhere else to go."

That is *the prayer of the bended knee and the outstretched hand*, the prayer of the man for whom there is nothing left to say but: "God help me! God help me!"

There are sorrows which none but God can comfort. There are problems which none but God can solve.

There is a strength which none but God can give.

There are times when every man reaches the limit of human effort and human endurance.

Then he can only stretch out his hands to God that God may give him the strength to pass the breaking point and not to break.

STANDING TO ATTENTION                                          September 12

Here is another of the lessons to be learned from the way people pray.
*Once Jesus prayed to God in the garden of Gethsemane and when he prayed his sweat was as drops of blood.*

At that moment the Cross was facing Jesus. He was only thirty-three. No man wishes to die at thirty-three, and least of all does he wish to die upon a cross.

That is *the prayer of the man who wrestles in prayer.*

Sometimes we know what is right, but it is desperately hard to do it.

Sometimes we have to face things which are apparently impossible to face.

Sometimes a man has to wrestle in an agony of prayer until in the end he can say: "Thy will be done."

Sometimes a prayer can be an agony of a struggle to gain that self-conquest which will make us accept the will of God. But when we do reach acceptance, then comes peace.

One of the most gallant exploits of the South African War was the defence of Ladysmith.

The leader who was responsible for that brave defence was Sir George White. It was his courage, his cheerfulness, his leadership which made his garrison hold out. When he came back to England, he was regarded as a hero.

Everyone was eager to learn the secret of his continual fortitude, his continual cheerfulness, and his continual vigour. He would never say, but one day, when he was pressed even more strongly than usual to say how he got through the strain and tension of those days of siege, he answered: "Well, if you want to know, every morning every day, I stood at attention before God."
This was *the prayer of a man of faith.*

What a difference it would make to life if we always began the day with God; if, before we met men, we had met God, if each day we took our orders from God.

This is the fourth lesson we learn from the way people pray.

No man could possibly begin a day better than by standing at attention before God.

## ORDERS TAKEN!                                   September 13

"More things are wrought by prayer than this world dreams of," said Tennyson.

There is a prayer for every moment and for every need in life.

There is the prayer of the bowed head and the shamed heart, which can only stammer out a sorry tale, and humbly ask for God's forgiveness.

There is the prayer of the bended knee and the outstretched hand which pleads for the help which only God can give, and which will never be disappointed.

There is the prayer which wrestles with God in agony until it achieves the self-conquest which can say: "Thy will be done", and which after the battle finds the peace.

There is the pray-er who stands to attention before God in faith and takes his orders of the day from him.

No matter what a man's need may be, that need will find its answer in God.

## DEFENDER OF THE FAITH                          September 14

In ancient Greece the Spartans were always proverbial for their courage. They might lack the finer virtues of the more cultured Athenians, but no one ever questioned their courage and their loyalty.

In his life of Lycurgus, the Spartan king, Plutarch tells a great story.

There was a certain Spartan wrestler competing at the Olympic Games. An attempt was made to buy him off by the offer of a large sum of money. He completely refused it. After a long struggle he outwrestled his opponent and won his victory.

He was asked: "What advantage, O Spartan, have you gained from your victory?" He answered with a smile: "I shall stand in front of my king when I fight our enemies."

The greatest privilege of which the Spartan could conceive was to defend his king, if need be with his life, in the day of battle.

It must be so with the Christian.

The greatest privilege the Christian has is the privilege of being the defender of the faith, the champion of Jesus Christ.

## GIVE A REASON!                                          September 15

Are you a defender of the faith?

*We are always faced with the temptation to play down our Christianity.*

We are faced with the temptation, if not to attempt to conceal, at least not to stress the fact that we are Christian, and that we belong to Jesus Christ.

We may fear the laughter of the world. We may fear to be different from others. But the real Christian is the man who in any company says along with Paul: "I am not ashamed of the gospel of Christ" (Rom. 1:16).

*The Christian must defend the faith in his words and with his arguments.*

The opponents of Christianity know what they believe. They have been drilled and schooled into learning the tenets of the particular political or philosophical faith which they happen to profess.

Too often the Christian is a man who, to put it bluntly, does not really know what he believes.

Too often he is a man who has never even tried to think things out for himself.

Too often the Church has forgotten her teaching ministry, and has sent out her members ill equipped to meet the arguments and the criticisms of the opponents of the Church and the critics of Christianity.

If the Christian is to be a true defender of the faith, he must be ready to give to all who ask him a reason for the hope that is in him (1 Pet. 3:15).

## MY RULES FOR WORK                                      September 16

I have had a letter from "Raymond". He asks me how I get my work done!

It is going to make me sound very conceited to do it, but I shall try to give you the answer!

I think that, generally speaking, there are three rules that I want to mention —though I'm sure I have mentioned these on other occasions.

(i) *My first rule is BEGIN EARLY.*

I have just been looking at a concordance, and I find that the phrase "early in the morning" occurs about forty times!

Raymond is a Methodist, so it is easy to remind him that John Wesley preached forty-two thousand sermons in fifty-three years, that he averaged four thousand five hundred miles per year in travel, and that he wrote or edited four hundred and fifty books.

John always got up at 4.30 a.m.! I can't claim to emulate that! But, though my classes don't normally begin till 11.30 a.m., I always leave home at 8 a.m., getting to my desk at the University by 8.30 a.m.

Without these three morning hours, I can honestly say that I would not get any work done at all!

So in my experience, start early!

## (ii) *My second rule is KEEP GOING!*

One of the greatest time-wasters, I find, is the habit we have of saying: "I've only got twenty-five minutes. It's not worth starting." But I find it is always worth starting!

To return to John Wesley, *he* did most of his reading on horseback!

It is amazing how much you can get done in the odd quarter-hour or half-hour. There is no unit of time that cannot be used.

## (iii) *My third rule is KEEP TO SCHEDULE!*

I have no use for the idea of waiting for inspiration! If *I* waited for inspiration, this book (or that material on which it is based) would never have been written. (You may feel this is obvious, but don't say so!) But when I was a minister in a parish, I don't think I ever wrote a sermon after Thursday morning.

May I repeat here an incident I used in "Through the Year" as it is relevant to this very personal entry!

Beverley Nichols tells of a conversation he had with Sir Winston Churchill. Churchill asked him how long it took to write "Prelude". Nichols said that it was written in spasms over five months.

Churchill asked if he did not write regularly. Nichols said he had to wait for the right mood.

"Nonsense," said Churchill. "You should go to your room at 9 a.m. each day and say 'I'm going to write for four hours'."

"Suppose you can't," said Nichols.

Churchill replied: "You've got to get over that. If you sit waiting for inspiration, you'll wait till you are an old man."

He went on: "Writing is like any other job . . . like marching an army . . . If you sit down and wait till the weather is suitable, you won't get very far with your troops. Kick yourself, irritate yourself, but *write. It's the only way.*"

It is!

So that roughly is how I get it done, dear Raymond.

WORDS! WORDS! WORDS!                                   September 17

I am recovering from an attack of speechlessness. A week ago I lost my voice completely and could only communicate with the outside world in a hoarse and almost inaudible whisper. This failure of voice came upon me quite suddenly in the middle of a day's work.

On the way home I thought it would be a good idea if I called in at a chemist's shop and obtained something to gargle with; and so I did. I explained to the girl behind the counter what I wanted. I didn't need to tell her that I had lost my voice! She recommended what she thought would be most helpful.

As she wrapped up the bottle and handed it across the counter to me and took my money, she smiled brightly, and said: "You must have been talking too much!"

Her diagnosis was correct—far more correct than she knew, and correct in a far deeper way than she meant, because the basic trouble with everyone of us is that we talk too much.

Torrents of talk inundate this world. Floods of the highest sentiments flow over the world. Oceans of good advice are poured out, cataracts of sermons are unleashed.

There is enough Christian talk in this world to reform half a dozen worlds! The trouble is that for all the talk there is so little action!

I know that I am going to be accused of being a moralist, and of preaching that Christianity consists of doing good. I am quite content to be so accused, for that is what Jesus said.

Jesus insisted: "By their fruits ye shall know them. Not everyone that *saith* unto me, Lord, Lord, shall enter into the kingdom of heaven; but he that doeth the will of my Father which is in heaven" (Matt. 7:20, 21).

When Jesus painted a picture of the judgment of God, the basic question was simply had or had not a man been kind (Matt. 25:31-46).

James, whose epistle had the ill-fortune to be called "a right strawy epistle" by Martin Luther, laid it down: "Pure religion and undefiled before God and the Father is this, to visit the fatherless and the widows in their affliction, and to keep himself unspotted from the world" (Jas. 1:27).

This is a call, not for words, but for action.

Thomas Chalmers was one of Scotland's great orators. After a masterly speech in the General Assembly he was congratulated by all his friends. "Yes," he answered, "but what did it do?"

Had the words simply gone whistling down the wind?

There never was a time when religion was so much discussed as it is today. But someone has said that half the trouble is that people tend to think that they are being religious when they are discussing religious questions.

The Church is littered with discussion groups—and discussion groups can be intensely valuable, but they are not valuable if people are sitting talking when they ought to be acting, and if they do not result in any action to follow the discussion.

Florence Allshorn was one of the great missionary teachers. She was principal of a great women's missionary college. She was always infuriated by the type of person who suddenly discovered that her quiet time for prayer was due just when the greasy dishes were waiting to be washed in the kitchen.

There is not much virtue in discussing or even in praying when we ought to be giving a hand to make someone's work easier about the house.

Robert Louis Stevenson turned on someone who expressed the highest sentiments with no accompanying action with the words: "I cannot hear what you say for listening to what you are."

Am I being a little unfair? Perhaps. But this I do know—that people will remember a minister's kindness in a time of trouble when they have forgotten every sermon that he ever preached.

I also know that many of the finest advertisements for Christianity I have ever known would have been like fish out of water at a discussion circle which was sunning itself in its own intellectual brilliance.

I wouldn't say I was the only one who produced too many words and too few deeds to fit them.

ADVICE TO LOFTY                                    September 19

A minister I knew joined the Royal Navy in the First World War. He is a big man, easily the biggest in his squad. So he soon found himself with the nickname "Lofty".

In charge of the squad there was a cockney petty officer. This petty officer was also a champion navy boxer. He was a small man, and he wanted some special practice before a certain tournament.

It struck the petty officer that Lofty was the very man to give him some practice. The fact that Lofty was big and he was small would make the practice all the more useful.

He asked my friend if he would put on the gloves with him. The latter said he had never boxed in his life, but he would try it if he liked. So he put on the gloves, and the petty officer told him to bore in and try to hit him. Lofty bore in all right, but left himself wide open. The petty officer stopped him, and told him to cover up his chin, or he might get hurt.

They started again. This time Lofty's wide open chin was too much of a temptation for the cockney champion and he hit Lofty, and hit him so hard that Lofty hit the ground. Lofty jumped up ruefully rubbing his chin.

The little petty officer stopped him: "Lofty," he said, "if ever you're boxing, remember one thing—and don't forget it. Don't ever let your opponent see that you're hurt."

It is good advice for a boxer—and for any man.


GRIN AND BEAR IT! September 20

Don't ever let them see that you're hurt. The world seems to be so full of the people who are always getting hurt and telling all the world about it.

A man doesn't get his own way in a committee meeting—and he just won't play any more.

A Church member doesn't get things done the way he thinks they should be done—and he constitutes himself a kind of permanent opposition in the Church.

A choir member doesn't get the solo he or she thinks was due—and the voice that once made music becomes huffily silent.

Someone is not thanked for some bit of service, someone is accidentally omitted in a vote of thanks—and that person's feelings are not only hurt, they are lacerated, and the whole community hears about it. Someone is not invited to the platform party—and the injured one has a grievance which all the world can see.

Churches are all too full of people who get hurt and let everyone see it and know it.

There is a phrase which tells us "to grin and bear it". It is good advice.

In sport we admire the player who can take a knock and bounce up smiling.

In business we admire the man who can take a failure or a disappointment and come back still smiling and still fighting.

Do you remember how Kipling has it?

> If you can meet with Triumph and Disaster
> And treat these two impostors just the same.

Do you remember how he goes on?

> If you can make one heap of all your winnings
> And risk it on one turn of pitch-and-toss
> And lose, and start again at your beginnings
> And never breathe a word about your loss.

These things to Kipling were the sign of a man.
He was right.


## SOMEONE'S WATCHING

I stepped off a bus, my journey ended. Without thinking what I was doing, I threw my ticket away.

I was hurrying away when my eye was caught by an oldish man who had stepped off the same bus. He also had a bus ticket in his hand. But he didn't throw his away. He walked over to the little wire basket for litter which was attached to the nearest lighting standard and neatly dropped it in.

I found myself then running after my thrown-away ticket, retrieving it from the pavement and also neatly placing it in the litter basket.

What a power of good an example can be!


Human nature is essentially suggestible. King Edward accidentally left the bottom button of his waistcoat unfastened, and before very long, every well-dressed man was doing the same.

A certain statesman wears a certain kind of hat, and soon the hat becomes the uniform of the well-dressed businessman.

A certain film star adopts a certain hair style, and soon all women are doing their hair in the same way.

A certain comedian develops a certain catchword, and soon everybody is repeating it.

A certain "royal" uses a certain gesture, and soon everyone is copying it.


Example is one of the most powerful forces in this world.


## WHAT AN EXAMPLE!

H. L. Gee tells of a moving event which happened in the days of Dunkirk.
On the quay of an English port a number of French troops had been disembarked. The spirit had gone out of them, and they were lying there in a dull

lethargy of despair, for they knew that they had lost, not a campaign, but their country.

Another ship came in, and from it there disembarked a detachment of the Brigade of Guards. The Guards' discipline had never relaxed. In so far as it was possible their uniform was still perfect and their equipment precisely as it ought to be. On the quay they formed up, and marched away as if they had been changing the guard.

Some of the Frenchmen looked up listlessly. Slowly in their eyes a light began to be reborn. Stiffly they rose, squared their shoulders, and marched off after the Guards and before that movement had finished every one of the Frenchmen had fallen in and was on the march.

The power of an example had changed dispirited, defeated men into men who had got back their hope and their self-respect.

I do not think that we realise that someone is always watching us.

The little boy watches the big boy, and models himself upon him.

The child watches his father or mother, and unconsciously copies his or her mannerisms and actions.

The Sunday school scholar watches his or her teacher.

We all remember how the Pied Piper of Hamelin piped the children away, and as someone has put it, "Everyone pipes for the feet of someone to follow."

When Paul was writing to Titus, he told him what to say to other people about their Christian duty, and then he says: "In all things show yourself a pattern, a type, an example of good works" (Titus 2:7).

When he writes to Timothy, he says: "Be thou an example to the believers, in word, in conduct, in love, in spirit, in faith, in purity" (I Tim. 4:12).

Here is our responsibility.

A careless action of ours may make it easier for someone else to sin—and we may never know it.

A right action of ours may make it easier for someone to stay on the right road—and again we may never know it.

As Peter puts it, Jesus left us "an example, that we should follow His steps" (I Pet. 2:21), and he left us the responsibility of being just that so that others can follow in ours.

In every action of life we are making it easier or harder for someone else to do the right.

My wife attended a city clinic in Glasgow at one time for treatment for fibrositis. She had many talks with an old lady who came to the clinic from the other side of the city. As they were talking one day, the old lady asked my wife if she could lend her a penny.

In the afternoon old age pensioners get a concession fare on the tramcars, and the old lady had nothing but one single pound note, and she wanted the penny to pay her penny fare home on the tramcar, because she did not wish to bother the tram conductress by presenting her with a pound note for a penny fare.

My wife opened her purse and gave the old lady the penny she wanted; and then laughingly my wife pointed at all the money she happened to have in her purse at the moment—a ten-shilling note and two florins—and said by way of a joke: "Look! That's all I've got until Tuesday (this happened on a Friday) when I get my housekeeping money."

The old lady's reaction was immediate. She held out the pound note: "Take this, my dear," she said. "It'll help you over the weekend anyway, and you can give me it back when you get your money."

I haven't dressed up that story at all! Here was an old lady, an old age pensioner, offering her only pound note to someone she scarcely knew, because she thought that the stranger was worse off than herself.

If there is one thing that moves the human heart, it is generosity—especially spontaneous generosity.

## A TRUE GIVING

There is not only a generosity in money. There is also a generosity in talent, a giving of whatever gifts we have, to other people.

Bruno Walter tells how Kathleen Ferrier, that wonderful singer who died too soon, was in America. Because he himself had engagements in New York, he could not play the host to her when she was in Los Angeles as he would like to have done. So he did the only thing he could—he gave her the use of his house in Los Angeles that she might stay in comfort and in peace there.

He goes on: "When we came home after she had left, our faithful domestic helpers, a married Austrian couple, told us that Kathleen on her free evenings used to call them to the music-room, where she sat down at the piano, shed her shoes, and sang to them to their heart's desire, and, of course, to their utter delight."

A true giving!

## FIND THE POOR! September 26

You would not think that meanness could ever be a vice of a Christian.

It is James who speaks of God who gives generously to all men, and never grudges the gift (Jas. 1:5).

It is Paul who speaks of the Lord Jesus Christ who, though he was rich, "yet for your sakes he became poor, that ye through his poverty might be rich" (2 Cor. 8:9).

It is not a case of giving big gifts.

At the Feast of Purim the Jews have a lovely custom. It is laid down that at the Feast which is the time of the giving of gifts, even the poorest person must search for someone poorer than himself and give him a gift.

Sometimes we feel we live in a drab enough world, but the world's greyness is lit by every act of generosity.

For in every such act, there is the reflection of God.

## THE REAL TESTS September 27

T. H. Huxley, in one of his published essays, puts forward a very interesting point of view. He writes:

That which is to be lamented, I fancy, is not that society should do its utmost to help capacity to ascend from the lower strata to the higher, but that it has no machinery by which to facilitate the descent of incapacity from the higher strata to the lower . . . We have all known noble lords who would have been coachmen, or gamekeepers, or billiard-markers, if they had not been kept afloat by our social corks; we have all known men among the lowest ranks of whom everyone has said: "What might not that man have become, if he had only had a little education?"

So Huxley makes the point that we rightly do everything to enable a clever man to rise in the world, but we have no corresponding machinery to bring the foolish and the useless man down in the world.

The result is that there are people in the lower ranks of society who ought on merit to be in the higher, and there are people in the higher ranks of society who ought to be in the lower. We try to arrange things so that the first may be promoted, but we make no effort to arrange things so that the second may be demoted!

Character is always more important than birth.

What a man is in himself is more important than what he is from the point of view of a genealogical tree.

As Tennyson had it:

> Howe'er it be, it seems to me
> 'Tis only noble to be good.
> Kind hearts are more than coronets,
> And simple faith than Norman blood.

NOT A PEDIGREE, BUT POTENTIAL                              September 28

The value of a man lies not in his social status, but in his efficiency. The true value of a man lies in the contribution he can make to the community. The true aristocracy lies not in lineage but in service.

All social claims are valueless and baseless unless they are backed by usefulness in the community of men.

The important thing about any man is not his ancestry but his potential, not his past but his future.

Sir Linton Andrews, the famous journalist, tells of the editor who greeted all candidates for jobs, when they produced their references and their testimonials, by saying: "Never mind what you did last year, or even yesterday. What can you do today, and tomorrow and next year? It is your future work I have to assess."

The really important thing about a man is that he should be able to produce, not a pedigree, but a potential. This is not to say that blood and ancestry and heredity do not matter, but it is to say that the judgment of any man is based on what he is, not on what his fathers were.

The important things are not the honours and the status and the rank and all the externals which a man has been able to collect or to inherit. The important thing is the man in himself. That only God can see.

The possibilities only God can help a man to realise.

God sees what a man is; God knows what a man can be.
Only God can turn the one into the other.

In *Faith in Fleet Street*, Robert Moore tells of one of his early experiences as a journalist. He was sent out on a special story and assignment, and he could get absolutely nowhere with it.

He was worried about this and he was also not a little alarmed. The investigation had been asked for by Lord Beaverbrook personally on the information given to him by one of his senior editors.

In spite of the source of the story, Robert Moore knew that the story was inaccurate. In great trepidation he had to go back to his editor and say so.

The editor told him to drop the investigation at once, and then he went on to say something which, as a journalist, Robert Moore never forgot.

The editor said: "Anyone who spends his time and energies and his experience fully proving that there is not a story to write has done just as good a day's work as someone who proves that there is a story."

What the paper was interested in was not in getting a story but in getting the truth. So Robert Moore writes of "the temptations and opportunities for a journalist that are lined up on every bar counter; stacked high in every whisper and gossip and which sometimes shriek at him on that blank sheet of paper in his typewriter at which he has been staring seemingly for hours". He says:

"I can never, must never, say that my journalism is the truth, the whole truth, and nothing but the truth. But this I do say, that my journalism is the result of looking for the truth."

In the same book T. E. Utley writes: "The first business of a newspaper is to describe life as it is—remorselessly, accurately, and with fanatical detachment."

The journalist looks for the truth.
It is not a good story if it is not a true story.

NO REPETITION!                                        September 30

The ethics of the Christian should be equal to the ethics of the journalist. And yet it is so often true that the so-called Christian will repeat the story, the rumour, the piece of gossip, which he knows perhaps only by hearsay, and of the truth of which he is by no means certain.

The journalist has to resist the temptation to write the spicy and malicious story. Too often the Christian falls to that temptation, for there are no hotbeds of gossip like Churches and congregations.

There are two things we should never repeat.

*We should never repeat the story about the truth of which we are uncertain.*

During war-time there was actual legislation to punish, and to punish severely, the person who disseminated alarmist and defeatist rumours.

The proverb has it that three things can never come back—the spent arrow, the spoken word, and the lost opportunity. There is nothing so attractive as gossip, and there is nothing so dangerous as gossip.

We might well remind ourselves more often than we do that we shall one day give account for every idle word that we have spoken (Matt. 12:36).

*We should never repeat what we have been told in confidence, or what we have been privileged to see or to experience in some private moment of intimacy.*

One of the great institutions of the Roman Catholic Church is the confessional. It may have its abuses, but it is infinitely valuable to have some place in which a person can lay bare his soul in utter confidence that what he says will never be repeated. To betray a confidence is one of the lowest actions to which any man or woman can stoop—and yet it is repeatedly done.

As James was so well aware, there are few things in this world which can do so much damage as the tongue (Jas. 3:1–12).

Let us remember the strict ethic of the journalist regarding the repetition of any story, and let us as Christians be no less honourable in our speech.

# *October*

I have been looking at the advertisements again!
As Shakespeare had it, there are

> . . . Tongues in trees, books in the running brooks,
> Sermons in stones, and good in everything.

There are certainly sermons on the advertisement posters for him who has an eye to see!

There is a certain well-known washing agent which commends itself to the public in two words. Its claim is that it "adds brightness".

I don't know if there could be a better definition of the effect of the Christian life. If a person is a true Christian he or she will add brightness everywhere.

It was said of Alice Freeman Palmer, the great American teacher, by one of her pupils, "She made me feel as if I were bathed in sunshine."

Is it not of Phillips Brookes, the great American preacher, that a lovely story is told?
He was going down the street one winter day of snow and ice. He stopped to buy a newspaper from the scantily clad and shivering lad at the street corner. As he turned away he smiled at the boy and said: "It's cold today, isn't it?" Whereat the boy flashed back: "It was, sir, till you passed."

There is an unwritten saying of Jesus which states: "He who is near Jesus is to be in the presence of a warm comforting glow. And those who are

215

followers of Jesus should also bring to others this glow of warmth and they also should add this brightness to life."

## PEOPLE YOU CAN BOTHER

A brother minister rang me up on the telephone. He is one of the princes of the Church, a far bigger person than ever I will be, and he is a man with the grace of God on him. He wanted some information which he believed that I could give him.

After he had talked he apologised that he had troubled me—not that to speak to him could ever be any trouble. I made the conventional reply, but I did not mean it merely conventionally. I said: "It's a pleasure." And he answered: "It's a pleasure to me to have the right to bother you whenever I like."

It was only a great man's humility which made him speak to me like that, but it set me thinking, and I came to see that the really valuable people are the people whom you *can* bother—at any time!

It is so easy to get so immersed in work—work which may be very important —that we cannot be bothered with people, and that we find them a trouble.

"People," he says, "are always more important than footnotes," as Kermit Eby reminded us in our entry under July 15.

That is true.

## NUISANCES?

Luke has a wonderful incident in his gospel.

He tells how Jesus went round the north end of the Sea of Galilee to Bethsaida Julias.

"He went aside privately into a desert place."

He wanted some peace and quiet for himself and for his men.

But the people marked where he had gone and followed him in their hordes, and his peace was wrecked and stolen away.

Luke says: "And he welcomed them, and talked to them about the Kingdom of God, and healed them that had need of healing" (Luke 9:11).

It would have been so easy to regard the people who had invaded his privacy as nuisances. They had interrupted his rest and spoiled his chance of praying and teaching his disciples. But no—*he welcomed them.*

If we are to have this priceless quality in our lives, this precious ability to be bothered, we must have certain qualities.

*We must always be ready to welcome people at any time.*

*We must be really and truly interested in people.*

*We must come to see that individual people are the most important thing in the world.*

Every individual man is dear to God.

Our most precious right is that we have the right to bother God with our troubles at any time. The right God gave to us, we must learn to give to other people.

PRACTICAL VISION                                                    October 4

Roger Fry, writing on what he calls the "Artist's Vision", once said that anyone who is to be a great artist must have four different kinds of vision.

Not only the artist, but the Christian also needs the four different kinds of vision which Roger Fry thinks so necessary.

*The first necessity is practical vision.*

"Practical vision" sees what demands to be done in any given situation.

So many people can look at a situation, can look at someone's sorrow and need and distress, and the sight conveys no challenge to their hearts and no summons to their hands.

In the parable of Dives and Lazarus (Luke 16:19–31), Dives, the rich man, finishes up in hell, not because he was in any way deliberately cruel to Lazarus, the poor man, but because he simply accepted him as an inevitable part of the landscape and did nothing about it.

As someone has put it: "It was not what Dives did that got him into gaol; it was what he did not do that got him into hell."

The Christian has the practical vision to see what needs to be done, and the loving heart to do it.

CURIOSITY UNSEEN                                                    October 5

*The second necessity, Roger Fry says, is curiosity vision.*

"Curiosity vision" is the vision which moves a man to ask, "Why?"

"Curiosity," Plato said long ago, "is the mother of knowledge."

Many people have seen apples fall from trees, but only Newton asked, "Why?" In doing so, he discovered the law of gravity.

A man loses half his life when he loses that faculty of wonder which makes him seek and search for reasons.

The soul is half dead when we take things all for granted and stop asking, "Why?"

*The third necessity is aesthetic vision.*

"Aesthetic vision" is the vision which sees loveliness everywhere. There is loveliness everywhere for him who has the eyes to see it.

Henry Ernest Hardy, who wrote the loveliest poems under the name of Father Andrew, has some wonderful verses entitled "Mystic Beauty", in which he writes of the beauty that can be seen in any London street.

> I've seen a back street bathed in blue,
>     Such as the soul of Whistler knew;
> A smudge of amber light,
>     Where some fried fish shop plied its trade,
> A perfect note of colour made—
>     Oh, it was exquisite!

Here is the man whose eyes can see beauty and find value even in the glow of the window of the fish and chip shop.

CREATIVE VISION                                              October 6

*The fourth necessity, says Roger Fry, is creative vision.*

"Creative vision" is the vision which sees the possibilities in any situation.

Here are two men looking over a remote area in the Western Highlands. They look at the bracken and the bogs.

They look at the glint of the little lochs and the spume of the waterfalls on the hillside.

One man says: "What a wilderness! There is nothing on earth to be done with a waste land like this!"

The other man is a hydro-electric engineer. He says: "Let me build a dam here; let me harness these waters there; and I'll give you power to drive the machines and light the lamps of half a dozen cities."

Jesus saw the possibilities in every situation and in every man.

He loved men not only for what they were, but even more for what they could become.

His was the eternal optimism of God.

We ought to pray to God to give us that "creative vision" which will fire us with the sense of the vast possibilities of the situation in which we live.

Then pessimism will die and optimism will send the light of possibilities blazing across the most apparently hopeless situation.

## TIME TO GO October 7

I well remember the time when there came to me the summons to leave the one pastoral charge that I ever had. I had been with my people for more than thirteen years, and I was happy. I was torn in mind as to whether to stay in my parish, or to go to teach.

I was talking to an old man who was a member of my congregation. He was a most distinguished engineer, with a name known far beyond Scotland, but he had never lost the broad Scottish speech of his boyhood. I told him of my problems and of my indecision.

He was silent for a moment, and then he said quietly: "It's a wise man that kens when tae lay doon the barra'."

(Being translated into English and American, it means: "It's a wise man who knows when to lay down the barrow.")

There was a lifetime of wisdom there.
He is a wise man who knows when the time has come to go.
The man who hangs on too long is a sad spectacle.

When Macbeth had done the evil deed, he very soon recognises what he has done and Shakespeare makes him say:

> Had I but died an hour before this chance,
> I had lived a blessed time.

There is all the tragedy in the world in waiting just a little too long.

## RETIRING GRACEFULLY October 8

It is one of the lovely facts of life that the great men have always had the gift of retiring gracefully.

Once William Gerhardi was at a dinner party with H. G. Wells, when Wells was an old man. As they rose to leave the table to join the ladies, Gerhardi courteously stood back at the door to allow Wells to pass before him. "You first," said Wells. "You are tomorrow and I am yesterday."

When Sir James Barrie made one of his amazing speeches to the Rhodes Scholars, he said: "If to despise us helps you in your enthusiasm, then, gentlemen, continue. Far worse than your scorning us beyond reason would be your not having a cheery belief that you can do better. If in firing at some of our performances you feel that the straightest line is through our bodies, still fire."

And there is one tremendous instance of this in the New Testament itself. When Jesus emerged, John the Baptist said: "He must increase, but I must decrease" (John 3:30).

John had held the centre of the stage, but now he knew that it was time to go.

BUT WHEN? October 9

How shall we know when the time has come to go?
*The time has come to go when we begin to resent all new ideas and all new methods.*

J. Alexander Findlay in his book *Jesus and His Parables* tells how a friend once said to him: "When you come to a conclusion you are dead."

When a man's mind is shut, when a man's mind, like the old wine-skins, loses its elasticity, it is time to go.

When he cannot be bothered to examine a new theory, when he cannot be bothered to try out a new method, it is time to go.

*The time has come to go when we find ourselves becoming annoyed with younger people.*

When tolerance turns to irritation, it is time to go. When, instead of looking at the energy and the enthusiasm of youth with sympathy, we look at them with annoyance and irritation, it is time to go.

Miss Anna Buchan, in her autobiography, tells how her old grandmother, who was always young, used to say again and again: "Never daunton youth."

When we find ourselves instinctively ready with the cold water, it is time to go.

The time has come to go when we think of the things we have done rather than of the things we still want to do.

When a man lives in the sunset rather than in the sunrise, his day is at an end, although he may live a long time yet. It is common enough for the young men to see visions, but it is godlike for the old men to dream dreams (Joel 2:28).

There are young people waiting to take over. We must see to it that we do not keep them waiting too long. I said this once before,* but I will say it again! May God grant that some day I will remember in time what I have written in these words.

THE WRONG WAY                                              October 10

I had occasion to make the journey from Glasgow to London. I was travelling by the "Royal Scot" which did not stop at any station between Glasgow and London. More than once a railway inspector passed up and down the train calling out: "First stop London!"

Then just about five minutes before the train was due to leave he made his last tour of the train, and this time, as he went, he put his head into each compartment and said: "Make no mistake! London first stop!"

So I heard him going down the train calling into each compartment: "Make no mistake!" It was as if he said: "Remember where you are going to finish up if you start out on this train!"

Now that is a thing that life is always saying to us. Life is always saying to us: "If you start this way, remember where you're going to finish up!"

*There are some who discover too late that they have taken the wrong destination.*
Cardinal Wolsey was Henry's great Prime Minister. For a time he flourished; and then the policy of the king demanded that Wolsey be jettisoned. For a time Wolsey managed to buy security, but in the end his execution came.

As he lay in the Tower awaiting the end, he was talking to the Lieutenant of the Tower.

"Master Knygton," he said, "had I but served God as diligently as I have served the king, he would not have given me over in my grey hairs. But this is my due reward for my pains and study, not regarding my service to God, but only my duty to my prince."

Wolsey had made a mistake.
Wolsey had not realised where he was going.
The end was tragedy.

IDLE THREATS                                               October 11

There is in our days an extraordinary contempt for the law. It may well be that we are living in one of the most lawless ages in history, and we are

*In the entry for January 5 (Time Up!) in *Through the Year with William Barclay.*

living in a time when there is less confidence between the public and the guardians of the law than there used to be.

A good deal of this is to be explained by three facts about the law.

*An unenforceable law is a bad law.*

A law which cannot be enforced should not really be enacted. If the national or civic authorities are not prepared to enforce laws, then they should not lay them down.

*Every time a threat is made and not carried out, respect for the law grows less and less.*

No man bothers about a law which he is fairly certain that he can flout with impunity.

*Erratically applied law is the biggest cause of resentment and trouble between the authorities and the ordinary man.*

There can never be any satisfactory relationship with law and authority when the same action may be on one occasion punished and on another unpunished, or when the law punishes one man and lets another go free for precisely the same fault.

Let us bring this nearer home.

What we have been saying of the law is equally true of the family. The parent who lays down family laws which he cannot enforce, the parent who makes a threat and does not carry it out—and some parents are for ever doing just that—the parent whose justice is erratic and unpredictable, can look for nothing but family trouble.

A child is not a fool. He very soon sees when threats are not going to be carried out. A child has a vivid sense of justice and will soon resent erratic justice.

In the family and in the community, law must have respect. People must observe laws, or law and order will necessarily come into disrepute. Perhaps this is exactly what has happened.

NOT THE HAPPY WAY                                    October 12

*There are those who discover too late that the easy way is not the happy way.*

Once Cranmer stood for the real faith, but in face of Mary's persecution he signed his six recantations, by which he hoped to purchase his life.

But no sooner had he signed them than he was wretched.

In the end he recanted his recantations and went to be burned.

As he spoke to the people before he was burned he said:

"Now I come to the great thing that troubleth my conscience more than any other thing that ever I said or did in my life, and that is the setting abroad of writings contrary to the truth; which here I now renounce and refuse as things written by my hand contrary to the truth which I thought in my heart, and written for fear of death, to save my life, if it might be. And forasmuch as my hand offended in writing contrary to my heart, my hand therefore shall be the first punished; for if I come to the fire, it shall be the first burnt."

He came to the stake:

"This was the hand that wrote it," he said, "therefore it shall first suffer punishment." And holding it steadily in the flame "he never stirred nor cried" till life was gone.

Cranmer thought that the destination of the easy way was peace. It wasn't.

WRONG DESTINATION                                   October 13

*There are some who have known the way they were going, and who, because they knew the destination, did not care how hard it was.*

Barrie tells of the students who took the way to knowledge:

I knew three undergraduates who lodged together in a dreary house at the top of a dreary street. Two of them used to study until two in the morning while the third slept.

When they shut their books they awoke number three who rose and dressed and studied till breakfast time: among the many advantages of this system was that, as they were dreadfully poor, one bed did for the three of them.

Two of them occupied it at one time and the third at another. Terrible privation? Dreadful destitution? Not a bit of it. If knowledge was at the top of a 100 steps, if students occasionally died of hunger and hard work combined, if midnight oil burned to show a ghastly face, weary and worn, if lodging were cheap and dirty, and dinners few and far between, life was real and earnest, and it did not turn out an empty dream.

The students knew where they were going, and the hardness of the way was as nothing.

This is not a thing which affects only statesmen. It does not need to be as dramatic as Barrie makes it. In every decision in life, before we allow ourselves any pleasure or indulgence, before we take the first step towards developing any habit, we ought to ask:

"Where is this way going? What is its destination?"

It is better never to start than to arrive at the wrong destination.

## THE IMMORTAL PART                                            October 14

Epitaphs are often dull and even distressing things, but sometimes one comes across one which has a touch of genius.

In Liverpool Cathedral there is a tablet on the wall, part of which reads like this: "Here lies in honour all that could die of a pioneer in orthopaedics, Sir Robert Jones."

"Here lies all that could die".

Centuries before Horace, the Roman poet, had said: "*Non omnis moriar*", "I shall not all die."

There is a part of man which is laid in the tomb, and there is a part of a man which lives on.

*Sometimes a man's words live on.*

Horace wrote in his Odes: "I have completed my work, and I have raised a monument more lasting than bronze."

Shakespeare wrote in one of his sonnets:

> So long as men can breathe, or eyes can see,
> So long lives this, and this gives life to thee.

It is not only the words of the great which live on.

It can happen that the wise word of a parent can live in the heart of a child until that child becomes an old man. Over a lifetime that life has been kept nearer to God by such a good word.

## THERE CAME A MAN . . .                                        October 15

*Sometimes a man's teaching lives on.*

A great teacher marks his scholars. He lives in them. Some of these scholars may themselves become teachers, and they pass on the mark of their old teacher, and so an influence begins which passes from generation to generation.

A. J. Gossip reminds us that Principal John Cairns once wrote to his teacher, Sir William Hamilton: "I do not know what life, or lives, may lie before me. But I know this, that, to the end of the last of them, I shall bear your mark upon me."

This is true not only of teachers in colleges and in universities. It is true of the teacher in the day school. It is true of the teacher in the Sunday school. The great teacher lives on in those whom he or she taught, though that great teacher is a humble person who never dreamed of greatness.

*Sometimes a man's memory and influence live on.*

There are some people who are talked about whenever those who knew them meet together.

There are some people about whom we find ourselves thinking whenever we are up against it.

In the hard times and the sore times, their memory comes back.

There are certain influences which do not die.

It is, I think, Augustine Birrell who tells how once, when he was staying in a village in Cornwall, a fishing village, he was impressed by the atmosphere of sheer goodness in the place.

In talk with an old fisherman, he asked what the explanation was of the atmosphere of simple goodness which pervaded this village. The old man bared his head: "There came a man amongst us," he said. "His name was John Wesley."

THE SOUL GOES ON                                        October 16

Whatever else is true, a man's soul lives on. All that can die of him is placed in the tomb, but there is a part of him which cannot die.

That is what makes life so important.

Life is the training school of eternity.

Life is the apprenticeship for glory.

All the time we live in this world, we either fit ourselves or unfit ourselves for the greater life of the world to come.

In this life all our days we are either winning or losing a crown.

Life is always infinitely worth living, because on how we live life depends eternity.

FOR ALL                                                 October 17

In Cheltenham there was an inn called The Five Alls. And its sign was most interesting.

On the sign there was a king, with the motto: "I rule for all."

There was a bishop, with the motto: "I pray for all."

There was a lawyer, with the motto: "I plead for all."

There was a soldier, with the motto: "I fight for all."

And there was an artisan in working clothes, with the motto: "I work for all."

There indeed is a programme for all.

*I rule for all.*

If it should happen that we are in control of many people, the motive which should animate us is not our private profit, but the good of all.

If we are simple ordinary people, servants and not masters, there is one person whom we can rule, and that is ourself, for only he who is master of himself is fit to be the servant of others.

*I pray for all.*

Jowett, the great preacher, used to tell of a girl who came to join his church. She was a servant girl, not well off, and not well educated. He wished to make sure that she knew what she was doing and that she was in earnest about her profession, and he asked her how she proposed to live the Christian life.

"I haven't much time off, sir," she said, "and I can't attend many meetings or even many services."

"Well," said Jowett, "what do you do?"

"Well, sir," she said, "I always take the daily paper to bed with me at night."

Jowett was puzzled, as well he might be. "What's the good of that?" he said.

"Well, sir," she said, "I look at the first page and I read the birth notices and I pray for the babies that have been born; and I read the marriages and I pray that they may be happy and true; and I read the deaths and I pray that God's comfort may come to these sorrowing homes." Is it not a staggering vision—the waves of prayer which went out from that attic beneath the tiles?

*I pray for all.*
The servant girl did.
So can we.

CRUSADERS                                                    October 18

*I plead for all.*

The writer to the Hebrews has the most tremendous vision in the New Testament. He speaks of Jesus in the heavenly places and he says of him:

"He ever liveth to make intercession for us" (Heb. 7:25). Even in heaven Jesus is pleading for men.

*I fight for all.*

That is what the great lovers of humanity have all done. They saw some wrong, some iniquity, some oppression, some distress, some need and they fought that it might be removed.

Often they themselves were well-to-do and comfortable and lived in ease. The conquest in the struggle of social reformation was not going to profit them. But they spent themselves for the sake of others.

Where there was poverty, oppression, sorrow, distress, they must fight the battle for others.

It is too often the case that so long as things are well with us, we do not much mind what is happening to others.

The great men were the men who bore the sorrows of the world upon their hearts, and who were God's crusaders in the battle for the down-trodden and the under-privileged and the oppressed.

NOT FOR SELF                                                    October 19

*I work for all.*

Do we?

The tragedy of things today is that hardly anyone does! Some of us work for ourselves, a bigger bank balance, a television set, a refrigerator, a motor car—these are the things for which we work.

Some of us go a little further and work for our families, a better chance for our sons and daughters, a better start in life for them, a better job than we have—these are the things for which we work.

Some of us work for the class to which we belong, more privileges, higher pay, shorter hours, longer holidays, better conditions for ourselves and our mates—these are the things for which we work.

But there are so few, so very few, who work for *all*, who have the spirit of service which sees beyond the boundaries of self and selfish interest.

The social and the economic millennium will come when master and man work, not for self, but for God and for all.

God so loved the world . . .
His love is over all.
And we, who are his servants, must ever seek to be like him.

As I came north from England, I stayed for a night at Banbury. Naturally I was interested to see Banbury Cross, which the nursery rhyme connects with the fine lady on the white horse.

But Banbury has a very handsome church. I went into it in the morning before I left Banbury, and I saw a very wonderful thing.

As I came in through the front door the church looked very dark, for there was no lighting. Then my eye travelled to the faraway end of the building. On the altar there was a polished brass cross and that cross was shining like a star through the dark. There was no artificial lighting on it.

With its own light, that cross was shining so that it stood out in the dark, even from far away.

J. L. Hodson, in one of his war books, tells of a conversation he had with a fellow journalist on the morning after London's most devastating air raid.

The journalist said to him: "Did you see the cross on St. Paul's, old boy? Nobody has ever seen it shine and glow as it did that night. Clouds of smoke rolled by it, an unearthly beauty was over it."

In the destruction and the devastation, the cross shone out.

I remember when I was a parish minister in Renfrew on Clydeside, I was visiting friends in Clydebank in the days when Clydebank was devastated in two terrible nights. They stayed in an avenue which was next door to the railway line. In sight of their house there was a signal gantry; and the signal lights formed exactly the shape of a cross.

They said to me: "So long as that cross of lights is lit, we know that there isn't going to be an air raid; but when the lights are put out, we look for trouble."

The light of the cross meant safety to them.

The Cross means safety (or the same word, salvation) for us.

CLOTHED IN GLORY                                         October 21

*Our future depends on how we use this life.*

No scholar or student is allowed to pass to a higher class and a higher study until he has mastered the junior class and the more elementary study. Life is like that.

There is one sense in which each day is sufficient to itself.

The New Testament forbids the anxious looking forward of the worried mind and the distrustful heart.

But there is a sense in which a Christian man is always looking forward; for he must see life in the light of eternity.

If we will remember that, the tasks of this life are the tests by which we prepare ourselves for a higher service, if we learn to look on this life as the training ground for eternity, then even the smallest and the most routine tasks will be clothed with glory.

For then it will be literally true that, whatsoever we do in deed or word, we will be doing it in the name of the Lord Jesus (Col. 3:17).

FOR WHOM THE LIGHT SHINES                                October 22

The light which shines from the Cross has always brought wonders in the dark.

*It shone in the dark for the sick and the suffering and the weak.*
Dr. A. Rendle Short wrote in *The Bible and Modern Medicine*: "We know from Jerome's writings that the first hospital of which we have any record . . . was founded by a Christian lady, Fabiola."

He goes on to tell how the plague smote Carthage in A.D. 252. The heathen flung out their dead and fled.

But Cyprian, the Christian bishop, assembled the Christian congregation to care for the sick and to bury the dead, and so saved the city from desolation.

The love, the care, the tenderness that the sick and the ailing and the weakly and the deformed received was quite absent from heathen civilisation; it shines from the Cross.

*It shone in the dark for the morally helpless.*
The tragedy of the ancient world was not lack of knowledge of the good. It was powerlessness to do it. Seneca said that men loved their vices and hated them at the same time. He bewailed what he called "our inefficiency in necessary things".

Men knew that they were sinners, and yet were helpless to do anything about it.

But Paul can write to the Corinthians, making a list of the foulest sins and sinners—fornicators, adulterers, homosexuals, drunkards—and then at the end add triumphantly—"And such were some of you" (I Cor. 6:9-11). The Cross has always shone with power to overcome and to defeat the moral helplessness which has man in its grip.

The light of the Cross shines for the sick and the sinner.
Not all the darkness in the world can quench *that* light.


SECURITY ?                                                    October 23

In London there is a little row of houses between Westminster Abbey and
Dean's Court.

One day I was going along it and looked up to see its name.

Its name is a lovely name.

Its name is "The Sanctuary".

As I walked along it I glanced at certain of the buildings of which it is
composed, and quite suddenly I noticed that two of them stood out as
insurance offices!


Here is a parable of modern life. Men seek their safety in earthly insurance.
They seek a sanctuary in insuring themselves in material things.

Now, in one sense, there is nothing to be said against that, and everything
to be said in its favour, for once a man has acquired a wife and a family he
has, in the old phrase, "given hostages to fortune". And he is a reckless man
who, in the face of the chances and changes of life, will leave them entirely
unprovided for.

But there is a sense in which this modern identification of insurance and
sanctuary is a wrong thing.


In these days men are searching for security.

The real Christian has never sought security.

Think of the old days in the Roman Empire.

A man might say to a Christian preacher: "If I become a Christian, what
may I expect?" The honest answer would be: "You can expect imprison-
ment, crucifixion, the fight with the beasts in the arena, the stake and
the flames. You will become an outlaw and your life will never be safe
again."

Unamuno, the Spanish mystic, used to pray for those he loved: "May God
deny you peace and give you glory."

There is a great prayer of the Christian Church which runs like this:


O Jesus Christ, the Lord of all good life who hast called us to build up
the city of God, do Thou enrich and purify our lives, and deepen in us our
discipleship.

Help us daily to know more of Thee, and, through us, by the power of
Thy Spirit, show forth Thyself to other men.

Make us humble, brave and loving; make us ready for adventure in Thy cause.

We do not ask that Thou shouldst keep us loyal, who for us didst face death unafraid and dost live and reign for ever and ever.

Ready for adventure?

A man came to Tertullian with a problem. His problem was the difficulty of earning a living in a heathen world.

What if the mason was asked to build a heathen temple?

What if the tailor was asked to make clothes for a heathen priest?

What if the soldier must daily burn his pinch of incense on the altar of the camp?

The man finished up by saying: "I must live."

And Tertullian answered him in one immortal question: "Must you?"

If it came to a choice between our Christian principles and our job, honestly, what would we do? Have most of us ever really taken a risk for our Christian faith in all our lives?

When we do seek for security, we seek for it in the wrong place.

We seek for it by taking earthly and material precautions.

We seek to ensure earthly security by earthly insurance.

But there is a safety far beyond that, and it is this other safety that matters.

In the 1914–18 war Rupert Brooke wrote his poem "Safety".

> Safe shall be my going,
> Secretly armed against all death's
>     endeavour;
> Safe though all safety's lost; safe where men fall;
> And if these poor limbs die, safest of all.

The Roman Catholic cardinal threatened Martin Luther with all kinds of vengeance. He told him that his present supporters would soon leave him in the lurch.

"Where will you be then?" he demanded menacingly.

"Then as now," said Luther, "then as now—in the hands of God."

There is not much use in a man insuring his life unless his life is safe with God.

The way to be safe with God is always to take the risk of staking everything on Jesus Christ.

BREAKING IN                                                         October 25

I know a lady whose household moved to a new house in a part of a town not very far away from where her home used to be. She is not young and she is not old. She is by no means shy. She is a good talker and meets all kinds of people with the greatest of ease. She was brought up in the Church and has always had the closest connection with the Church.

Now, I have always believed as a matter of principle that a family ought to go to the church of their parish or their community area, and that to travel long distances to maintain an old connection is neither wise nor right.

I said to this lady: "I suppose you will be leaving your church and you will be joining a congregation nearer at hand."

"No," she said, "I am going to stay in the church of which I am a member just now."

"Why's that?" I asked, surprised.

She looked at me and said: "I just couldn't bear to make the effort to break into another congregation."

The effort to *break into* a congregation!

It was not as if this lady had not changed her congregation before. More than once she had had to leave one town for another. It was not as if she was shy or a stranger to churches. Yet she was daunted by the effort which she felt was required to break into another church!

Is the Church as welcoming as it ought to be?

Are Christians not all brothers and sisters because they are all sons and daughters of the one Father?

Yet the difficulty remains.

It shouldn't!

WHERE DO I GO?                                                      October 26

Does the Church welcome sinners as it ought to welcome them?

Suppose someone has made a mess of things, suppose someone has fallen into some of the sins into which a passionate nature may bring a man or a woman, is that person likely to receive a warm welcome, if he or she tries to break into a Church?

Hugh Redwood somewhere tells a terrible story.

There was a woman in the dock district of London. She associated with a Chinese and bore him a half-caste child.

She found her way to a women's meeting in a certain church, taking her child with her. She liked it and she came back. She came back a third time. The minister of the church came up to her. Awkward and embarrassed, he said to her: "I'm very sorry but I must ask you not to come to this meeting again."

"Why can't I come?" she said.

He answered: "The other women know about you, and they say that, if *you* keep on coming, *they* will stop."

The woman looked at the minister with poignant sorrow on her face. "Sir," she said, "I know I'm a sinner but isn't there anywhere a sinner can go?"

Fortunately the Salvation Army got hold of her. But "the Church" had slammed the door in her face.

I have felt that if I made a shipwreck of life, the Church is the last place to which I could go. There are many good people in this world, but you could not go and weep out a sorry tale on their shoulder. If you tried to do so, you would freeze. They would be embarrassed.

It is not a question of taking sin lightly, but it is a question of remembering that Jesus said: "Him that cometh unto me I will no wise cast out."

THE SHY STRANGER                                             October 27

Does the Church welcome strangers as it ought to welcome them?

Does a stranger feel a stranger when he enters a church, or does he feel he has come among friends?

One of the great tributes that Homer paid to one of his characters was: "He dwelt in a house at the side of the road, and he was the friend of way-faring men."

Can we really say that about the Church?

Was it not Sir Walter Scott about whom they used to say that when he shook hands with you, he was never the first to withdraw his hand?

Does the Church give you a welcome like that?

One of the strange, disturbing features of many churches is the "possession" of pews by their members.

There is something radically wrong, something totally unchristian in the sight of any man having an exclusive right to eighteen inches or two feet of seating accommodation in any church.

True, in most cases the stranger will be shown to a pew—as if he was there by grace and favour. In most cases he will receive some kind of welcome. But there is a kind of malign fate which will sometimes lead him to the one pew where he will be met with blank hostility.

It is not a case of a back-slapping, vociferous, overwhelming welcome. It is just a question of Christian kindliness to the stranger in a strange place.

Does the Church welcome shy people as it ought to welcome them? There are far more shy people in this world than we realise.

Sometimes I wonder if young people who leave home, and then stop going to church, do stop going just because they are too shy to go.

Surely we ought to try to meet people half-way.

Surely we ought to try to get alongside them better than we do.

Surely we ought to make the family of God the one place where shyness is at home.

Will you think of all this?

Is your church a place where it needs an effort to *break in*?

I hope not!

## "MY CHOICE" October 28

My parents were Gaelic-speaking West Highlanders, and their native place was Fort William.

When I was a small boy most of our holidays were spent in Fort William.

One of the great delights in my life was when we rowed across Loch Linnhe and had a picnic on the opposite shore at Trieslaig.

Now the West Highlands are very beautiful, but they are also very wet.

One day we planned to cross the loch and to picnic on the other side. We had waited to get the newspapers from the morning train and after that we proposed to set off.

The morning had dawned most beautifully; but the mist and the rain came down and clearly there could be no picnic that day. We left the station and we were walking along the main street and I was very disconsolate.

We came to one of the shops and, at the door there was standing its owner, an elder of the Church. We stopped to talk to him, and I told him of our plans and of our disappointment because the rain had come. He looked down at me from what was then to me his vast height, and fixed me with a peculiarly unsympathetic eye, and then he said with all the unconscious arrogance of age: "Boy, if God sends rain, rain's my choice."

By that time I had decided to become a minister, but that man's words came very close to stopping me from entering the ministry, because I felt that, if the Church was run by people like that, I didn't want anything to do with it.

It was not that the man was not right. What he said was no doubt a laudable thing to say; but it was the smug, self-righteous, unsympathetic way in which it was said.

No doubt he spoke the truth, but he certainly did not speak the truth in love, as Paul would have us to do.


## THE EVIDENCE OF THE TONGUE                    October 29

I have quite frequently had to go to towns and cities to which I have never been before. It therefore happens that often I have to stop complete strangers to ask them the way to the place which I am trying to find.

I can usually tell something about the man from whom I ask directions by the directions he gives me.

The person who gives me directions will usually tell me that when I see such-and-such a place I will be near my destination. He very naturally gives me directions on the basis of the landmarks which stick out in his mind.

If he says to me, "When you see such-and-such a church, you are getting near where you want to go," I know that man is a churchman, because he directs me in terms of churches.

If he says, "You will see such-and-such a cinema on your left," I know that that man is a cinema-goer because he directs me in terms of cinemas.

If he says to me, "You get off the bus after such-and-such a garage," it's a fair guess that that man is a motorist or that he is at least interested in motor cars because he directs me in terms of garages.

If he tells me that I must make for such-and-such a public-house, I know that he is not unacquainted with such places because he directs me in terms of public-houses.

In every case the man's directions give him away.

It *is* true that our speech betrays us!


## "TRY IT AND SEE"                    October 30

There is a limit beyond which permissiveness cannot be allowed to go.

We live in a permissive society. There are those who declare that this is one of our great advances. They declare it to be a good thing that the controls are slackened, the restraints removed, and that young people are allowed to order life for themselves and to say for themselves what they shall do and what they shall not do.

There is a sense in which this is true. But permissiveness must never go to the length of allowing any person to destroy himself or to corrupt others by his actions.

No one in his senses would hold that it is a good thing to stand back and watch a man walk over a precipice.

No one can claim that any man ought to be allowed to introduce any other man to practices which are demonstrably ruinous.

There is a line beyond which permissiveness cannot go, unless we think it right to stand back and watch a person throwing away happiness, and health and even life itself.

It is never wise to play with fire. The man who plays with fire will in the end be burned.

It is not so much that we plead with people, and especially young people, to play safe. It is simply that we plead with them not to throw life uselessly away.

"Try it and see" is a good motto in many cases, but there are many things in this world that we do not need personally to try to know that they are ruinous.

That has been settled long ago, and to defy the sum total of experience is not to be adventurous. It is to be a fool.

A CREED REVISED                                             October 31

Ernest Bacon tells—very disapprovingly—how in 1859 F. D. Maurice wrote of Spurgeon as if the staple of his preaching was "hell and the devil".

Maurice wrote of Spurgeon: "If he should waken up to the perception of a God of absolute love, his popularity would probably vanish."

This is no doubt unfair to Spurgeon personally, but the omission of the Love of God from the basic beliefs is strange.

We might well look again at the revised creed presented to the United Free Church Assembly in 1926, and quoted in A. B. Macauley's *The Death of Jesus*:

"I believe in God, the Father Almighty, Maker of heaven and earth, holy and wise, Whose loving will and purpose all things serve; and in Jesus Christ, His Son, our Lord and Saviour, Who by His life on earth, His death for our sake upon the Cross, and His rising from the dead, wrought salvation for the world, and is now exalted Lord over all.

And in the Holy Spirit of God, Who evermore reveals the Son in love and power to men, awakening them to repentance and faith, assuring them of the forgiveness of sins through Jesus Christ, and enabling them to know and obey the will of God.

I believe in the fellowship of the redeemed, the one Church of the Lord Jesus Christ, called to show forth his glory by worship and service; in judgment to come; in the triumph of the Kingdom of God; and in the life everlasting."

To rescue that 1926 creed from oblivion would be a useful service.

You cannot talk about the Christian Gospel and leave out that God is love.

# *November*

One of the hero stories of modern times is the story of the Scottish poet, William Soutar. He died in 1943 at the tragically early age of forty-five.

He died after twenty-five years of illness and ten years of complete help-lessness.

There was a time when he could do nothing more than move his head.

That situation Soutar met with gallantry. When at twenty-five he knew that he was doomed, he said: "Now I can be a poet."

When he became increasingly helpless, as helpless as a child, he said: "One's core of manliness must be preserved."

"Life," he said, "demands something more from a man than a handful of lyrics," and life received more from William Soutar.

The story of that life was admirably written recently by Alexander Scott in his biography of Soutar entitled *Still Life*.

In that book two sayings of Soutar are quoted.

The first is an incident related by Soutar himself. He was thinking of his earliest memories and he describes the "first important symbolic episode in his life".

He and his mother had set out for a walk one afternoon when he was about three years old. Suddenly the walk was interrupted, when the little lad ran from his mother with the words which he flung over his shoulder: "Get back, get back, I don't require a mother."

There was the child's desire for independence.

But this very same William Soutar was later in his manhood also to say:

239

"If I have been privileged to catch a more comprehensive glimpse of life than many other men, it is because I have stood on the shoulders of my parents."

There is the declaration not of independence, but of dependence.


November 2

William Soutar was not only one of the great Scottish poets. He was also a prose writer of more than ordinary distinction, often with a touch of wit and humour.

Sometimes he used to write parables.

Here is one of them.

There was once a woodcutter's wife who forgot to salt her husband's porridge, and when the woodman reproved her she retorted that he was a fool to make a fuss about so small a thing.

This angered the woodman and, coming to his task, he began to smite at a tree furiously, so that in a backswing his axe-head flew off to a great distance and injured a favourite horse of his master's which was being led to be reshod.

Now on that day this very horse was to have borne the nobleman to a meeting of noblemen who were gathering to discuss their grievances against the king.

It was therefore in a disgruntled mood that the woodcutter's master joined his peers; and under compulsion of his anger, eloquently counselled his confederates to revolt.

In the subsequent tumult many were slain by the sword, pestilence and famine; and for a generation afterwards the people bowed under the burden of great taxation.

There came a rebellion, and a generation of suffering all because a woodman's wife forgot to salt her husband's porridge!

This is a parable of the greatness of little things.

"Who hath despised the day of small things?" said Zechariah (Zech. 4:10).


November 3

*There are times when small things can save a man.*

This was something William Soutar found out himself. In his increasing helplessness, it was inevitable that more and more things should vanish from his life.

He writes: "So much can wither away from the human spirit, and yet the great gift of the ordinary day remains; the stability of the small things of life, which yet in their constancy are the greatest."

Again and again a man finds salvation in the things of every day. In sorrow, worry, indecision, there is nothing which so saves a man's sanity and life as simply to go on with the ordinary routine things of life.

To sit down amidst regrets, to sit and do nothing but worry is fatal.

Ordinary duties enable us at these times to go on.

*There are times when small things can ruin life.*

A habit beginning from the smallest of things can spoil life. A rank growth can come from the market seed.

The point of Soutar's parable told yesterday is the way in which the small things can cause widespread disaster. Their effect can be like that of a stone on a still pond. The waves can go out and out and reach people who do not even know where the waves came from.

A lost collar stud can send a man out in a frame of mind which bodes trouble for a whole office or class or shop.

A trifling upset can make a woman begin a day in a way which disrupts the whole family.

A dispute, an argument, a difference at a breakfast table can produce repercussions all over a city in the different places in which the various members of the family work.

If we are to make life tolerable for ourselves and for others, we must learn something of the great virtue of serenity.

We can learn that from Jesus.

THE PARENT'S TASK                                           November 4

There are in the two sayings of William Soutar which we have quoted a summary of the task of the parent—and it is a task almost impossibly difficult and hard.

There is a time when the child is utterly dependent. Everything has to be done for him or he would literally die. There is a time when the lad or girl, or the youth or the maiden has to be gently but firmly guided and controlled. But all this dependence and all this guidance have but one end—the production of a person who some day will be able to stand up and meet life on his own two feet.

In life there is nothing more difficult than the duty of the parent to guide and control and yet to render strong and independent his child. And today that duty is infinitely more difficult than it used to be.

So often the tendency is to hold on to people too long, to try to keep them dependent, consciously or unconsciously to resent the day when they must live their own lives and come to their own conclusions.

I went to hear one of my own former students preach some time ago. He preached on laying aside every weight (Heb. 12:1), on the things that must be laid aside, on the things we must learn to let go.

It was an admirable sermon, with an amazing maturity.

We must let go material things; we must let go preconceived notions and ideas. So far these are conventional preaching points. But then this young man added something startling—*we must let people go.* We must never hang on to people when the time has come for them to be themselves.

We must never smother them when they ought to be breathing a larger air.

We must never try to make them dependent when they ought to be independent.

There is a wonderful text in Deuteronomy 32:11: "As an eagle stirreth up her nest, fluttereth over her young, spreadeth abroad her wings, taketh them, beareth them on her wings, so the Lord alone did lead him."

The eagle has to teach her young to risk the adventure of flight. At first she rouses them; takes them on her broad wings; carries them; but then bit by bit she withdraws her wings and the young eagles find themselves in the sky alone. She carries them—but only to launch them out in flight for themselves.

Those of us who are older, and those of us who are parents, must remember that we have a double duty—*the duty of guidance and of control*, and yet at the same time *the duty of making our young people independent*, able to live their lives on their own.

ALL OR NOTHING                                                   November 5

There is no finer storehouse of stories than classical literature. Let us think then of some of the great stories of the Romans and the Greeks.

The greatest of all the Greek kings was Alexander the Great, the man who before he was thirty wept because there were no more worlds left to conquer.

The most illuminating story of Alexander comes from his Persian campaigns.

He had put Darius into a position in which ultimate defeat was certain. Darius recognised this and offered Alexander terms which were very favourable. He offered Alexander a great ransom for the captives which had been taken, a mutual alliance, and the hand of one of his daughters in marriage.

All this Darius offered, if Alexander would halt and stay his hand and be content with that which he had won. Alexander told Parmenio, his chief of staff, of the terms which had been offered.

Parmenio said: "If I were you I would accept them." And Alexander replied: "So would I—if I were Parmenio."

Alexander was Alexander, and for him there was nothing less than absolute victory. A lesser man would be content, and well content, with lesser things, but for Alexander it was all or nothing.

Great men have always had a sense of their own greatness.

Napoleon's plans and schemes had led him into conflict with the Pope.

He had an uncle who was a cardinal. The uncle protested against Napoleon's actions, and warned him to be content with less. The uncle was an old man and dim-sighted. It was night time.

Napoleon led him to the window and pointed into the night.

"Do you see that star?" he asked.

The dim-sighted old cardinal answered: "No, sir."

Napoleon answered: "But I see it; you may go."

Napoleon could see the star; the cardinal could not.

Therein lay the secret of his greatness.

THINK GREATLY! November 6

To be great one must have a sense of greatness. This we have said. But this is a very different thing from conceit.

How shall we get that sense of greatness?

*We get it from self-respect.*

When Nehemiah was urged to seek a cowardly safety in the hour of his danger, his answer was: "Should such a man as I flee?" (Neh. 6:11).

Many a man has been compelled to greatness, because he respected himself, and would not let himself down.

*We get it from the fact that others are thinking of us, hoping for us, believing in us, praying for us.*

George Washington once said: "I shall not despair so long as I know that one faithful saint is praying for me."

We carry upon us the hopes and the prayers and the dreams of those to whom we are dear.

*We have God behind us.*

Every time we say good-bye, and every time we use the word "good-bye", we are listening to the words, or we are saying the words: "God be with you!"

We go in the strength of the Lord.

The world needs men and women who can think and act greatly.

In Manchester Exchange Station there was a tea bar. It was typical of that station at that time that there was not even room there in which to drink your cup of tea. There was a makeshift counter and one or two comfortless forms. But it was a wonderful experience to have a cup of tea there.

Why?

Because the station sparrows try to share it with you! They were so tame that they hopped about on the counter within inches of you to ask for crumbs and to eat them.

I shall never forget the friendly sparrows in Manchester Exchange Station.

Now no sooner had I got home here to Glasgow than a minister friend of mine came to visit me.

He told me that he had been with his wife on holiday in Paris. He went into one of the great parks in the centre of the city. There he saw a man feeding the sparrows.

The man had a long French loaf in his hand. He would break off a piece, crumble it between his finger and thumb, and the sparrows would fly on to his hand and eat it. And the curious thing was that the sparrows were queued up in single file, coming one at a time in strict order for their crumbs!

Once two sparrows flew up together, and tried to get at the same crumb. The man looked rebukingly at one of the sparrows and muttered, and, lo and behold, the sparrow went back to the end of the queue! Then after a while the man chirruped to the sparrow, and the queue-jumping sparrow came up to get his piece of bread.

My friend asked the man how he had managed to make the sparrows so tame. He said that for years and years at his lunch time he had been coming to feed the sparrows, and they had got to know him so well they were no longer frightened of him.

My friend added that he *must* have been coming for years, because he noticed the man's fingers. Like many Frenchmen he was swarthy-skinned. But the finger and thumb with which he crumbled the bread were quite white, whitened by the bread, and hacked with the pecks that the birds had given him.

GOD AND THE SPARROWS                                   November 8

Jesus would have liked the stories about the sparrows I told in yesterday's entry. He too said something about sparrows.

Matthew and Luke tell it differently.

Matthew says: "Are not two sparrows sold for a farthing? And one of them shall not light on the ground without your Father" (Matt. 10:29). (It's not a case of the sparrow falling dead; it's a case of the sparrow hopping on the ground; God sees even that.)

Luke has it: "Are not five sparrows sold for two farthings, and not one of them is forgotten before God?" (Luke 12:6). Something wrong with the arithmetic? Two sparrows for one farthing—five sparrows for two farthings—someone slipped up in counting? No! In Palestine two sparrows cost a farthing, but if you were prepared to spend two farthings, an extra sparrow was flung into the bargain for nothing.

A sparrow that was literally worth nothing—and yet God sees and cares for that sparrow!

Jesus used that saying for a purpose. If, he said, God cares for sparrows like that, if God cares even for the sparrow that is worth nothing at all, the sparrow that is just flung into the bargain and given away as worthless, how much more will he care for you?

God cares for the sparrows.

Are you not of more value than many sparrows?

SCRAPE AN ACQUAINTANCE!                                November 9

In the ancient world of Greece and Rome, the public baths were the places where everyone met. Aristocrat and commoner met there. The baths were far more clubs than merely places of washing.

It was there that the gymnasts trained; and it was there that the philosophers like Plato met and talked to their friends and discussed the greatest things.

It is from the Roman baths, and from an incident which happened there, that we get a famous phrase which we still very often use.

One day Hadrian the Roman Emperor visited the baths. In those days bathers used scrapers to scrape off the oil with which they anointed their bodies after bathing.

In the baths Hadrian noticed an old soldier. The old veteran was too poor to buy a proper scraper made of bone or ivory or metal, and he was using an old piece of broken pottery as a scraper.

Hadrian said nothing, but that very night he sent the old veteran a sum of money, not only to buy a scraper, but also to relieve his poverty.

The story of the Emperor's generosity very naturally got about. Soon after word went round that Hadrian was to visit the baths again. When he arrived, the baths were crowded with bathers using pieces of broken pottery to scrape themselves, in the hope of arousing the Emperor's generosity again. Hadrian looked at them and smiled gently: "Scrape on, gentlemen," he said, "you will not scrape an acquaintance with me!"

From that incident we get our phrase which speaks of "scraping an acquaintance" with someone.

That incident is a lesson in giving.

THE LINGUIST                                              November 10

There was once a Welsh girl who went to work in an English town.

In the English city there was a Welsh church, but it was a long journey from where the girl worked and stayed, yet Sunday by Sunday, she made the long journey to worship with her own people in her own tongue.

The people with whom the girl stayed and worked were kindly people, and they invited her to save herself the trouble of her long Sunday journey and to come with them to their own church. The girl courteously refused, saying that she would rather make the journey to share in worship in the tongue which she knew and loved so well.

Not at all critically, and in no spirit of fault-finding, but very gently the master of the house said to the girl: "You must remember that Jesus wasn't a Welshman."

The girl answered: "I know that, sir, but it is in Welsh that he speaks to me."

On the day of Pentecost the thing that amazed the listening people was that every man heard the message of the gospel in his own tongue (Acts 2:8).

Jesus speaks to every man in the tongue and the language that he can understand.

*Jesus speaks to men of every nation.*

Christianity is the one thing which can overpass all national barriers and boundaries. The Church is not a human institution which belongs to any one land or nation or continent or colour.

Within the Church all nations are gathered.

Christ comes to every man in that man's own tongue.

*Jesus speaks to men of every condition.*

The philosopher with his wisdom, and the simple man who has no book learning, the great man with the cares of great affairs upon him, and the humble man of whom no one has ever heard, the saint who walks in holiness and the sinner who is soiled with sin—Jesus Christ speaks to each in a language that he can understand.

*Jesus speaks to men of every experience.*

The man who has succeeded and the man who has failed, the man whose dreams have come true and the man whose dream has never been realised, the child, the youth, the man in the mid-time and the man far down the vale of years, the man for whom the sun shines in joy, and the man for whom life is wet with the tears of sorrow—Jesus Christ speaks to each in a language that he can understand.

The reason? The language that Jesus Christ speaks is the language of love.

There is an old and often-quoted five lines of verse.
It goes like this:

> The wise men ask: "What language did Christ speak?"
> They cavil, argue, search, and little prove.
> O sages, leave your Syriac and your Greek!
> Each heart contains the knowledge that you seek;
> Christ spoke the universal language—Love.

It is the wonder of Jesus Christ that he speaks to every man in his own tongue.

He is the spiritual linguist.

In any day and in any week and all through life you get the rough and the smooth, the sunshine and the shadow, the prizes and the spots.

Life is bound to be a mixture.

It is of the greatest importance to remember that life *is* a mixture and to accept it as it comes.

*In life there are things we can do and things we cannot do.*

There is nobody in the world who can do everything equally well. Each of us has his abilities and each of us has his inabilities.

One of the great secrets of life is to realise what we can do and to do it, and to see our limitations and to accept them.

One of the unhappiest spectacles in life is to see a man pining for a job or a post or a position that is not for him and for his abilities.

One of the happiest spectacles in life is to see a man who has realised both his capabilities and his limitations, and who has made the best of them.

*There are pleasures we can have and pleasures we cannot have.*

That is more than a matter of merely being able to afford them. One of the strange features of life is that in every pleasure there is an element of danger.

It is so very easy for a pleasure to become an addiction, and for a habit to become a master, and even a tyrant.

It is a wise man who realises the pleasures which are not for him.

*There are things in life that we get and things that we do not get.*

In this world there are two kinds of people. There are the people who are constantly surprised that life has been so good to them—and they are by no means always the people who have the most. And there are the people who are always bitter and resentful because life has—as they see it—withheld so much from them.

There are a great many things which may not be for us, so it is well to begin to count the blessings which are for us.

The number of them will surprise us!

Life is always a mixture. Life is never of the one colour. "Life, like a dome of many coloured glass, Stains the white radiance of eternity," as the poet had it. Or to use a much more homely simile, life is like a patchwork quilt.

Yet the strange thing is that the colours in a stained-glass window and the colours in a patchwork quilt for all their diversity can make a harmony. Life can be like that for those who have learned to accept life and to make the best of it as it is.

Life has its prizes and life has its blots. It has the things we can do and the things we cannot do, the pleasures we can have and the pleasures we can not have, the things we get and the things we do not get.

But for those who love God it can still be harmony, for God always works things together for good to them that love him (Rom. 8:28).

DREAMS November 14

The fable of Perette and her milkpail is one of the oldest fables in the world. You will find it in La Fontaine, in Dodsley, in Rabelais, and even in *The Arabian Nights*.

Perette was a girl who worked on a farm, and one day the farmer's wife gave her a whole pailful of milk for herself. So Perette put the pail of milk on her head, for that is where they carried things in those days, and she set off to the market to sell it; and as Perette went she was dreaming her dreams.

Perette's dreams went something like this.

"I'll sell this pail of milk, and with the money I get for it I'll buy some eggs, and I'll soon have some chicks, and I'll keep them and I'll fatten them, and when they are grown into hens, I'll sell them. And with the money I get for the hens, I'll buy a little pig, and I'll keep him and I'll fatten him and I'll sell him."

And then she began to smile with anticipation. "And with the money I get for the pig, I'll buy a real silk dress; and I'll put on my dress, and I'll go to the dance, and Robin will be there, and when he sees me all dressed in silk, he'll ask me to marry, but I'll show him how particular I am; I'll toss my head and—"

And there and then, in her dream, she tossed her head, as she would do at Robin, and when she tossed her head, off fell the pail, and the milk all spilled, and all Perette's dreams were gone.

The castle in the air had come tumbling down.

THE INTERPRETER                                            November 15

Like all fables, the story of Perette has its lessons for life.

*We cannot do without our dreams.*

It was the tragedy of the days of Eli that there was no open vision in the land (1 Sam. 3:1). As the writer of the Proverbs had it: "Where there is no vision, the people will perish" (Prov. 29:18)—which may be a wrong translation, but which none the less, even if it be by accident, contains a great truth.

All the men who have done great things have had their dreams, dreams of the distant places, dreams of a new world, dreams of the defeat of pain, dreams of harnessing new power.

Always behind the action there lie the dreams.

*But the dream needs an interpreter.*

The complaint of Pharaoh's butler and baker, when they were in prison, was: "We have dreamed a dream, and there is no interpreter of it" (Gen. 40:8).

The interpretation of the dream can make all the difference. A man's dream may drive him to selfish ambition or may move him to selfless ambition or may move him to selfless service—it all depends how he interprets it.

The greatness of the dream may drive a man to paralysed despair or to heroic action—it all depends how he interprets it.

One of the great things about Jesus Christ is that he is the interpreter of men's dreams.

In him men find again and again the satisfaction of their highest longings, the fulfilment of their deepest desires, the meaning of their dream.

THE TEST                                                   November 16

The dream will not realise itself; the dream remains an unsubstantial picture in the mind, until action is brought to it.

*When a man has had the dream, when he has found the interpretation of it, the final thing that the dream needs is action.*

It is there the test comes. The dream may come in a flash, but the turning of the dream into reality may take more than half a lifetime.

The road to the fulfilment of the dream will certainly be through sweat and toil.

The greater the dream, the longer and the harder the road to it.

Nothing can happen without the dream. The dream can take the wrong way unless the right interpreter can be found. The realisation of the dream may take a long, long time; and it is pleasanter to sit dreaming than it is to set to working!

If a man does nothing but sit dreaming, then in the end he will wake up with nothing—not even the dream.

But if he spends the toil and the perseverance and the sacrifice, he will be the happiest of men, for he will be the man whose dream came true.

WHAT IS THE POINT?                                    November 17

*What is the point* of so much of our business and of our hurry and our worry and our effort and our anxiety?

We strive so hard to get a little more money, to get a little farther up the ladder—but in the end, what's the point of it all? What good is it *really* going to do us?

We worry about this and that and the next thing—and in the end, what's the point about it all? Even if the things we worry about do happen, the heavens won't collapse. As a friend of mine often says, "it will be all the same a hundred years from now".

We would do well just to stand still sometimes and ask the question: "What *is* the point of what I'm doing?"

I do sometimes wonder what the point is of many of the arguments that go on in committees and all kinds of Church bodies. We get so hot and bothered about a comma in a report. A trifle can be magnified into a matter of epoch-making principle.

We would save time and trouble *and* wear and tear, if, before we started an argument, we would say: "*What's the point* of it anyhow?"

AGAIN, WHAT'S THE POINT?                              November 18

I hope that I won't be misunderstood, if I say that there is a great deal of scholarship of which one is sorely tempted to ask: "*What's the point* of it anyhow?"

There are many books which have undoubtedly taken years of research, and which, regarded as pure scholarship, are monuments of erudition, but what's the point of them?

Epictetus used to say: "Vain is the discourse of philosophy by which no human heart is healed."

It is an interesting test.

If it were applied, quite a number of erudite works would emerge as vanity.

But there is a bigger question than any of these—*What's the point* of life?

The point of life is to know Jesus Christ, and through him to be ready, fearlessly, to meet the call of God when that call comes.

If we saw life that way, then all other things would take their proper place.

Once Elijah ran away when things were difficult. Let no one blame him! But out in the desert there came God's voice to him: "What doest thou here, Elijah?" (I Kgs. 19:9).

It might be no bad thing if every now and again we stopped and said: "What am I doing here?"

*What's the point* of it all?

It might enable us to see a little better what things are important and what things, ultimately, really do not matter.

SILENCE IS GOLDEN                                                 November 19

There is nothing worse than talking at the wrong time. There is nothing so valuable as knowing when to keep quiet.

It was said as a tribute to a great linguist, not that he could speak seven different languages, but that he could be silent in seven different languages.

There are times when we ought to keep silent.
*We ought to keep silent when we are angry.*

If we speak when we are in the grip of anger, we will say things which will hurt others and hurt ourselves, when we remember them.

Many and many a friendship has been wrecked because some one spoke too much, and many and many a friendship has been saved, because someone knew how to hold his tongue in the moment of anger.

*We ought to keep silent when we want to criticise.*

Most criticisms are better never uttered. No one has the right to criticise at all, unless he is prepared himself to try to do better what he criticises.

It is a good rule never to be slow with praise and never to be quick with criticism.

*We ought to keep silent when we are criticised.*

When we are criticised, it is a natural instinct to spring to our own defence; and that is the very kind of thing that is so apt to lead to quarrels and to breaches which are hard to heal. Pills and criticism are sometimes hard to swallow, but sometimes both of them can do us good.

Anaximenes, the old Cynic philosopher, used to say that there are only two people who can tell us the truth—an enemy who hates us bitterly and a friend who loves us dearly.

The truth can hurt.

It is sometimes better to suffer in silence.

*There is certain company in which we ought to keep silent.*

Boswell tells how once Dr. Johnson was enjoying himself with freedom of jest and talk in a company of friends. He saw a foolish man approaching.

"Let us be silent," said Johnson. "A fool is coming."

There are some people in whose presence it is dangerous to talk. They will repeat our confidences. They will twist our words. They will broadcast in public that which was said in private. In the presence of such people—and it is not long before we are able to identify them—a wise silence is better than words.

*There is need for silence, if ever we are to hear the voice of God.*

It is quite possible that we hear the voice of God so seldom because we listen for it so seldom!

Sometimes we may feel that God does not speak to us. But "Do you ever give him the chance to speak to you?"

The Psalmist heard God say: "Be still and know that I am God" (Ps. 46:10).

There is a little book of prayers entitled *God's Minute*. A minute of listening in the morning and in the evening, at the day's beginning and at the day's ending, would make a world of difference to our over-talkative life.

There are times when words are needed, and when not to speak is to fail both men and God, but on the whole it is true to say that speech does far more harm than silence.

It is harder to learn not to speak than it is to learn to speak.

WHOM TO KNOW                                                November 21

It is knowing people that matters. Compared with knowing people, knowing things is not of any very great importance.

*It is from knowing people that certainty comes.*

It would be quite possible to have an argument with an atheist, or an agnostic, or a communist about Christ and about Christianity, and to be quite unable to meet and to counter the arguments he advanced against Christianity. But, if we know someone who is really and truly a Christian, a person in whom Christ lives again, then we can say: "I know that I can't meet your arguments. But I know so-and-so, and so-and-so is the living and indestructible argument that the Christian faith is a fact."

A human being is always the best argument for the Christian religion.

*It is from knowing people that comfort comes.*

When we are up against it, when sorrow comes, when life is bewildering and the heart is sore, it is possible to read books about life and heaven and immortality. It is possible to read books of comfort. It is even possible to read the Bible, and to get no comfort at all. At such a time it is possible for a dear friend to come, and, with a few words, to bring the comfort for which our heart is craving.

People can do what print can never do.

God sends his comfort through people much more than through any written word.

*It is from knowing people that courage comes.*
    It is always easier to walk some frightening road, to do some difficult thing, to meet some hard situation, if there is someone there to meet it with us.

    Loneliness is the great begetter of fear. At such a time it is often possible to know all the promises of God and of Jesus Christ, and to believe them in a kind of way; but again and again they come alive in a person.
    It is through the company and the influence of somebody that we really lay hold upon them.

    It is God's way to work through people. Blessed are those who know the people who can bring us certainty and comfort and courage.
    It is never enough to know the creeds; it is not even enough to know the print of the Bible. It is only enough to know him whom the creed seeks to define, and him of whom the Bible tells. Jesus himself said it: "This is life eternal, that they might know Thee the only true God, and Jesus Christ whom Thou hast sent" (John 17:3).
    Christianity never consists in knowing what; it always consists in knowing whom.

    It is good to know the creeds and the doctrines and the written book, but it is better yet to know the One of whom they tell, and to whom they all point.

THE LENGTH OF LIFE       November 23

    There are many living things in this world whose life-span is far beyond the life-span of a man. Man is by no means like the living creature with the longest life on earth.
    So length of life is not the most important thing about life.

    Shelley, Keats, Rupert Brooke, Schubert, Mozart (as we have noted earlier) all died long, long before they had attained even middle age.
    Jesus himself died at thirty-three.

*The value of a life lies in the intensity of its living.*
    It is better to live for a shorter time with a kind of passionate intensity, stretching out eager hands to grasp life, enjoying life to the uttermost, living

life to the full, than it is to live for a much longer time with care and prudence and careful calculation never to become excited and never to do too much.

Sir Walter Scott used the famous lines as a chapter heading in *Old Mortality*:

> Sound, sound the clarion, fill the fife;
> Throughout the sensual world proclaim,
> One crowded hour of glorious life
> Is worth an age without a name.

The people we remember with grateful hearts are the people who had the joy of living, even if their time was short.

CALLED TO HIGHER SERVICE                                          November 24

*The value of a life lies in the way in which it is spent, not in the way in which it is hoarded.*

The people whom the world remembers with gratitude are the people who poured out life with a prodigal hand, not the careful souls who jealously hoarded it, lest they should make too much of an effort.

Philip James Bailey's epic "Festus", is long since forgotten except for its four famous lines:

> We live in deeds, not years; in thoughts, not breaths;
> In feelings, not in figures on a dial.
> We should count time by heart-throbs. He most lives
> Who thinks most, feels the noblest, acts the best.

The question about life is not how we have managed to save it, but how we have managed to spend it.

Life is the one possession in which reckless extravagance is better than cautious economy.

*In assessing the value of any life, it must always be added to the reckoning that no life stops here.*

Rita Snowden tells of two workmen who were discussing the death of Dick Sheppard, that man of God who was also the friend of the people, and who died—from the human point of view—too soon.

"Poor Dick Sheppard's dead," said the one.

"None of your poor Dick Sheppard," said the other, "God will be right glad to have him."

It is not just a religious conventional platitude to say of someone that he has been "called to a higher service". Somewhere there will be things to do for those whose intensity wore them out, and for those who spent life so lavishly that they had none of it left for themselves.

"Whosoever shall seek to save his life shall lose it; and whosoever shall lose his life shall preserve it" (Luke 17:33)—that is the word of him who is the Lord of all good life.

FLESH ON THE BONES                                    November 25

Edwin Muir, in his autobiography, tells how one of his continental friends, Mitrinović by name, once said to him of Bertrand Russell: "When he die, the angels they find nothing to eat on his bones."

In some people there is a strange kind of fleshlessness, a kind of inhumanity, a kind of cool detachment from the sorrows and the problems and the passions of mankind.

I have a friend called James Thomas Williams.* I have never met him in the flesh, but sometimes he writes to me. He sends me poems he has written, and there are times when his lines are very near the heart of things.

He sent me a poem entitled "The Skeleton", which, with his permission, I pass on:

> With prayer and supplication
>     and so much preparation,
> they were so still,
>     with so much to be,
> through constant consecration.
> Without adequate preparation,
>     one's life is all peroration,
> there's not much bones
>     in a life without prayer—
> only continual evaporation!

There are things in life whose very design it is to keep us human, and to preserve us from, or to make us unlearn, this detached inhumanity.

*James Thomas Williams is in fact the editor of *Kingsway*, the magazine of the West London Methodist Mission of which Lord Soper is Superintendent.—Ed.

*Sorrow is designed to make us human.*

Edwin Muir quotes a wonderful line of poetry:

A deep despair hath humanized my soul.

The Arabs have a proverb: "All sunshine makes a desert."
The land needs the rain and life needs its tears.

*Love is designed to make us human.*
W. B. Yeats says of an Irish writer called Todhunter: "If he had liked anything strongly, he might have been a famous man."

Edwin Muir tells of a period when he lost his religious faith. One of the devastating effects of that loss was that he saw men and women as animals. He would look at them on the street, in a bus or a subway or a tramcar, and as he looked he saw them as animals. The experience was so terrible that he could not endure to live in this animal world. Then his faith came back, and he writes: "I can see men and women as really human only when I see them as immortal souls."

We never really see people as they are, and very certainly we can never help them at all, unless we see them with the eyes of the love of God. One of the great tests of love is that a real and a true love should make us suddenly discover that we love, not only one person, but all men and women everywhere.

*The whole experience of life is designed to make us human.*
That is why the "pure" scholar, the man who lives for ever surrounded by books in a library, can never be really human.
It is only when we have lived amongst men, when we have shared their sorrows, met their temptation, been involved in their sins that we become human.

J. S. Whale talks of a modern habit. He says that we are so apt to scurry round taking photographs of the burning bush from suitable angles instead of taking our shoes from off our feet, because the place whereon we stand is holy ground.
We are apt to sit in an armchair, pipe in mouth, feet on the mantelpiece

and talk about theories of the atonement, instead of bowing down before the wounds of Christ.

Long ago Ezekiel saw the valley of dry bones, and heard the voice of God saying to him: "Son of man, can these bones live?" (Ezek. 37:3). They did live because the breath and the Spirit of God moved upon them.

Love, sorrow, the human sense of human failure and of human sin are meant to humanise us.

We only become really human when the divine heart of Jesus Christ becomes the heart with which we meet all the experiences and all the people of this life.

NEVER EXPENDABLE                                            November 28

My eye caught the headlines at the top of a column. They read: "Only 80 casualties; only 20 dead." And suddenly I caught my breath—"Only 20 dead."

To the high command twenty dead were as nothing, a very satisfactory figure. But somewhere in Britain there were twenty broken hearts and maybe more.

In military strategy there is a very terrible word. Sometimes when an attack is launched, or when a situation has to be desperately defended, so many men are said to be "expendable". That is to say, the high command have worked it out that they can afford to lose men up to that number.

The dreadful thing in any war is that it is always assumed that the death of a certain number of men does not matter.

I remember something I read in that wonderful volume *A Doctor's Casebook in the Light of the Bible*, by Paul Tournier.

Dr. Tournier writes: "There was one patient of mine, the youngest daughter in a large family, which the father found it difficult to support. One day she heard him mutter despairingly, referring to her: 'We could well have done without that one!' You can guess the effect of such a remark," says Dr. Tournier, "not wanted by her parents, not wanted in life."

If the New Testament teaches one truth with the greatest definiteness, it is that in God's sight no human being is expendable.

We *all* matter.

Jesus drove home in his preaching the value of every one.

There was the woman who had the ten silver coins and who lost one. Does one in ten matter so very much? It mattered to her. And she lit a candle and swept and searched until she found it, and, when she found it, she was so happy that she called in her neighbours to share her joy (Luke 15:8–10).

There was the shepherd who had a hundred sheep and one went lost. What was one in a hundred? Did one foolish sheep more or less matter so much? It mattered to him. And the man risked his life on the mountain-side and amidst the crags and gullies until he found the sheep that was lost (Luke 15:3–7).

Sometimes we may be apt to look at some peculiarly unpleasant person, or sometimes on the streets we may catch a glimpse of some wretched, dirty, degraded creature; and there goes through us a kind of shudder of disgust; and we wonder how anyone could care for a creature like that.
God does.

Sometimes we get a feeling of our own uselessness, our own ineffectiveness, and sometimes when we are feeling misused and disgruntled, we wonder if we matter very much to anyone at all.
We do—to God.

The dignity of human life comes from nothing else than the fact that each individual man is dear to God.
No Christian can ever despise a fellow-man, for that man, no matter what he is like, is dear to God.
No Christian can ever ultimately despise himself, for, in his black moments, he must ever remind himself that he is a child whom God cannot do without, and that, even if he matters to no one else, he matters to God.

THE DEATH OF FEAR                                         November 30

From beginning to the end of Scripture the word is the same.

"You will not fear," says the Psalmist, "the terror of the night, nor the arrow that flies by day" (Ps. 91:5).

Across the waters Jesus comes to his disciples with the words: "It is I; do not be afraid" (John 6:20).

In the heavenly places the words of the Risen Christ to the John of the Revelation are still the same: "Fear not, I am the first and the last, and the living one" (Rev. 1:17).

In truth Christianity means the death of fear.

# *December*

T. H. Huxley wrote to Herbert Spencer, the philosopher: "You and I, my dear friend, have had our innings, and carry our bats out while our side is winning. One could not reasonably ask for more."

He wrote to John Skelton: "I got my son-in-law to build me a cottage here (at Eastbourne), where my wife and I may go downhill quietly together."

He wrote to a man called Donnelly: "I feel myself distinctly aged—tired out body and soul . . . I feel as if another year of it would be the death of me. Next May I shall be sixty."

By the time he was sixty, Huxley felt an old man and that life was no longer tolerable.

I have been re-reading R. C. Robertson-Glasgow's autobiography *46 Not Out*. He writes of his grandfather, when that indomitable character was seventy:

"His activity was inexhaustible, his interest universal. Into each month of life he crammed a year. He laughed at time and distance. To preach in his own Church, teach in the Sunday school, carve the joint, try out a new pony, visit the cook's declining father, walk six miles each way to preach in another Church, return to calculate his accounts and dictate his diary—this was just an average Sunday to him."

Even at seventy he was setting out to emigrate to Canada to see what it was like!

But even that record pales into insignificance with John Wesley's statement on his eighty-sixth birthday that by that time he found it difficult to preach more than twice a day!

Too old at—?

263

Age is a very undefinable thing. It certainly has very little to do with the date which happens to be entered on your birth certificate.

Some people are never really young, like the schoolboy on whose annual report his headmaster entered the comment: "Would make an excellent father."

Other people are never really old, for there are people of more than mature years of whom we can say that they have never really grown up.

The ancients had their proverb: "Whom the gods love, die young." This did not mean that those whom the gods love are taken from this life in their youth and their early years. It means that, if the gods love a man, no matter what age he is, and even if he goes well over the three score years and ten, he still has the gift of essential youth.

Where does this essential youth come from?

There has been a good deal of research lately into the problem of retirement. In an ageing population, and with social security pensions, there are many more people who now retire from work, because they have to, while they have still a fair time to live. In such retirement, the researches show, there is a good deal of unhappiness, and most of it has its source in boredom.

The thing which keeps a man young and the thing which keeps him really alive is *interest*. If a man wishes to stay young, the more things he is interested in the better, especially if these things are outside his own job.

The elixir of eternal youth is *wonder*. So long as a man can find new things at which to wonder, he need never grow old. In this world of God's, and in the world of human relationships, he need never lack for that.

Learn to be interested and stay young!

STAY AS YOU ARE!                                        December 3

In one of his addresses Pope John XXIII said a very wise thing. He said: "To be guided by Christian principles does not mean to be reconciled with stagnation in obsolete positions; nor does it mean giving up all efforts at progress."

This is well said. There is an approach to Christianity where the instinct is to look back and to keep things as they are.

*There can be stagnation in the statement of belief.*

It is not that the truth changes; it is that the expression of it in every age must change. Truth has to be expressed in the categories of the age to which it is addressed.

Take the idea of "substance"; the old creeds say that Jesus is of the same "substance" as God.

One feature of Greek thought was that it was in the literal sense materialist. It had no real conception of "spirit" other than that "spirit" was infinitely fine matter. And when it said that Jesus was of the same "substance" as God, it literally meant that Jesus was made of the same stuff as God.

We can understand what they were getting at; but we can no longer use this way of speaking!

Every age has to find its own way of expressing the relationship of Jesus to God, and, if that new way of expression is different from the old way, no one should immediately set up a shout of heresy.

To do so is to vote for stagnation.

STAGNATION                                              December 4

*There can be stagnation in language.*

For some quite unintelligible reason, religious language petrified in 1611. When the New Testament was first written, it was absolutely colloquial and contemporary. It was written in the everyday language of everyday people. And it must go back into that language. Otherwise, however beautiful it is, it has stagnated into a language which no one now speaks.

*There can be stagnation in worship.*

Worship for so many has got to be in the language of the Authorised Version of the Bible. But surely a twentieth-century man speaks to God in twentieth-century English. The biggest barrier to prayer is the stagnation which insists on a special prayer language which is quite out of date.

But in worship there is also stagnation in the order of service. For the person within the Church, and brought up within the Church, no doubt the accepted and traditional orders of service are hallowed and dear. But when a man comes in from outside the Church, we cannot afford to go through the long preparation of prayer and praise and reading, or we lose him.

We must talk to him almost at once.

After all, the Church must be concurred for the man outside.

There are fewer and fewer inside!

*There can be stagnation in method.*

Religious institutions change their methods too late. Even today, for instance, we think of evangelism in terms of Moody and Sankey.

One good custom can corrupt the world, as Tennyson said.

One of the most significant stories in the Old Testament is the story of Nehushtan, the brazen serpent. It was originally made by Moses to bring healing to the people bitten by serpents, and it was made at the command of God (Num. 21:4-9). But in later times the people came to worship it as an idol and in the end Hezekiah had to destroy it for ever (2 Kgs. 18:4).

That which had originally been given by God ended up as a menace because people made it an idol. That has been happening in the Church ever since.

The sad thing about the Church is that it is for ever fighting these rearguard actions. It is seldom out in front. It is always resisting change, seldom initiating it, and rarely welcoming it. It so often confounds stagnation with loyalty to principle.

"Change and decay in all around I see", says the hymn, but there is a real sense in which it is not "Change *and* decay". It is "Change *or* decay".

For stagnation leads to death.

I have come across two very interesting and significant incidents in two recent biographies of very great Christians.

The first is from Ernest W. Bacon's biography of Spurgeon.

One of Spurgeon's great enterprises was the founding of a college in which students might be trained for the ministry.

One of the earliest students, the Rev. D. J. Hiley, tells of an encounter with Spurgeon when he was a student in that college. He and Spurgeon met one day in the corridor.

"Is that your best coat?" Spurgeon asked.

"Yes, sir," Hiley answered.

Spurgeon was silent for a moment and then he said: "I wonder if you would render me a little service."

Hiley said that he would be delighted to render Spurgeon any service.

The service which Spurgeon required was the delivery of a note at a certain tailor's shop.

Hiley goes on: "I was to wait for an answer. For reply—the tailor measured me for a new suit of clothes and an overcoat, and sent me away with a hat-box!"

Spurgeon had seen that the impecunious student needed a coat and a suit, and did something about it.

The other incident is from Richard Collier's biography of William Booth, although the story itself is of Bramwell Booth, when Bramwell had succeeded his father as General of the Army.

Collier writes:

"The Army ... had become his life ... His officers' welfare was always paramount; once, lynx-eyed as always, he noticed that several officers taking tea with him bit on only one side of their jaws. Promptly, at his own expense, he sent them to his dentist."

Bramwell Booth saw that his officers needed dental treatment and saw that they got it.

Here we see the same kind of attitude to others in Spurgeon and in Bramwell Booth, who both saw the need.

THE UNIVERSAL EXPERT                                        December 7

I saw an advertisement recently which first of all amused me and then made me think. The advertisement was that of a firm of painters and decorators, and it said: "Specialists in all kinds of painting and decorating."

At first sight it seems ridiculous to claim to be an expert in everything. To claim to be an expert in everything seems to be a contradiction in terms.

It has been said that a specialist is a man who knows more and more about less and less. If we go to a medical specialist, we go to a man who is an expert on some particular part of the body, like the heart or the lungs, or the ear, the throat at the most.

In stamp-collecting a specialist is a man who has made a detailed study of the stamps of one particular country, or even of the stamps of one particular issue of one country.

We do not expect a musician to be a specialist on all instruments; we do not expect a man to be an expert on the piano and the trumpet, or on the violin and on the trombone.

In sport we do not expect a cricketer to be a specialist in batting, bowling and wicket-keeping; he is a specialist in one branch of the game. We do not expect an expert goal-keeper to be an equally expert centre-forward.

Yes, indeed, the idea of a universal specialist sounds queer indeed. A man can be jack-of-all-trades and master of none.

But there is another side to this. We speak of the all-rounder, and a very useful person the all-rounder is. He can bat well enough, and he can take his turn with ball, and if need be he can take the pads and the gloves and keep wicket.

In the football team the all-rounder can play a good game anywhere. There have been exceptional people who represented their country at cricket, tennis and golf, all three.

Even in medicine we have the general practitioner who is at least expert enough to recognise most of the things that are wrong with us.

There is a case for the man who is a kind of specialist in everything.

JACK-OF-ALL-TRADES                                    December 8

This kind of universal specialism is the sort of thing that people expect from a minister or a parson.

He must be a good preacher and an able pastor.

He must know something about teaching young people.

He will be better to know something about music.

He must be a good administrator and it will help if he knows something about law and architecture.

He must be able to be master of ceremonies of a social occasion and chairman at an important meeting.

When you think of what people expect from the minister or the parson, you begin to think that the man must be an expert in all kinds of things!

But we can go further than that. The Christian has to be a kind of expert in all the conditions of life, a spiritual jack-of-all-trades.

He must be able to meet sorrow without despair.

He must be able to meet difficulty without defeat.

He must be able to meet success without pride.

In the storm or in the calm, in the sunshine or in the shadow, in sorrow or in joy, in success or in failure, in youth, in maturity and in age, he must be the expert who can cope with anything in life.

This is the very thing that Paul claims: "I have learned, in whatever state I am, to be content. I know both how to be abased and how to abound; in any and all circumstances I have learned the secret of facing plenty and hunger, abundance and want. I can do all things in him who strengthens me" (Phil. 4:11–13).

Yes, Jesus can make a man an expert and a specialist in every circumstance in life.

TRUST IN GOD AND . . . December 9

A friend of mine was telling me of a notice her son saw displayed in a garage. It ran like this: "In God we trust; all others pay cash."

At the back of that jesting notice there lies one great truth—the truth that God is the only completely trustworthy person in the universe.

The biblical writers have a great many things to say about whom not to trust.

*They warn against trust in riches.*

"Put no confidence in extortion; set no vain hopes on robbery; if riches increase, set not your heart on them" (Ps. 62:10). Tragic is the fate of the men "who trust in their wealth and boast of the abundance of their riches" (Ps. 49:6). The man who "would not make God his refuge, but trusted in the abundance of his riches, and sought refuge in his wealth", is doomed in the end to become the laughing-stock of wiser men (Ps. 52:7). "He who trusts in riches will wither," says the Sage, "but the righteous will flourish like a green leaf" (Prov. 11:28).

A man is a fool if he trusts in something so easily lost as money.

The biblical writers are impressed by the way in which human friendship can fail. It is the complaint of the Psalmist that "the bosom friend in whom we trusted", the friend who ate bread with him, has turned against him (Ps. 41:9). "Put no confidence in a neighbour," says Micah, "have no confidence in a friend" (Mic. 7:5).

It is a grim thought, but the Psalmist, like the realist he was, did not forget that the closest human relationship is fallible.

But you can trust in God . . .

HOW ACCIDENTS HAPPEN December 10

I have been driving a car of some sort since February 1933, and I have been thinking back across the years to see if I could discover out of my own experience, what the main causes of accidents are.

I think they are three. Two of these we shall think about today.

*There is irritation with the other driver.*

Someone wants to pass us and we do not want to be passed, so we take steps to hinder the other man every time he tries. We get behind a slow-moving vehicle and in the end we lose patience and take a risk. We try to pass and there is a smash. This, that and the next thing irritate us, and an irritated driver is a bad driver.

This is true of all life. There is nothing which obscures judgment like anger and irritation. Three times Psalm 37 (verses 1, 7, 8) gives us the advice: "Fret not yourself." "Fret not yourself," it says, "it tends only to evil."

We should all pray that we do not lose our tempers!

There is a second cause of accidents which every driver must have experienced, and that is a momentary wandering of attention. There can hardly be any driver who has not found himself within a hair's breadth of disaster because for a split second his attention wandered. But, of course, with the speed of the modern car, not even a split second of inattention is safe.

What is true of driving is just as true of life. It is so often true that it is the unguarded moment which brings life to shame or even to ruin.

One of the basic demands of the New Testament is: "Watch!" (Matt. 24:42).

Life can end in disaster for the man who is even momentarily off his guard.

SPOILING THE BEST                                December 11

Romans 14:16 has many different translations.

The *Authorised Version* has: "Let not your good be evil spoken of."

The *Revised Standard Version* has: "Do not let what is good to you be spoken of as evil."

Moffat has: "Your rights must not get a bad name."

The *New English Bible* has: "What for you is a good thing must not become an occasion for scandalous talk."

*J. B. Phillips* has: "You mustn't let something which is all right for you look like an evil practice to someone else."

This text comes from the passage in which Paul is pleading that the man who is strong in the faith must deal very gently and understandingly with the man who is weak in the faith and whose conscience is over-sensitive and over-scrupulous. I think the best translation of all would be: "You must not do the right thing in such a way that it gets you a bad reputation."

The idea here comes from the same circle of ideas as one which I never tire of stressing. The favourite New Testament word for "good" is the word *kalos*, and *kalos* is also the word for "beautiful".

Christian goodness is not only good; it is also attractive.

What Paul was saying was this: Don't do a thing which in itself is a good thing in such a way that it becomes ugly and unattractive.

Too often Christianity is rendered unattractive by the misuse of good things.

It is a miracle to turn water into wine.

It is a tragedy to turn wine into water.

ABSURDLY HAPPY                                            December 12

Christianity has a high moral code, but that must never be made a reason for making Christianity look as if it consisted entirely of "thou shalt not's". It must never issue in an attitude of unsympathetic disapproval.

There are still too many people whose Christianity is negative. And there are still too many Christians who exude an attitude of disapproval.

There are older Christians who in their attitude to young people seem perilously near to a policy of, "If they want it, don't let them have it."

Nothing could be higher than the moral code of the Christian, but it is quite wrong to express it in an endless series of prohibitions, and in an attitude of consistent disapproval.

Christianity takes life seriously, but that is not to say that it takes life with gloomy solemnity. The black clothes, long-faces conception of religion dies hard. It must never be forgotten that *joy* is one of the commonest New Testament words.

It was said of Robert Burns that he was "haunted and not helped by his religion".

That is still true of too many.

Russell Maltby once said that Jesus promised his people three things—that they would be in constant trouble, completely fearless, and absurdly happy.

A Christian should be enjoying life, and he should look as if he was!

IT'S GREAT TO KNOW THE GREAT!                             December 13

One day, motoring south from Glasgow to London, I stopped at Penrith in the Lake District of north England in order to get out and stretch my legs.

As I walked along the main street, my eye was caught by a little metal tablet on the side of a shop window. It was erected by the Penrith Urban District,

Council, and it said: "William and Ann Cookson, grandparents of William and Dorothy Wordsworth, lived here."

I had never heard of William and Ann Cookson before. I don't suppose that anyone would ever have heard of them or remembered them now if they had not been the grandparents of William Wordsworth, one of the princes of English poetry.

The greatness and the memorableness of William and Ann Cookson lay not in themselves. It lay in their contact with William Wordsworth.

Sometimes a quite simple and ordinary person becomes great, not because he is great himself, but because of some contact with greatness.

Muirhead Bone tells of an old man in the Inns of Court in London. He was long past his work and a little in his dotage. But people still let him come about the place. If anyone spoke to him, before the conversation was five minutes old, he would say to them: "*I* was an office boy to Charles Dickens."

The one thing he remembered of which he was proud was his contact with greatness.

I think it is Leslie Church, that very great preacher, who tells that he was preaching somewhere. After the service a very ordinary little man came round to see him, a little insignificant creature. "Sir," said the little man, "you mentioned Nelson in your sermon. My grandfather held him in his arms as he died on board the *Victory*."

That little man seemed to grow in stature as he remembered his one, remote contact with greatness!

That is what the Christian is like.

Peter and Andrew and James and John were fishermen from the Sea of Galilee. Who would ever have heard of them but for their contact with the greatness of Jesus Christ?

Matthew and Zacchaeus were traitors and quislings. Who would have ever known their names but for their contact with the splendour of Jesus Christ?

We have no greatness of our own. We are ordinary, sinful people. Our only greatness is that somehow, in the infinite love of God, we have had our contact with Christ.

Let us too remember our contact with greatness.

Let us too live as men who have touched the hand of their King.

Remember an astonishing saying of Jesus in the Fourth Gospel. He speaks of the works that he did himself, and then he speaks of the man who in the future will believe in him, and he says: "*Greater* works than these will he do!" (John 14:12).

It's great to know the great!

When I read newspapers, I find myself reacting in the same way over and over again.

I see a headline which tells of some disaster—a train or aeroplane crash, a death, a murder, a shipwreck. If the event took place in this country, I read on with interest and with feeling. But if the event took place in Europe, or Africa or America, I find myself not reading beyond the first line; I move on to something else without even completing the reading of the paragraph. If the disaster is near at hand, it grips me. If far away, it leaves me cold.

I am far from being pleased about this. I set it down as a regrettable fact— but a fact which has started me thinking.

There are certain things to be said for our attitude to the near and the far away.

*It is true that charity should begin at home, but there is something very far wrong when charity ends at home.*

To be interested in nothing but our own home and our own parish and our own congregation is all wrong.

There are two reasons why it is wrong.

First, broken hearts and smashed lives are broken hearts and smashed lives wherever they happen. No broken heart or smashed life should ever be unimportant to anyone who is trying to be a Christian. Trouble should matter to me, whoever is the victim.

Second, there never was a time when the world was more one than it is today. As things are now, there is no far away. Mankind is bound up in the bundle of life as he never was before. We are now living in one world, and distress, wherever it is, should matter to me.

The congregation which never looks beyond its own activities and its own needs is not a Christian congregation.

But there is another side to the near and the far-away.

We are living in a world where the far-away has frequently made people forget the near at hand. There are people who are impassioned about the sufferings in Vietnam—as they ought to be—but who are completely indifferent to the slum conditions in which many people have to live in in any great city today.

There are people who are passionate about the rights of coloured people in Rhodesia who do nothing to help the colour problem in our own country.

To come nearer home, there are people who are on half a dozen and more worthy committees who fail in their duty to their own homes. There are men and women so involved in Church work that they neglect their own families every day.

It is far more important for a mother to put young children to bed herself than it is for her to serve on any number of committees.

It is far more important for a father to be the friend of his own children than the leader of youth work amongst other people's children.

Let this not be misunderstood.

These outside activities are of importance.

Someone has to do them.

But they must never become a form of escapism from the duties which lie within the home.

The Christian has a double duty.

He must be a citizen of the world, for all men everywhere are his brothers in Jesus Christ.

But he must also be supremely interested in that little piece of the world in which life has set him to live and to work.

In other words, we have to hold the balance between the far-away and the near at hand.

Jesus did this.

For thirty years he answered the claims of home before he went out to the world; and on his Cross, when he was dying for all mankind, he was not forgetful of his mother (John 19:26, 27).

SOMEONE LIKES YOU!                                    December 16

There is nothing which *someone* doesn't like. Even if we ourselves think something entirely unpleasant, there will be someone who likes it.

I remember an astonishing passage in Sextus Empiricus' work on the Sceptic philosophers. The Sceptics said that you can never be sure of anything, because quite possibly the opposite can be equally true. He went on to say that the words "good" and "pleasant" can have no standard meaning, because they mean quite different things to different people.

He cites examples: "An old wife of Attica, so they say, swallowed thirty

274

drams of hemlock and took no harm, and Lysis took four drams of poppy juice and was none the worse for it. Demophon, Alexander's butler, used to shiver when he was in the sun or in a hot bath, but felt warm in the shade. Athenagoras the Argive took no hurt from the stings of scorpions or poisonous spiders."

Rufinus of Chalcis drank hellebore like someone drinking a cup of lemonade.

Andron the Argive was never thirsty, not even when crossing a desert, and never drank water.

Tiberius Caesar could see in the dark.

So Sextus Empiricus gives us his extraordinary list of people who like unpleasant and even poisonous things.

I have myself known people who love undiluted lemon juice in all its bitterness, and who actually enjoy drinking castor oil!

All this is interesting, but what is more important is that it is the same with people.

*There is no one whom someone does not love.*

## "THE KING LOVES ME"                                    December 17

Love does not see the faults and the failings and the uglinesses which spring to the eyes of other people. That is one of the meanings of the Greek saying that "love is blind".

It is one of the loveliest and tenderest things in the human situation that often a parent will love most of all a child who is in some way handicapped.

When Bunyan was under threat of death, the one thing that haunted him most of all was the thought of his little blind daughter.

During the First World War the King and Queen (King George V and Queen Mary) at least on one Christmas sent Christmas cards to all the soldiers in the army.

There was a soldier who had no friends and no relations; he was alone in the world. He had received nothing at Christmas. Then the royal Christmas card came. "Even if no one else remembers me," he said, "my king and queen do."

The Psalmist had it: "For my father and mother have forsaken me, but the Lord will take me up" (Ps. 27:10).

Everyone has someone to love them, even if the closest ties on earth are broken, and that someone is God.

In *Race: A Christian Symposium*, edited by Clifford S. Hill and David Mathews, there is one section which is specially significant for the Church. It is a brief section in which an Indian immigrant, a West Indian Social Worker, and an African student in turn take a brief look at Britain.

I want to quote just one sentence from what each of them wrote.

The Indian immigrant writes: "Christianity (in Britain) as a way of life seems practically non-existent, at least not the full-blooded commitment that distinguishes good Christians in India."

The West Indian social worker writes of British Church leaders: "Too often the Church reflects rather than formulates opinion."

The African student writes: "The biggest shock we receive is in the field of Christianity." He writes of British landladies: "'Knock and the door shall be slammed in your face' is their policy with African students."

This is indeed an indictment.

It is said that in British Christianity there is no commitment. T. S. Eliot wrote:

> Our age is an age of moderate virtue
> And of moderate vice
> When men will not lay down the Cross
> Because they will never assume it.

A man cannot lay down a cross which he will not even take up.

When it was discovered from his diary that Dag Hammarskjold, the once secretary-general of the United Nations Organisation, had been in many ways a Christian mystic, a Swedish writer wrote: "In a half de-Christianised country the most elementary features of Christian discipleship are unknown, or regarded as presumptuousness or blasphemy."

Is it true that we are approaching a day when there will be none left to say: "Jesus Christ is Lord"?


LOOK HARD!                                                December 19

It is always easier to go with the crowd, to swim with the tide, to run before the wind. This must be the conclusion from these quotations from the Symposium on Race, yesterday.

It is always dangerous and lonely to stand alone for some great truth or principle which men do not wish to hear.

The first way may be the way to an easy popularity, and the second way may be the way to an agonising martyrdom; but it will be a bad day for the world when there is no one left to defy the world and to stand alone with God.

George Bernard Shaw makes Joan of Arc say: "It is better to be alone with God. In his strength I will dare and dare until I die." Is there in the Church no one left to say: "We cannot but speak of what we have seen and heard"? (Acts 4:20).

The third charge in the quotation is that, in this country too, apartheid may well be practised.

It is by no means impossible to find the apartheid of snobbery and the apartheid of racial prejudice.

It is perfectly true that the coloured person will have difficulty in finding lodgings or a house, or just promotion in his job. Have we forgotten that in Christ Jesus we are all sons of God, and that in him there is neither Jew nor Greek, slave nor free, male or female? (Gal. 3:26–8).

Others have come into this country and have looked at us and have not liked what they saw.

Perhaps we should take a long, hard, honest look at ourselves sometimes.


A MAN WITH A WELCOME                                    December 20

It must have been very hard for Ananias to forget the savagery with which Saul had attacked the Church in Jerusalem. It must have been very hard for him, knowing as he did why Saul had come to Damascus, to believe that Saul really was a changed man.

It must have been very hard to stifle the suspicion which must have lurked in his mind. And yet the first two words that Ananias spoke to Saul are amongst the most astonishing words in the New Testament. The words were: "Brother Saul" (Acts 9:17; 22:13).

No breath of suspicion, no moment of hesitation, no hint of recrimination, simply the open heart, and the outstretched hand, the man with the welcome.

Just because of this, we know a great deal about Ananias.

Let's mention one point today.

Ananias was clearly a man who believed in conversion.

Many a person would have bluntly stated that they believed it to be impossible that Saul the persecutor should ever become Paul the chosen vessel. Not so Ananias.

The supreme sin of the pastor or the missionary or the preacher is to think anyone is hopeless.

Ananias is the example of a man who insisted on believing that there are no limits to the grace of God.

He was right.

## THE MEANS TO GRACE                                    December 21

Here are two more points about Ananias.

Ananias was a man who was prepared to forget and to forgive the past. He might well have said: "Even if this Saul is converted, we want nothing to do with him in Damascus. He'll have to work his passage before we believe that the man who came to murder us has changed like this."

Whatever Paul's past was like, Ananias was prepared to believe that there was a grace which made all things new.

Because Ananias was as he was, he had the joy of introducing to the Church a man who was to prove far greater than himself.

It has often happened that some simple and unlettered person has been the means whereby someone was brought into the Church who was due to do great things for the Church.

No man can do a greater thing than to bring someone else to Jesus Christ.

When he does that, he never knows the possibilities he has opened up.

Ananias certainly did more than he understood when he helped to give us Paul.

## THE MIDDLEMAN                                    December 22

Tychicus appears four times in the Letter of Paul (Eph. 6:21; Col. 4:7; 2 Tim. 4:12; Titus 3:12), and on every one of these occasions Paul is sending him somewhere with a letter or with a message.

Quite clearly, Tychicus was one of Paul's most trusted go-betweens. We never find Tychicus speaking or writing in his own name; he is always speaking and writing in the name of Paul.

He is Paul's middleman.

The world needs its go-betweens and its middlemen.

*The world needs the middleman between person and person.*

In the New Testament one of the basic meanings of the word "peace" is right relations between person and person. To produce a right relationship between two people, especially if they were estranged, was according to the rabbis one of the greatest things that a man could do.

It was something which brought him joy in this world and honour in the life to come.

Jesus said: Blessed are the peacemakers (Matt. 5:9).

Blessed indeed are the middlemen, who bring people together.

There are people who go about doing things, saying things, repeating things which cause divisions between people. They are doing the devil's work. There are people whose whole presence and influence is towards uniting others, and bringing others together. They are doing Jesus's work, and earning his blessing.

Blessed are the middlemen.

*The world needs the middleman between the scholar and the ordinary people.*

This is in fact the function of the preacher.

The world needs a middleman between God and man. We need someone to bridge the gulf of estrangement and fear which stretches between God and man. And we have that person in Jesus.

More than once the New Testament calls Jesus *mesites*. *Mesos* is the Greek for "in the middle"; and a *mesites* was one who stood in the middle, and who brought two estranged people together.

This is exactly what Jesus does with us and God.

He is God's middleman between men and their God.

"SHE DID WHAT SHE COULD"  December 23

In the giving of any gift, there are two things which make all the difference. *There is the timing of the gift.*

When everything is prospering and flourishing, an extra gift may not make so very much difference; but at a time when we are discouraged and disheartened and in trouble someone's gift may make all the difference in the world.

If we know anyone who is going through such a time, it would be a kindly and valuable thing to give him some gift—even if it is nothing other than a word of cheer.

*There is the spirit in which the gift is given.*

The money price of a gift has nothing to do with the value of a gift. The value of a gift lies entirely in the love which prompted the giver to give it.

Many a mother will wear, with more pride, a little piece of artificial jewellery, than she would a spray of diamonds, because it was bought with a child's saved pennies, and given with a child's love.

The most costly gift is valueless, if there is no love in the giving.

The cheapest gift is priceless, if it comes from the love which could give no more.

Once when he was very near the end a woman gave Jesus a gift, and there were some to find fault with love's extravagance.

But Jesus paid her the finest of all compliments, "She hath done what she could," he said (Mark 14:8).

And he meant it!


## ON CHRISTMAS EVE                                      December 24

Julian B. Arnold tells of something that happened to himself. He is an Englishman, and on one occasion he found himself all alone in Edinburgh on Christmas Eve.

He walked along Princes Street feeling very much alone, and finally went into a brightly lit restaurant to eat a lonely dinner. He took a table and sat all by himself.

At the end of the meal he summoned the waiter and asked for his bill.

The waiter said: "Sir, a gentleman sitting at a table near by instructed me to tell you that he gathered you were a stranger in our city, and therefore he had ventured to give himself the honour of being your unknown host upon this Christmas Eve. He hoped that you would pardon this wish of his to offer you his own good wishes, and the courtesy of his country."

Someone's generosity had lit up a lonely Christmas Eve for a stranger in a strange land.


## WIDE AS THE WORLD                                     December 25

I have come across two sayings of two men who were widely different, and who yet had the same vision of the task of Christianity.

Richard Collier, in his great biography of William Booth, paints a picture of the General at a rally of London Salvationists.

"How wide is the girth of the world?" he shouted. "Twenty-five thousand miles," came the answer. "Then," roared Booth, "we must grow till our arms get right round about it."

Nothing less than the world for Christ would do.
This is the message of Christmas.

Vincent A. Yzerman's selection from the speeches of Pope John XXIII opens with a picture of Pope John on the second night of the Vatican Council.

"Pope John XXIII stood in the window of his private study, smiling at thousands and thousands of cheering Romans below in St. Peter's Square. He quieted them. He spoke to them. 'Go home,' he said, 'and make love grow from here to everywhere.'"

It is the same message.
Nothing less than a world united in the love of Christ will do.
"Love came down at Christmas."
To create love.

A SIGH                                                                December 26

The desire of the Christian is to take in, not to shut out.
It is a grievous and a tragic thing to see how many Christians in these days are concerned to shut the door rather than to open it; they are concerned rather to narrow the circle than to widen it.
Their policy is withdrawal from others rather than co-operation with them.

There are people whose aim it is to depopulate heaven. In the picture of the Holy City in Revelation 21:16 the city is a square, each side of which is 12,000 stades, which is 1,500 miles. The area of such a city is 2,250,000 square miles.
There will be room for many there.
Inclusion, not exclusion, is the watchword of the true Christian.

The accent of the true Christian is love, as we said on Christmas Day.
The sternest things that Jesus ever said are in Matthew 23:13–36, where again and again he says: "Woe unto you, Scribes and Pharisees." But that passage ought never to be read, as if it had been spoken in an accent of scarifying anger and bitter condemnation.
The word for "woe" is *ouai*; the very sound of it is a sigh.
Jesus spoke on that occasion, not with the accent of anger, but with the accent of sorrow.

This is not denunciation.
It is the appeal of love.

I like this story . . .
"There was a little Indian girl at school today," announced my son proudly.
"Does she speak English?" I asked.
"No," came the reply. "But it doesn't matter because she laughs in English."

Laughter is the universal language.
You can laugh in any language and it will be understood.
Keep laughing!

> There is a tide in the affairs of men,
> Which, taken at the flood, leads on to fortune;
> Omitted, all the voyage of their life
> Is bound in shallows and in miseries.
> On such a full sea are we now afloat.
> And we must take the current when it serves,
> Or lose our ventures.

So wrote Shakespeare in *Julius Caesar*.

James Russell Lowell, the American poet, in his poem "The Present Crisis'
said the same thing:

> Once to every man and nation
>    comes the moment to decide,
> In the strife of Truth with
>    Falsehood, for the good
>       or evil side.

As Lowell saw it, God sends to each man some great cause, some new
Messiah.

> Offering each the bloom or blight
>    And the choice goes by for
> ever twixt that darkness and
>    that light.

To every man there comes what we call the psychological moment.
The All-important moment.
It must be recognised.
And used.

*Opportunities do not return.*

I can't say this too often.

There is a time to speak a word; there is a time to perform a deed; there is a time to learn something; or to acquire some skills; and, if that time is allowed to pass, it very often does not return.

The law of life is that, if a thing is not said or done, in its own moment, the opportunity to say or do it does not return.

Life is for ever saying to us: "Now is the time."

*A man cannot seize an opportunity unless he has fitted himself to receive it before it comes.*

The understudy in a play cannot step into the part unless he has learned the part.

The reserve for a team cannot step into the team, unless he is physically fit and physically trained for the game.

When the offer of some great task or some important post comes to a man, he cannot accept it, unless he has trained himself in the skill and in the character demanded.

The great task of life is to fit oneself for the opportunities when they come, as come they will.

Two things are necessary for this. One is the patient preparation of body, mind and spirit to fit ourselves for life's opportunities, when they will come, and the other is decision of mind to seize them, when they have come.

On your marks!

SEE YONDER LIGHT? December 30

Everyone remembers the passage in John Bunyan's *Pilgrim's Progress* in which Bunyan saw Christian in a time of indecision.

Christian "looked as if he would run, yet he stood still, because, as I perceived, he could not tell which way to go".

Then Bunyan, in his dream, saw Evangelist come up to Christian, and he goes on in the immortal passage.

"Then," said Evangelist, pointing with his finger over a very wide Field, "Do you see yonder Wicket-gate?" The Man said, "No . . ."

"Do you see yonder shining light?" Evangelist said. He said, "I think I do."

"Then," said Evangelist, "keep that light in your eye, and go up directly thereto, so shalt thou see the Gate; at which when thou knockest, it shall be told thee what thou shalt do."

This is the message for a New Year.

We may not see the goal, but we need have no doubt as to the direction in which we should be travelling.

The gate, Christian could not see; the light, he could see.

If he went towards the light, he would surely find the gate.

He knew the direction, and for the time being that was enough.

There are certain directions in which we should be travelling all through this year.

They are forward, outward, upward.

FORWARD! OUTWARD! UPWARD! December 31

Forward, outward and upward—these are the directions in a new year.

We should be travelling forward.

*We should be travelling forward.*

When David Livingstone volunteered for missionary service, they asked him where he was willing to go.

"I will go anywhere," he said, "so long as it is forward."

The daunting thing about life is that so often the end of one year finds us no farther on than the end of the year before. We have still the same faults; we are still making the same mistakes; we are still falling to the same temptations.

Let us resolve now to go forward.

*We should be travelling outward.*

If we look out instead of in, if we think of others instead of self, if concerned care for others takes the place of selfishness, then obviously life will be more useful, and certainly life will be happier.

It is said that in certain places in Africa, when an African gets a very heavy burden to carry, he puts it at one end of a pole. He then gets a stone of equal weight to the burden and puts it on the other end of the pole. He then puts the pole with burden and stone across his shoulders and goes off.

The stone balances the burden, and that is the easiest way to carry it.

Often the easiest way to carry our own troubles is to carry someone else's as well.

To take thought for the troubles of others is the surest way to forget our own.

*We should be travelling upward.*

In a sense we cannot help doing that, for every day brings us nearer the end of this life and nearer the entry to the next life.

We would see things very much more clearly and in their true proportions if we lived with that perspective.

We would see the difference between the things which are important and the things which do not matter, if we looked at them in the light of eternity.

See yonder light?

Keep climbing!